Exploring
Galatians
and
Ephesians

Other books by George R. Knight (selected):

Exploring
Galatians
and
Ephesians

A DEVOTIONAL COMMENTARY

GEORGE R. KNIGHT

REVIEW AND HERALD® PUBLISHING ASSOCIATION
HAGERSTOWN, MD 21740

The author assumes full responsibility for the accuracy of all facts and quotations as cited in this book.

All Bible texts quoted are the author's translation unless otherwise noted.

Bible texts credited to ESV are from the *English Standard Version* of the Bible, copyright © 2001, by Crossway Bibles, a division of Good News Publications. Used by permission.

Texts credited to Message are from *The Message*. Copyright © 1993, 1994, 1995, 1996. Used by permission of NavPress Publishing Group.

Texts credited to NASB are from the *New American Standard Bible,* copyright © 1960, 1962, 1968, 1971, 1975, 1977, 1994 by the Lockman Foundation. Used by permission.

Scriptural quotations marked NIV are from the *Holy Bible, New International Version.* Copyright © 1973, 1978, 1984, International Bible Society, used by permission of Zondervan Bible Publishers.

Bible texts credited to Phillips are from J. B. Phillips: *The New Testament in Modern English,* Revised Edition. © J. B. Phillips, 1958, 1960, 1972. Used by permission of Macmillan Publishing Co.

Texts credited to REB are from *The Revised English Bible*. Copyright © Oxford University Press and Cambridge University Press, 1989. Reprinted by permission.

Scripture quotations marked RSV are from the *Revised Standard Version of the Bible,* copyright © 1946, 1952, 1971, by the Division of Christian Education of the National Council of the Churches of Christ in the U.S.A. Used by permission.

This book was
Edited by Gerald Wheeler
Cover designed by Left Coast Design
Cover illustration by Jerry Blank
Electronic makeup by Shirley M. Bolivar
Typeset: 11/14 Bembo

PRINTED IN U.S.A.

09 08 07 06 05   5 4 3 2 1

R&H Cataloging Service
Knight, George R.
    Exploring Galatians and Ephesians: a devotional commentary.

    1. Bible. N.T. Galatians and Ephesians—Criticism, interpretation, etc.   I. Title.

227.87

ISBN 0-8280-1896-0

Dedicated to

the memory of
Professor Lewis H. Hartin,
a skilled teacher
who first inspired me
with a love for Paul's epistles

Contents

Book I: *Exploring Galatians*

Book II. *Exploring Ephesians*

Exploring the "Exploring" Idea

Exploring Galatians and Ephesians joins Exploring Hebrews and Exploring Mark as the third volume in what is becoming a series of user-friendly commentaries aimed at helping people understand the Bible better. While the books have the needs and abilities of laypeople in mind, they will also prove beneficial to pastors and other church leaders. Beyond individual readers, the "Exploring" format will be helpful for church study groups and in enriching participation in midweek meetings.

Each volume is best thought of as a devotional commentary. While the treatment of each passage seeks to develop its exegetical meaning, it does not stop there but moves on to practical application in the daily life of believers in the twenty-first century.

Rather than focusing on the details of each verse, the "Exploring" volumes seek to give readers an understanding of the themes and patterns of each biblical book as a whole and how each passage fits into its context. As a result, they do not attempt to solve all of the problems or answer all the questions related to a given portion of Scripture.

In an effort to be user-friendly these devotional commentaries on the Old and New Testaments present the entire text of each biblical book treated. The volumes divide the text into "bite-sized" portions that are included immediately before the comments on the passage. Thus readers do not have to flip back and forth between their Bibles and the commentary.

The commentary sections aim at being long enough to significantly treat a topic, but short enough for individual, family, or group readings.

The translation of each biblical book is my own, and claims no special merit. Although I have based it on the original languages, in making it I have conferred with several English versions. While not being a "technical achievement," the translation has sought to take every significant translational problem and issue into consideration and to remain as close as possible to the original text of the Bible. In order to accomplish that goal the translation employs word-for-word translation wherever possible but utilizes thought-for-thought translation when word-for-word fails adequately to carry God's message from the original languages and cultures into modern English.

George R. Knight
Andrews University
Berrien Springs, Michigan

Foreword

Galatians and Ephesians are two of the brightest pearls in the Pauline writings. In their own way both focus on the great theme of salvation for both Jews and Gentiles and both highlight the changed life that comes about through a relationship to God through Jesus. Both letters have immensely enriched the Christian community for the past 2,000 years. And both will transform and enhance our personal and corporate lives as we let the Holy Spirit speak through them to our hearts and minds.

These two relatively short Bible books not only meant much to people in the early church, but they continue to be relevant two millennia later. They are books that tell us how we are saved in Christ, how to walk with Him in daily life, and how to live together as Christians. Thus they have universal appeal and meaning.

This devotional commentary can be read as a freestanding book or it can be utilized with the on-line study guide developed to accompany it. The study guide to *Exploring Galatians and Ephesians* will provide those who use it with an opportunity to let the biblical books speak to them personally through structured questions before they turn to the commentary itself. (To download and print the free study guide, go to www.Adventist BookCenter.com, find the book *Exploring Galatians and Ephesians,* then "Click for Details" and follow the instructions near the bottom of the page for downloading the study guide.)

I would like to express as always my special appreciation to Bonnie Beres, who year after year manages to transform my rather "interesting" handwriting into typed copy; to Gerald Wheeler, who again supplied his editorial expertise; to Jeannette R. Johnson, who continues to encourage me in my writing; and to the administration of Andrews University, who have provided me with support and time for research and writing.

Exploring
Galatians

Introduction
to the Letter to the Galatians

Galatians, Leon Morris writes, "is a passionate letter, the outpouring of the soul of a preacher on fire for his Lord and deeply committed to bringing his hearers to an understanding of what saving faith is" (Morris, p. 26). In turn, Paul's "passionate letter" has ignited passion in the hearts of its readers down through 2,000 years of Christian history. Before turning to the letter itself, it will be helpful to examine a few background issues.

Purpose of Galatians

In order to understand the book of Galatians it is important to comprehend the crisis that provoked the apostle's fiery response.

Paul had previously preached the gospel in Galatia and a number of people had responded to it with enthusiasm (Gal. 4:13, 14; 1:9). Besides accepting the gospel as set forth by the apostle, the Galatian believers had also received the Spirit of God, who had worked miracles among them (3:2, 3, 5). They had had a genuine Christian experience.

But sometime after Paul established the gospel in Galatia, certain Jewish Christians had arrived and taught the apostle's Gentile converts that it was necessary to be circumcised and belong to the Jewish people in order to have God's full blessing (2:12-14; 5:2; 6:12, 13).

In the process of making such assertions the Jewish Christian teachers had declared that they had the backing of the Jerusalem church and had apparently even "claimed" that the authority of the original apostles stood behind their teachings. And those apostles, they declared, possessed higher authority than Paul—a latecomer who had never known the earthly Jesus personally. As a result, the mission of the teachers from Jerusalem undermined both Paul's authority and his theology.

The apostle did not take such an attack sitting down. His letter to the Galatians is his passionate response to what he viewed as a first-order crisis. The purpose of his epistle was to set the record straight on both his apostolic authority and the nature of the gospel.

Galatians' Major Themes

Galatians has four major theological themes. The first two chapters deal with the issue of authority, the next two with salvation, and the last two with holiness. Running throughout all six is the overarching importance of the unity of God's people.

1. *Apostolic Authority.* Authority is a fundamental issue in Galatians. How would the Galatians solve the theological issues facing them? On the one hand was the apostolic authority of Paul. On the other was the authority of the Jewish Christian teachers (the Judaizers) who claimed to have the support and prestige of the Jerusalem church behind them and even (more dubiously) that of the original apostles. Both sides appeared to have good credentials and were represented by upright and persuasive individuals. Who should the Galatian believers listen to?

Paul's answer was to assert his own apostolic authority. Whereas the Judaizers boasted an ecclesiastical authority coming from the Jerusalem church, Paul argues that both his message and mission originated not from the church but from Christ Himself. Paul sets forth his answer in Galatians 1 and 2, wherein he asserts that his credentials came not from any group of people in Jerusalem but directly from Christ.

"Conscious of his apostolic authority," John Stott observes, "Paul expects the Galatians to accept it. They had done this on the first missionary journey, receiving him 'as an angel of God, as Christ Jesus' (4:14). . . . The original message, which he had preached to them (1:8) and which they had received (1:9), was to be normative. If anybody preached a gospel contrary to this, however august a personage he might be, 'let him be accursed'" (Stott, p. 186).

In his argument Paul set forth a principle that will exist until the end of time: we must test all teachings against the apostolic message as set forth in the Bible. Ellen White reflected upon that same insight when she penned that "the Bible is the only rule of faith and doctrine" (*Review and Herald,* July 17, 1888, p. 449).

2. *Salvation in Christ.* The fact that the Judaizers were preaching "another gospel"—a perverted one at that—especially incensed the apostle. For him there was only one gospel. In his letter to the Galatians he will emphasize two of its major aspects.

One is the *cross of Christ.* Jesus, he notes in his introduction, "gave himself for our sins to deliver us from the present evil age" (Gal. 1:4, RSV). Beyond that, "Christ redeemed us from the curse of the law, having become a curse for us—for it is written, 'Cursed be every one who hangs on a tree'" (3:13, RSV).

Paul described his own ministry as portraying the crucified Christ before his hearers (3:1), and he claimed that he never boasted except "in the cross of our Lord Jesus Christ" (6:14, NIV). At the very center of his experience was the "Son of God, who loved me and gave himself for me" (2:20, RSV).

The second major aspect in the gospel according to Paul in Galatians was *justification by faith* in the Christ who had died for their sins. Faith is the means by which people appropriate the blessings of Christ's sacrifice on the cross. Such faith unites believers to Christ, through whom they receive justification (2:16), the gift of the Holy Spirit, and adoption into the Abrahamic covenant promise (3:26-4:7).

Standing over against the validity of faith in getting right with God in Galatians is law. It is faith rather than law that provides the only way a person may be justified. After all, "by works of the law shall no one be justified. . . . For if justification were through the law, then Christ died to no purpose" (2:16, 21, RSV).

Believing rather than doing is the sole ground of justification in Galatians. And the object of that belief is the Christ who died for each person on the cross. One function of the law is its condemnation of those who don't keep all of it (3:10). A second is to lead God's people to Christ so that they might be justified by faith (3:19-24). The law has important roles, but it is not the agent of salvation.

3. *Holiness.* Even though justification comes through faith apart from works of law, that does not mean that Christians are free to disregard the

law. Or, as Paul puts it, "do not use your freedom as an opportunity for the flesh" (5:13, RSV). To the contrary, faith will "express itself in love," which is the heart and summary of the law (5:6, 14, Phillips). Those who are free in Christ will avoid the works of the flesh (fornication, idolatry, jealousy, anger, envy, and so on—5:19-21). "Those who belong to Christ Jesus have crucified the flesh with its passions and desires" (5:24, RSV).

Instead of the works of the flesh, Christians will let God develop in them the fruit of the Holy Spirit—"love, joy, peace, patience, kindness, goodness, faithfulness, gentleness, self-control" (5:22, 23, RSV). They are to live as God's holy people. And holiness will characterize their relationships with others (5:13-15; 5:25-6:10).

4. *The Unity of God's People.* G. Walter Hansen is correct when he writes that "in Galatians Paul develops his argument for justification by faith in order to correct a social problem: Gentile believers have been excluded from fellowship with Jewish believers because they did not observe the law. Paul demonstrates that justification by faith means that Gentile believers are included within the people of God; on the basis of this doctrine Gentile believers have the right to eat at the same table with Jewish believers [2:11-16].

"Paul uses the Old Testament story of Abraham's faith to show that faith in God is the mark of belonging to Abraham's family. The conclusion of his argument from Scripture in Galatians 3 declares the unity and equality of all in Christ: 'There is neither Jew nor Greek, slave nor free, male nor female, for you are all one in Christ Jesus' " (Hansen, p. 25).

The unity of God's people across time and racial and other divisions is a major theme in Galatians. Faith unites individuals with God's people in both the past and in the present.

Structure of Galatians

The structure of Galatians is quite straightforward. After an introduction (Gal. 1:1-10), the epistle's six chapters fall into three well-defined sections. C. K. Barrett aptly labels them as history, theology, and ethics. "Paul's first step in dealing with the troubled situation in his Galatian churches," Barrett observes, "is to set straight the record of the past; till that is done there can be no hope of securing the future" (Barrett, p. 3). Thus the first two chapters deal with history.

But history isn't an end in itself. After dealing with the past he moves on to theology in chapters 3 and 4 as he sets forth the proper understandings upon which the future must rest. But even good theology isn't his ultimate goal. In chapters 5 and 6 he caps off his letter with ethics. For Paul, right thinking always leads to right living. In the Epistle to the Galatians Paul's "theology of freedom" leads directly to an "ethics of obligation" *(ibid.)*.

Outline of Galatians

I. Introducing the threat to Christian liberty (1:1-10)
    A. Greetings (1:1, 2)
    B. The gospel of deliverance (1:3-5)
    C. The occasion of the letter: the invasion of "another gospel" (1:6-10)
II. History: Paul's authority as an apostle of liberty (1:11-2:21)
    A. The divine origin of Paul's authority (1:11-17)
    B. Humans added nothing (1:18-24)
    C. Paul's divine commission accepted by the Jerusalem church (2:1-10)
    D. Paul's authority demonstrated in the conflict with Peter (2:11-21)
       1. The conflict (2:11-15)
       2. The underlying issue: justification by law or faith? (2:16-21)
III. Theology: Justification by faith as the basis for Christian liberty (3:1-4:31)
    A. The Galatians were deceived away from faith (3:1-5)
    B. Abraham was justified by faith (3:6-9)
    C. The law can condemn but not redeem (3:10-14)
    D. The Abrahamic covenant comes through Christ (3:15-18)
    E. The function of the law: beyond condemning sin it points to Christ and justification through faith in Him (3:19-25)
    F. All who have faith in Christ are united as children of Abraham (3:26-29)
    G. God's gift through Christ sets believers free to know God as Father (4:1-7)
    H. But the Galatians are rejecting freedom and opting for slavery (4:8-20)
       1. They are returning to the bondage of the law (4:8-11)
       2. Paul appeals to the Galatians to be like him rather than like

A Note on Authorship, Recipients, and Date

Unlike some biblical books that do not identify their author (Hebrews and Mark, for example), Galatians' very first verse makes the claim that it is the work of "Paul an apostle." That claim has been almost universally accepted down through Christian history, not only because of its own assertion but also because Paul's style and theology are evident throughout the epistle.

The virtual unanimity of agreement regarding the authorship of Galatians breaks down when it comes to the topic of the letter's recipients. The problem arises because the term "Galatia" can mean two different things. First, the region in north central Asia Minor (today's Turkey) that was home to the ethnic Galatians. Second, the Roman province of Galatia that stretched from northern ethnic Galatia down through central Asia Minor to include such southern cities Iconium, Lystra, and Derbe (see map on p. 14). The evidence favors the southern or Roman province theory, since the book of Acts clearly reflects Paul's ministry to the southern cities but makes no reference to any preaching in the north (see Acts 13, 14).

Major battles have raged over the destination of Paul's letter to the Galatians. But the good news is that "the outcome has little if any effect on the interpretation of the major themes of the letter" (Hansen, p. 16).

Of more consequence are the struggles over the date of the book's composition. The central issue here is trying to line up Paul's visits to Jerusalem in the autobiographical sections of Galatians with Luke's record. Galatians records two visits (1:18—first post-conversion visit, 2:1-10—conference with leading apostles visit), while Luke reports five (Acts 9:26-30—first post-conversion visit, 11:30—famine relief visit, 15:1-30—Jerusalem council visit, 18:22—quick visit, and 21:15-17—arrest visit).

It has seemed quite natural to equate the first post-conversion visit of Galatians 1:18 with that of Acts 9:26-30 and the conference one of Galatians 2:1-10 with that of Acts 15:1-30. That seemingly natural equation, however, runs up against two problems. First, it skips over the Acts 11 visit, which seems strange in a Galatians passage in which Paul lists his journeys to Jerusalem as he defends the point that he got his apostolic commission directly from Christ rather than from the Jerusalem apostles.

More seriously, we find no mention of the Jerusalem council of Acts 15 in Galatians. That is especially significant since the Acts 15 council convened to make an authoritative ruling as to whether Gentiles needed to undergo circumcision and live according "to the custom of Moses" (15:1, RSV). The council's decision was a resounding "no" on both counts (verses 19-21). Thus, as Leon Morris points out, "it is not easy to see why Paul should have omitted all reference to the Council in this letter if it had already taken place, for . . . it would have given him splendid support. Specifically, it is difficult to see why he should have failed to quote the decrees of the Council which had direct reference to the question of circumcision (Acts 15:19-21). His opponents in Galatia were clearly arguing that Peter (among other people) was in favour of circumcising new Christians, a position at variance with the Council's position that Gentile converts need not be circumcised. The obvious conclusion is that the Council had not yet taken place" (Morris, p. 21).

The most natural result is that we should equate the first post-conversion visits of Galatians 1:18 and Acts 9:26-30 and regard the second visit of Acts 11:30 as a brief mention of the visit reported more extensively by Paul in Galatians 2:1-10. That would date the Acts 15 council after he wrote the letter to the Galatians. And that makes sense, since the church convened the council to rule on the very problems that Paul faced in Galatia.

With the above facts in mind, Paul's letter to the Galatians must have

Chronology of Paul's Visits to Jerusalem		
1. First post-conversion visit—after 3 years	Acts 9:26-30	Galatians 1:18
2. Second visit—after 14 years	Acts 11:30	Galatians 2:1-10
3. Jerusalem council visit—to solve some issues Paul had to meet in the letter to the Galatians	Acts 15:1-30	Post-Galatians

been one of his early writings. Assuming that he had his Damascus road encounter about A.D. 34, his reference to going up to Jerusalem after 14 years (Gal. 2:1) takes us to A.D. 48 or so. That would place the writing of Galatians most probably in the late 40s or very early 50s.

Galatians' Relevance for the Twenty-first Century

Galatians is perpetually relevant because it deals with issues central to the Christian faith throughout its history. One of those perennial issues is that of authority. Believers in every age must decide on the foundation of theological decision making. Who or what determines what should be believed? Is it the "church," tradition, Scripture, or some other form of authority? Galatians' forceful answer is that every teaching must be tested by the teaching of the apostles of Christ. "Indeed," John Stott observes, "this is the only kind of apostolic succession we can accept—not a line of bishops stretching back to the apostles and claiming to be their successors . . . , but loyalty to the apostolic doctrine of the New Testament. The teaching of the apostles, now permanently preserved in the New Testament, is to regulate the beliefs and the practices of the church of every generation," including ours (Stott, p. 187).

A second theme of continuing relevance is the plan of salvation, the greatest need of every person in every generation. Along with the book of Romans, Galatians is Paul's most intensive treatment of the topic. In both books the apostle forcefully states that justification is by grace alone through faith (Gal. 2:16; Rom. 1:16). But also in both he points out that obedience to God's great law of love is the natural response to the gift of salvation (Gal. 5:1-6:10; Rom. 1:5; 6:1-14; 13:8-10; 16:26). Thus Paul maintains a consistent balance between grace and our response to it.

It is the lack of such balance that has repeatedly led to crisis throughout Christian history. On the one hand are those so focused on justifying grace that they neglect the obedient response. On the other hand are those who are so concerned with obedience that they confuse it with the path to justification. It is the carefully integrated balance between gospel and law, faith and works, that makes Galatians such an important document for twenty-first century believers.

A third item vital to believers today is Paul's concern with unity. The church always faces potential division over racial, gender, economic, and marginal theological and lifestyle issues. Galatians in one sense is primarily a response to those differences. Its message is that we need to avoid majoring on the marginal and that ethnic and other differences should mean nothing to those who are one in Christ through faith (Gal. 3:26-29). As G. Walter Hansen points out, "if a church does not defend in practice the equality and unity of all in Christ, it implicitly communicates that justification is not by faith but by race, social status or some other standard" (Hansen, p. 25).

A fourth relevance is Galatians' uplifting of the law of God as centered on love (Gal. 5:14, 22; cf. Rom. 13:8-10; Matt. 22:37-39). Like most congregations today, those in Galatia had their share of differences. Yet, in spite of the problems, the book of Galatians emphasizes the fact that "the love which fulfills the law is the love active amidst dissension, pride, and envy (5:14-15, 26)" (Cousar, p. 11). It is no accident that in Galatians Paul lists the first aspect of the fruit of the spirit as love (5:22). It is that very attribute that we most need in our day.

Lastly, Galatians has missiological lessons that the church still needs to learn as it moves into new cultures and racial groupings. The sending organizations too often still seek to make converts to Americanism or some other ism as it brings people to Christ. But one of the great teachings of Galatians (and Acts and several of Paul's other letters) is that it is important to distinguish between the core of the gospel and the cultural baggage of those who present it.

List of Works Cited

Arichea, Daniel C. and Eugene A. Nida. *A Handbook on Paul's Letter to the Galatians,* UBS Handbook Series. New York: United Bible Societies, 1976.

Barclay, William. *The Letters to the Galatians and Ephesians,* 2d ed. The Daily Study Bible. Edinburgh: The Saint Andrews Press, 1958.

Barrett, C. K. *Freedom and Obligation: A Study of the Epistle to the Galatians.* Philadelphia: Westminster, 1985.

Barton, Bruce B. et al. *Galatians.* Life Application Bible Commentary. Wheaton, Ill.: Tyndale House, 1994.

Betz, Hans Dieter. *Galatians: A Commentary on Paul's Letter to the Churches in Galatia.* Hermeneia—A Critical and Historical Commentary on the Bible. Philadelphia: Fortress, 1979.

Boice, James Montgomery. "Galatians." In *The Expositor's Bible Commentary,* Frank E. Gaebelein, ed. Grand Rapids: Zondervan, 1976, X:407–508.

Bring, Ragnar. *Commentary on Galatians.* Eric Wahlstrom, trans. Philadelphia: Muhlenberg, 1961.

Bruce, F. F. *The Epistle to the Galatians: A Commentary on the Greek Text.* The New International Greek Testament Commentary. Grand Rapids: Eerdmans, 1982.

Burton, Ernest De Witt. *A Critical and Exegetical Commentary on the Epistle to the Galatians.* The International Critical Commentary. Edinburgh: T. & T. Clark, [1920].

Calvin, John. *The Epistles of Paul the Apostle to the Galatians, Ephesians, Philippians, and Colossians.* T.H.L. Parker, trans. Calvin's Commentaries. Grand Rapids: Eerdmans, 1965.

Cole, R. Alan. *The Epistle of Paul to the Galatians.* Tyndale New Testament Commentaries. Grand Rapids: Eerdmans, 1965.

Cousar, Charles B. *Galatians.* Interpretation: A Bible Commentary for Teaching and Preaching. Louisville: John Knox, 1982.

Cullman, Oscar. *Peter: Disciple, Apostle, Martyr: A Historical and Theological Essay.* Floyd V. Filson, trans. New York: Meridian, 1958.

Danker, Frederick William, ed. *A Greek-English Lexicon of the New Testament and Other Early Christian Literature,* 3rd ed. Chicago: University of Chicago, 2000.

Duncan, George S. *The Epistle of Paul to the Galatians.* The Moffatt New Testament Commentary. New York: Harper and Brothers, [1934].

Dunn, James D. G. *The Epistle to the Galatians.* Black's New Testament Commentary. Peabody, Mass.: Hendrickson, 1993.

Findlay, G. G. *The Epistle to the Galatians.* The Expositor's Bible. New York: A. C.

Armstrong and Son, 1902.

Fung, Ronald Y. K. *The Epistle to the Galatians*. The New International Commentary on the New Testament. Grand Rapids: Eerdmans, 1988.

George, Timothy. *Galatians*. The New American Commentary. Nashville: Broadman & Holman, 1994.

Guthrie, Donald. *Galatians*. New Century Bible Commentary. Grand Rapids: Eerdmans, 1974.

Hansen, G. Walter. *Galatians*. The IVP New Testament Commentary Series. Downers Grove, Ill.: InterVarsity, 1994.

Hawthorne, Gerald F., and Ralph P. Martin, eds. *Dictionary of Paul and His Letters*. Downers Grove, Ill.: InterVarsity, 1993.

Hunter, Archibald M. *The Letter of Paul to the Galatians, The Letter of Paul to the Ephesians, The Letter of Paul to the Philippians, The Letter of Paul to the Colossians*. The Layman's Bible Commentary. Richmond, Vir.: John Knox, 1959.

Keener, Craig S. *The IVP Bible Background Commentary: New Testament*. Downers Grove, Ill.: InterVarsity, 1993.

Kittel, Gerhard, and Gerhard Friedrich, eds. *Theological Dictionary of the New Testament,* 10 vols. Grand Rapids: Eerdmans, 1964–1976.

Knight, George R. *Exploring Hebrews*. Hagerstown, Md.: Review and Herald, 2003.

_____. *I Used to Be Perfect: A Study of Sin and Salvation,* 2d ed. Berrien Springs, Mich.: Andrews University Press, 2001.

_____. *My Gripe With God: A Study in Divine Justice and the Problem of the Cross.* Washington, D.C.: Review and Herald, 1990.

_____. *The Pharisee's Guide to Perfect Holiness: A Study of Sin and Salvation.* Boise, Ida.: Pacific Press, 1992.

_____. *Walking With Paul Through the Book of Romans.* Hagerstown, Md.: Review and Herald, 2002.

Ladd, George Eldon. *A Theology of the New Testament.* Grand Rapids: Eerdmans, 1974.

Lenski, R.C.H. *The Interpretation of St. Paul's Epistles to the Galatians, to the Ephesians, and to the Philippians.* Minneapolis: Augsburg, 1961.

Lightfoot, J. B. *The Epistle of St. Paul to the Galatians.* Grand Rapids: Zondervan, n.d.

Longenecker, Richard N. *Galatians*. Word Biblical Commentary. Dallas: Word, 1990.

Lührmann, Dieter. *Galatians*. O. C. Dean, Jr., trans. A Continental Commentary. Minneapolis: Fortress, 1992.

Luther, Martin. *A Commentary on St. Paul's Epistle to the Galatians.* Philip S. Watson, ed. London: James Clarke, 1953.

_____. *Luther: Letters of Spiritual Counsel.* Theodore G. Tappert, ed. and trans. Philadelphia: Westminster, 1955.

McDonald, H. D. *Freedom in Faith: A Commentary on Paul's Epistle to the Galatians.* Old Tappan, N.J.: Fleming H. Revell, 1973.

McGrath, Alister E. *Justification by Faith.* Grand Rapids: Zondervan, 1990.

McKnight, Scot. *Galatians*. The NIV Application Commentary. Grand Rapids: Zondervan, 1995.

Morris, Leon. *Galatians: Paul's Charter of Christian Freedom.* Downers Grove, Ill.: InterVarsity, 1996.

Nichol, Francis D., ed. *The Seventh-day Adventist Bible Commentary,* 7 vols. Washington, D.C.: Review and Herald, 1953-1957, VI:929-990.

Ramsay, Wm. M. *A Historical Commentary on St. Paul's Epistle to the Galatians.* Grand Rapids: Baker, 1979.

Rendall, Frederic. "The Epistle to the Galatians." In *The Expositor's Greek Testament.* Grand Rapids: Eerdmans, n.d., III:121-200.

Ridderbos, Herman N. *The Epistle of Paul to the Churches of Galatia.* The New International Commentary on the New Testament. Grand Rapids: Eerdmans, 1953.

Rogers, Cleon L., Jr., and Cleon L. Rogers III. *The New Linguistic and Exegetical Key to the Greek New Testament.* Grand Rapids: Zondervan, 1998.

Shanks, Hershel, and Ben Witherington III. *The Brother of Jesus.* San Francisco: HarperSanFrancisco, 2003.

Stott, John R. W. *The Message of Galatians: Only One Way.* The Bible Speaks Today. Downers Grove, Ill.: InterVarsity, 1968.

Warfield, Benjamin Breckinridge. *The Person and Work of Christ.* Philadelphia: Presbyterian and Reformed, 1950.

White, Ellen G. *The Acts of the Apostles.* Mountain View, Calif.: Pacific Press, 1911.

_____. *The Desire of Ages.* Mountain View, Calif.: Pacific Press, 1940.

_____. *Education.* Mountain View, Calif.: Pacific Press, 1952.

Williams, Sam K. *Galatians.* Abingdon New Testament Commentaries. Nashville: Abingdon, 1997.

Witherington, Ben, III. *Grace in Galatia: A Commentary on St. Paul's Letter to the Galatians.* Grand Rapids: Eerdmans, 1998.

Wuest, Kenneth S. *Wuest's Word Studies From the Greek New Testament,* 4 vols. Grand Rapids: Eerdmans, 1998.

Ziesler, John. *The Epistle to the Galatians.* Epworth Commentaries. London: Epworth, 1992.

Part I

Introducing the Threat to Christian Liberty

Galatians 1:1-10

1. The Gospel of Deliverance

Galatians 1:1-5

> *¹Paul an apostle (not from men nor through man, but through Jesus Christ and God the Father, who raised Him from death) ²and all the brothers with me,*
>
> *To the churches of Galatia:*
>
> *³Grace and peace to you from God our Father and the Lord Jesus Christ, ⁴who gave Himself for our sins so that He might deliver us from the present evil age, according to the will of our God and Father, ⁵to whom be glory for ever and ever. Amen.*

The opening words of Galatians are anything but a casual greeting. Rather, they are like a cannon shot in the first salvo of a barrage that will extend throughout the six chapters of Paul's letter.

The apostle doesn't beat around the bush in his salutation. He wastes no time in commending the virtues of his readers, as he does in Romans 1:8, 1 Corinthians 1:4, and in most of his other epistles. To the contrary, he jumps right into the issues at hand—his authority and his gospel. Verses 1 and 2 take up the first of those topics and verses 3 and 4 the second.

Paul asserts his apostleship in the letter's first phrase. That is no accident. His authority challenged, he claims the title that certain false teachers who had invaded the Galatian congregations were evidently denying him. After all, they had undoubtedly pointed out, Paul certainly wasn't one of those whom Jesus had personally commissioned as one of His 12 apostles. Beyond that, he had savagely persecuted the early Christian church. To put it bluntly, Paul, for all of his virtues, had lesser authority than the Jerusalem apostles. It was therefore a mistake to stake too much on his teachings.

In the epistle's very first verse Paul moves right to the heart of the accusations against him. He was, he asserts, an apostle indeed, one appointed by the risen Jesus Himself. Here Paul refers to his commissioning on the road to Damascus (see Acts 9:1-22).

It is no accident that Paul describes Jesus as the risen one in Galatians 1:1. After all, it was the resurrected Jesus who had personally commissioned him, and, in addition, one of the agreed-upon marks of true apostles is that they had to be able to witness to the resurrection of Jesus (Acts 1:22). Paul, since the Damascus road event, had had that special characteristic. As he put it in 1 Corinthians 15, after He had revealed Himself to the apostles and others, Jesus "last of all, as to one untimely born, . . . appeared also to me" (verses 5-8, RSV).

The Greek word for apostle, *apostolos,* means one who is sent. In the Jewish world it signified a special messenger with a unique status who had a commission from a higher body. Thus, writes R. A. Cole, "a Jewish apostolos would normally be sent from a group (perhaps the Sanhedrin) and would have received his commission from the high priest or some similar high official. When Paul went on his journey to Damascus his apostolate was of this nature (Acts ix.2)" (Cole, p. 31). But not so now. Instead, he unapologetically asserts, his commission is from none other than Jesus the Christ, the one whom God had raised from the dead (Gal. 1:1).

But why, we need to ask, did Paul feel the need to assert and defend his apostleship so aggressively? "Was he," queries John Stott, "just a braggart, inflated with personal vanity? No. Was it from pique that men had dared to challenge his authority? No. It was because the gospel that he preached was at stake. If Paul were not an apostle of Jesus Christ, then men could, and no doubt would, reject his gospel. This he could not bear. For what Paul spoke was Christ's message on Christ's authority. So he defended his apostolic authority in order to defend his message" (Stott, pp. 14, 15).

Following his initial defense of his apostleship in verse 1, in verses 2 and 3 Paul pronounces his usual blessing of grace and peace on the Galatian congregation. Both are distinctly Pauline words and both are pregnant with meaning. Grace *(charis)* is that which fills with joy (Kittel, vol. 9, p. 360). And in a Christian context, nothing can bring more joy than what God has done for us in Christ.

The word "peace" is also directly related to what the Lord has done for Christians through the life, death, and heavenly ministry of Jesus. It was a word of great importance to Paul, who taught that all people were under the curse of the penalty of the broken law but that "Christ redeemed us from the curse of the law, having become a curse for us" in His sacrifice on Calvary (Gal. 3:10-13, RSV; cf. Rom. 6:23; 3:21-25). For the apostle, the result of accepting Christ's sacrifice by faith is both justification and peace with God (Rom. 5:1). Those who have accepted Christ have been "reconciled to God by the death of his Son" (5:10, RSV). They are no longer God's enemies but have peace with Him (verse 10) and, by extension, with other people and with their own selves. It is no accident that Paul frequently combined grace and peace in his greetings. Both were at the heart of his understanding of the gospel.

That gospel comes to the front in Galatians 1:4, in which Paul writes of "Jesus Christ, who gave Himself for our sins so that He might deliver us from the present evil age, according to the will of our God and Father." To Martin Luther "these words are very thunderclaps from heaven against all kinds of [self-]righteousness; like as is also this sentence of John: 'Behold the Lamb of God, that taketh away the sins of the world'" (Luther, *Commentary,* p. 47).

The heart of Paul's gospel is that Jesus "gave Himself for our sins" that we might be delivered. Salvation is not the result of our actions but of His. It is not the consequence of some great thing that we as human beings do as an offering to or an appeasement of God, but something done for us by Jesus who bore our sins and took our place on the tree of Calvary (Gal. 3:13). Here we have the core of Paul's understanding of the good news. "The gospel," he writes to the Corinthians, is that "Christ died for our sins in accordance with the scriptures, that he was buried, that he was raised on the third day" (1 Cor. 15:1-4, RSV).

The very foundation of the gospel is that salvation rests on what God has done for us in Christ rather than on something we must do for Him. It is that teaching that the false teachers who have invaded the Galatian congregations now challenge.

They have thrown down the gauntlet, and Paul has picked it up. As a means of discrediting his gospel they question his apostleship. Paul, on the other hand, will defend his apostleship as the vindication of his understanding of the gospel. In the vigorous epistle to the Galatians he will aggressively attack until he has his enemies pinned to the wall.

In the process, Paul provides us in Galatians 1:4 with what F. F. Bruce suggests "is probably the earliest written statement in the NT about the significance of the death of Christ" (Bruce, p. 77). That significance not only relates Christ's death to the forgiveness of His peoples' sins but also to their deliverance "from the present evil age" (Gal. 1:4). The Jews believed that history divided into two ages: the present one and the age to come. The early Christians adopted that idea. Thus, for Paul, Christians have in a sense already been saved. God has rescued, delivered, and emancipated them from a state of bondage, from this "present evil age." As a result, Cole suggests, "what Christ's death has done is to transfer the Christian from the sphere of Satan's power to that of God. While still living in this world, therefore, he enjoys already that life of the age to come" (Cole, p. 35).

If that is so, then "Christians are not meant to live in bondage to the ideas and the manner of life of those among whom they find themselves. Christ died to deliver them from such bondage" (Morris, p. 37).

We will discover in our study of Galatians that Paul's gospel is a radical one. It not only spells out redemption through grace without works of law, but it sets forth an ethic in chapters 5 and 6 that pits the ways of the present age (the flesh) over against the ways of the future age (the Spirit). God's people, according to Paul, have already been delivered from both the penalty of sin through justification by faith (Gal. 2:16) and the power of sin through the work of the Holy Spirit (5:22; 3:3, 5). In that condition they await their delivery from the presence of sin when Jesus comes in the clouds of heaven to complete the salvation process.

2. Troublers of the Church

Galatians 1:6-9
> *⁶I am astonished that you are so quickly turning from the One who called you by the grace of Christ, for a different gospel, ⁷which is not really another. But there are some who are troubling you and who desire to pervert the gospel of Christ. ⁸But even if we or an angel from heaven should preach a gospel to you contrary to that which we preached to you, let him be accursed! ⁹As we have said before, and now I say again, if anyone preaches a gospel to you contrary to that which you received, let him be accursed!*

What a brutal paragraph! It is hardly one that I would want to find in the mail.

Many writers have noted a major difference between Galatians and Paul's other epistles. After his greeting in every other letter, for example, he then commends his readers, prays for them, or praises God. Even in those in which he will eventually use strong words of warning and rebuke, he still restrains himself until after he has said something positive. Thus, though the church in Thessalonica has problems that he will have to address, he first shares his appreciation of their growing faith (1 Thess. 1:2-4; 2 Thess. 1:3, 4). Even with the troublesome church in Corinth, in which Paul quickly jumps into the issues dividing it, he has a few words right up front in which he thanks God for their spiritual gifts and their general walk in Christ (1 Cor. 1:4-9).

But things are different in his greetings to the Galatians. "Instead of a word of praise, the Epistle opens with an abrupt and passionate outburst. . . . Not for a moment can the apostle keep back what presses so heavily on his soul" (Duncan, p. 15). "These words," writes G. G. Findlay, "were well calculated to startle the Galatians out of their levity. They are like a lightning-flash which shows one to be standing on the edge of a precipice" (Findlay, p. 35).

And just what was it that they needed to be shocked into realizing? That is the topic of verses 6-9. Paul begins by saying that he is "astonished" at the change taking place among the believers. Generally the word "astonished" conveys the idea of surprise. But as Paul uses it here the word has connotations of "irritation" and "rebuke" (Rogers, p. 421). Hans Betz notes that Paul is employing "a device which was used in the rhetoric of law courts and politics" that signaled "indignant rebuttal and attack of things the opposition party has done and is about to do" (Betz, p. 47).

The thing that his Galatian converts had done to upset him so was to turn away from the gospel of grace to a different gospel (1:6). The word Paul uses for "turning from" is the same one employed to describe soldiers who revolt or desert, people who change sides in politics and philosophy, or individuals who turn their back on one religion for another. In its context in Galatians 1:6 it is desertion from the very thing that saved them (God's grace in Christ) to a different way of salvation.

Paul's gospel—the one he had preached to the Galatians and elsewhere—was "the gospel of the grace of God" (Acts 20:24, RSV). It proclaimed that "by grace you have been saved through faith; and this is not your own doing, it is the gift of God—not because of works, lest any man should boast" (Eph. 2:8, 9, RSV; cf. Gal. 2:16). His gospel declared that "no human being will be justified in his sight by works of the law" (Rom. 3:20, RSV), that all are "justified as a gift by His grace through the redemption which is in Christ Jesus; whom God displayed publicly as a propitiation in His blood through faith" (verses 24, 25, NASB). Above all, it clearly taught that Jesus had made full provision for salvation by bearing our sin and becoming a curse for us on Calvary's tree (Gal. 3:13).

And what was this "different gospel" being preached in Galatia that was not in fact a gospel at all, but rather a perversion of the only Gospel (1:6, 7)? It apparently had something to do with Gentile converts needing to become circumcised and follow the Mosaic law before they could become full members of the Abrahamic covenant and the people of God (6:12; 5:11; 3:29, 16-18; 4:21-31). The preachers of this "different gospel"

were undoubtedly those teaching the Gentiles that "unless you are circum-
cized according to the custom of Moses, you cannot be saved" (Acts 15:1,
RSV), a position that would soon lead to the Jerusalem council in which
Paul and Barnabas met with the leaders of the Jerusalem church. At that
important meeting the church at large would officially reject the "different
gospel" of the Judaizers (see Acts 15). But in the meantime, Paul had to
deal with the perverters of the gospel in Galatia.

His real problem was that they appeared to be good Christian leaders.
In fact, his allegations against the Judaizers probably would have shocked
the Galatian church members. After all, R. Alan Cole points out, they
"certainly preached salvation through Christ. They never denied, as far as
we know, that it was necessary to believe in Jesus as the Messiah and
Saviour" (Cole, p. 39). How could Paul possibly claim that they had a different gospel? That question is especially pertinent since "it is highly likely
that the Judaizers observed no customs other than those observed by the
bulk of the church at Jerusalem; and Paul certainly never accused James or
John or Peter of preaching 'a different gospel'" (ibid.). Why did Paul get
so upset with this particular group of Jewish/Christian teachers?

Again, the answer lies in the fact that the Judaizers were instructing
Gentile believers that accepting Christ by faith was not enough to be justified, that they as Gentiles had to be circumcised and observe the Jewish
law if they wanted to be a part of God's covenant people. The aspect that
Paul fought was their teaching that the preaching of Christ alone was insufficient for their salvation, that they needed to add their works to that
of Christ.

"But," asks Charles Cousar, "is this really a serious issue? Would it not
be the better part of wisdom to thank God that they were not advocating
sacred prostitution or divinely ordered sedition against Rome or something more destructive than circumcision? After all, circumcision was a rite
established with Abraham; it had a good Old Testament precedent (cf.
Gen. 17:9-14). For Paul, however, the issue is urgent. An addendum,
when absolutized, negates the very nature of the gospel itself. What may
seem like a harmless addition turns out to be a gross contradiction"
(Cousar, p. 20).

For Paul, any addition to the gospel of God's free grace made it no
gospel at all. It was rather a total perversion of the gospel (Gal. 1:7). The

word translated as "perversion" can also mean "to reverse." With that meaning in mind, we see that the false teachers were not merely corrupting the gospel, but reversing it, turning it about from its preordained mission. To preach such a doctrine eroded the very heart of the Christian message. After all, Paul will say later, "if justification were through the law, then Christ died to no purpose" (Gal. 2:21, RSV). In short, to add anything to grace as God's way of justification is to destroy the very idea of grace itself. From his perspective, God's justification in Christ is not a bargain between Him and human beings, but a gift. Thus the seemingly harmless additions of the Judaizers in actual fact negated the entire gospel message.

That still holds in our day. We will always encounter those "good" people in the church who want to add works to faith. Then again, we meet those who would subtract the substitutionary aspect from the gospel (3:13). To all such in every age the apostle Paul blazes forth in indignation. He accepts no perversions of the gospel in terms of either subtraction or addition. It is faithfulness to the gospel message, he argues, that defines who is a genuine Christian teacher. If they do not have the gospel message straight, then their authority and message does not come from God, even if they be "an angel from heaven" (1:8) or the most impressive preacher possible. The message validates the messenger rather than the messenger authenticating the message. For Paul, being straight on the gospel of grace is the test of everyone who claims to have a message from God. From his perspective, if people are off here, they are not just nice individuals who

The Church's Greatest Enemies

"The two chief characteristics of the false teachers are that they were troubling the church and changing the gospel. These two go together. To tamper with the gospel is always to trouble the church. You cannot touch the gospel and leave the church untouched, because the church is created and lives by the gospel. Indeed, the church's greatest troublemakers (now as then) are not those outside who oppose, ridicule and persecute it, but those inside who try to change the gospel" (Stott, p. 23).

have imbibed a bit of error. To the contrary, they are dangerous to the very essence of what Christianity is all about. They are in all of their goodness and religiosity "the worst enemies of Christ" (Findlay, p. 46).

The apostle reserves his strongest words for such teachers. Twice in verses 8 and 9 he says "let him be accursed!" The Greek word used for accursed is *anathema*. One expert on the Greek languages claims that *"may he be condemned to hell!* captures the intensity of the original phrase" (Arichea, p. 14).

G. G. Findlay points out that "commentators have been shocked at the Apostle's damning his opponents after this fashion, and have sought to lighten the weight of this awful sentence. It has been sometimes toned down into an act of excommunication or ecclesiastical censure. But this explanation will not hold." Rather, Paul's anathema "contemplates the exclusion of the offenders from the Covenant of grace, their loss of final salvation" (Findlay, pp. 43, 44).

Paul could have used no stronger words. The Galatian heresy was dangerous because both the glory of Christ and the salvation of souls was at stake. To him nothing was more central than the gospel message that justification is by grace alone through faith alone without works of law. The apostle recognized only one gospel, one way to God. Any "good" church member that had a different theology was *anathema* in his eyes.

3. Set Free to Slavery

Galatians 1:10

*¹⁰Now, am I now seeking the favor of men, or of God? Or am I try-
ing to please men? If I were still pleasing men, then I would not be a
slave of Christ.*

Some students of Galatians see verse 10 as the beginning of the long autobiographical section that runs from 1:11 to 2:14, while others regard
it as the concluding remarks of the letter's opening remarks (verses 1-9).
It is best viewed as both, a bridging text that binds the introduction to
what follows.

One translator has rendered the verse's opening question as, "Does this
sound as if I am trying to win man's approval?" (Arichea, p. 15). The obvious answer is no, but, as R.C.H. Lenski observes, "like a flash the questions" in verse 10 "reveal the charges the Judaizers had launched against
Paul in order to discredit him and his gospel. They alleged that Paul toned
down the rigorous legal requirements of the original gospel in order to
gain the approval of the Gentiles, to make the gospel palatable to them, to
curry favor with them. In his ambition to build churches and to gain a
great following he had emasculated the gospel and stripped it of essential
parts. The Judaizers came to Galatia in order to restore the gospel to its
true content. Paul's gospel of liberty was a piece of conscienceless accom-
modation to Gentile reluctance in accepting Jewish law. O yes, the
Judaizers also preached Christ, but in the full legal setting without which
the Galatians could not be saved!" (Lenski, p. 43).

Such were the implications behind the implied accusations of verse

10: "Am I now seeking the favor of men, or of God? Or am I trying to please men?"

And it probably looked to his detractors as if he was trying to please human beings. After all, didn't his philosophy indicate that Paul was willing to be "all things to all men"? (1 Cor. 9:22, RSV). Part of the insinuation might have been that when he was among Jews he taught the need of circumcision and lawkeeping in order to be on their good side. For example, didn't Paul at one time have Timothy, who had a Greek father, circumcised "because of the Jews that were in those places"? (Acts 16:3, RSV). But when he spoke to Gentiles, so the accusation ran, he curried their favor by preaching freedom from circumcision and related Jewish teachings.

Such an accusation intimated that Paul was more of an ecclesiastical politician than a true servant of God, that he was playing the numbers game, and that he sought greater and greater influence. To achieve his goal he attempted to make religion easy. And such an argument made sense from the Pharisaic position of the Jews opposing him (Acts 15:1, 5). After all, normal adult males don't generally stand in line so that they can get circumcised. That being so, circumcision provided a certain and objective test for those who wanted to become a part of the Abrahamic covenant. Yet here is Paul, so eager to be a popular preacher and fill his churches that he ignores the basic sign of God's covenant with His people since the time of Abraham (see Gen. 17:10).

All such accusations and intimations Paul meets with his rhetorical questions of Galatians1:10. The answers to them are obvious. How could anybody that was seeking to please other people meet them with the anathemas of verse 9? The same can be said for much of the rest of the letter. What people pleaser, for example, would address readers as "foolish Galatians" who had been "bewitched" (Gal. 3:1, RSV)?

In actuality, it is the Judaizers who want to please other people. Playing to their audience back home in Jerusalem, they had presented themselves as those who had the "real truth" as opposed to Paul with his wishy-washy emphasis on grace and faith. Such individuals would be heroes to a certain type of Christian who wanted to be faithful to what they saw as the straight testimony of the old ways.

It is the Judaizers who had made things easy in order to curry the praise of other church members. "After all," William Barclay points out, "if religion consists in being circumcised and in fulfilling a mass of rules and regulations, it is, at least theoretically, possible to satisfy its demands. But look what Paul is saying—he is holding up the Cross and he is saying, 'God loved you like that.' And so religion becomes a matter, not of satisfying the claims of law, but of trying to meet the obligation of love. A man can satisfy the claims of law, for they have strict and statutory limits; but a man can never satisfy the claims of love" (Barclay, p. 10).

Put in another way, it is possible to get the victory over diet and bad habits, but it is quite another thing to love all one's enemies all the time and to pray on a regular basis for those who despitefully use us (see Matt. 5:43, 44; Gal. 5:14, 22-24). One of the tragic paradoxes of the Pharisees of all ages is that by uplifting behaviors and rules they have actually lowered the requirements of God's law of love. Thus the church has down through the ages faced Sabbathkeepers, and even vegetarians, who are meaner than the devil. Such church members have the laws and rules and regulations, but they have neglected the foundational principle of the law (Gal. 5:14; Matt. 22:37-40; Rom. 13:8-10). We must never forget that it was strict lawkeepers who put Jesus on the cross because He didn't uphold the Sabbath according to their expectations (Matt. 12:9-14; Mark 2:23-3:6).

One of the sad facts of religious history is that it is those who emphasize certain types of religious obedience who are people pleasers, since humans are tempted to feel a bit of pride even in their religion. That is why Paul added the words "not because of works, lest any man should boast" right after his great saying on salvation by grace through faith in Ephesians 2:8, 9 (RSV). Humans love to boast in their religious accomplishments. But in the shadow of the cross and God's redeeming grace we find no place for boasting (Rom. 4:2) except in the cross of Christ (Gal. 6:14). That truth goes against the Pharisaic spirit so prevalent among the "religious" elite of every church and every generation.

That thought brings us back to Paul who quite frankly states that "if I were *still* pleasing men, then I would not be a slave of Christ" (Gal. 1:10). The word "still" is of particular interest. It implies that there did exist a time when his goal was to please other people. "Before his conversion to Christ," Timothy George writes, "he was on a fast track toward the highest echelons of the Jewish rabbinic establishment. His entire career, including his persecution of the Christians, was designed not only to justify himself before God but also to curry the favor of those in power so as better to advance his own ambitions. But this kind of self-serving, time-serving endeavor was forever shattered when Saul of Tarsus and Jesus of Nazareth collided outside Damascus" (George, p. 100).

The New Testament makes it clear from beginning to end that serving Christ and pleasing other people are diametrical opposites rather than compatible goals: *"If* I were still pleasing men, then I would not be a slave of Christ." It is one or the other. "No one," said Jesus, "can serve two masters" (Matt. 6:24, RSV). By definition a Roman slave could have only one master. Paul knew who his previous master had been (the approval of other people), and he had no doubt as to his new master—Jesus Christ. He had gone through the same conversion experience that each Christian must pass through. To be a Christian is to be a slave of Christ.

Many modern translations seek to soften the word "slave" by rendering it as "servant." But the Greek word *doulos* primarily means "slave." Paul tells us that he is not a hired man working with Christ for wages, but a slave who totally belongs to Him.

It may seem strange that he speaks of being a slave of Christ in a letter emphasizing freedom. In Galatians 4:9 and 5:1, for example, he urges his readers not to return to bondage. Paul's meaning becomes evident as we trace out his logic. "Real freedom," Ragnar Bring asserts, "is not used in such a way as to give an opportunity for the flesh, but rather so that men serve one another in love (5:13). To be a servant of Christ and to serve in love is to be free, free from what really enslaves man: covert slavery to self, to the flesh, to a false use of the law. . . . We may say paradoxically that according to Paul slavery to Christ is not slavery but a total commitment to a power which gives man the greatest freedom he can attain; while freedom from Christ means slavery under all the powers that de facto enslave life. Slavery under Christ can therefore be likened to adoption as sons. Complete commitment to Christ can be likened to a son's entry into his inheritance after he has come of age, and it signifies therefore the most complete freedom (cf. 4:1ff.)" (Bring, p. 36). Freedom in Christ is freedom from the condemnation of the law so that Christians have liberty to serve God and others in the spirit of the law of love (Gal. 5:13-15).

Part II

History: Paul's Authority
as an Apostle of Liberty

Galatians 1:11–2:21

4. The Call of God

Galatians 1:11–16a

> *¹¹I want you to know, brothers, that the gospel preached by me is not according to man. ¹²For I neither received it from a person nor was I taught it, but it came through a revelation of Jesus Christ.*
>
> *¹³For you have heard of my former manner of life in Judaism, how I persecuted the church of God intensely and tried to destroy it. ¹⁴And I advanced in Judaism beyond many of my agemates in my country, being extremely zealous for the tradition of my ancestors. ¹⁵But when God, who had set me apart even from my mother's womb and called me through His grace, was pleased ¹⁶to reveal His Son in me, so that I must preach Him among the Gentiles, I did not immediately consult with flesh and blood.*

Have you ever been unjustly charged? Have you had your motives impugned or your honesty called into question? Such accusations can be devastating, especially when you have willingly given of your time and done your best to tell the truth in your desire to help others. Those who have gone through such an experience can begin to grasp the feelings of the apostle Paul, who realizes that not only is his person being challenged but also the validity of the message that means so much to him.

He responds with a vigorous autobiographical defense in which he hopes to clear both himself and, more importantly, his gospel message. Up through Galatians 1:10 Paul had only mentioned himself once—in verse 1 in which he had introduced himself as an apostle of Christ. But from verse 10 up through Galatians 2:14 he will provide an account of his personal experience from his conversion up to the time of writing as he seeks to disprove the false charges and insinuations of those attacking him.

To Paul the differences between him and his opponents is not some small difference of opinion. It is a matter of life and death without any middle ground. The Judaizers are preaching a false message that by no stretch of the imagination can be considered a gospel at all. Paul has gone so far as to claim that not only is his gospel the correct one, but that it is the *only* one, that believers should judge all other so-called gospels by his.

Such a stupendous claim raises the question of the origin of Paul's gospel. Where did it come from? Did he just dream it up? Or did he get it from the apostles in Jerusalem and then change (pervert) it (the position that the Judaizers seem to hold)?

In verses 11 and 12 he will declare that his gospel came directly from God, a parallel assertion to that of verse 1 in which he stated that his apostleship had its origin straight from God and Christ. His claim has nothing backward or humble about it. As John Stott puts it, his gospel was not "'his' because he had made it up but because it had been uniquely revealed to him." In fact, "his message is not his message but God's message, . . . his gospel is not his gospel but God's gospel" (Stott, p. 30).

But such a claim demands proof. It is to the task of documenting it that he turns in verse 13. As his first line of argument he points to the incontrovertible evidence of the change in his life. No one is on record as being a more violent and persistent enemy of the early Christian church than Paul. He himself claims that he "persecuted the church of God intensely and tried to destroy it" (Gal. 1:13). The word he uses for "destroy" is the same employed to describe utterly sacking a city, while the word I have translated as "intensely" is variously rendered as "violently" (RSV), "savagely" (NEB), "furiously" (Moffatt), and "without mercy" (Arichea, p. 18). It implies "to an extraordinary degree, beyond measure, utterly" (Danker, p. 1032).

The book of Acts backs up Paul's self-evaluation. "Saul," Luke penned, "was ravaging the church, and entering house after house, he dragged off men and women and committed them to prison" (Acts 8:3, RSV). And when the authorities had them put to death, Luke reports Paul as casting his vote against them (26:10). The apostle was never one to do anything in a halfhearted manner.

But why, we need to ask, did he so hate the Christian church? Interestingly enough, his hostility probably centered on the crucifixion of

Jesus. "To Paul as to every other Jew," Ronald Fung writes, "a crucified Messiah [Christ] was not only an insult to his national-political messianic hopes, it was also 'incomprehensible absurdity,' since the Messiah was, almost by definition, one uniquely favored by God (cf. Isa. 11:2), whereas a hanged man was, according to the law, cursed by God (Dt. 21:23). . . . Paul must have seen in the cross the decisive refutation of the claim that Jesus was the Messiah. . . . The crucifixion at once rendered it unnecessary to give any serious consideration to the question of Jesus' messiahship. . . . And [the Christians'] further claim that he was risen could not be treated as anything but criminal deception" (Fung, p. 59).

No wonder the unconverted Paul sought to stamp out the new sect. To his mind they were a deceptive and dangerous band of utter heretics.

Yet now he was willing to give his very life to spread the message he had once sought to destroy. Why? Paul will argue that the change implies an adequate cause.

He will turn to that cause in Galatians 1:16, 17. But first he provides us with a second thumbnail sketch of his past in verse 14, noting that he "advanced in Judaism beyond many of my agemates in my country, being extremely zealous for the tradition of my ancestors." In plain words, *"he had been a fanatic for the law.* The law had been his life; it had been the one object of his study to know it; it had been the one effort of his life to keep it." Yet "now the one dominant centre of his life is *grace"* (Barclay, p. 12).

Once again we must marvel at the transformation. The man who had once destroyed people over issues of the cross, the resurrection, and grace now finds those three concepts at the very center of his existence.

The key word in verse 15 that highlights the change is *"but."* With that word the center of action shifts from what Paul had done (note the "I persecuted" and "I advanced" in verses 13 and 14) to what God had done in verses 15 and 16. In those verses it is God who

- set Paul apart before his birth,
- called him through His grace, and
- revealed His Son to Paul.

Only God could have transformed the strong-minded Saul of Tarsus. And when He did, it not only changed the man but also the history of the Christian church.

In Paul's mind his call was not something that God had done on the spur of the moment. To the contrary, it had all along been His plan to transform Paul's boundless zeal and energy into a ministry for the Gentiles. But when the apostle claims that God had set him apart even from his mother's womb and called him by His grace, Paul was not merely making a statement about himself. Even more importantly, he was rooting his call in the line of succession to the Old Testament prophets. Jeremiah, for example, reports God saying of his own call to ministry, " 'before I formed you in the womb I knew you, and before you were born I consecrated you; I appointed you a prophet to the nations'" (1:5, RSV; cf. Isa. 49:5, 6).

We should point out that the word Jeremiah used for nations is in the Greek version of the Old Testament the same one that Paul employed for Gentiles in Galatians 1:16 in reference to his own call. The parallelism between Jeremiah's (and Isaiah's) call and Paul's reporting of his own call reflects his consciousness that his apostolic call reflected that of God's Old Testament servants.

Two Divine Calls Demonstrating a Continuity of God's Delegated Authority

Jeremiah	Paul
"'Before I formed you in the womb I knew you, and before you were born I consecrated you; I appointed you a prophet to the nations'" (Jer. 1:5, RSV).	"He who had set me apart before I was born, and had called me through his grace, was pleased to reveal his Son to me, in order that I might preach him among the Gentiles [i.e., nations]" (Gal. 1:15, 16, RSV).

Paul's divine call, as noted above, was a summons to service—"that I must preach Him among the Gentiles" (Gal. 1:16). We find an important lesson here. Like Paul, each of us as converted Christians also find ourselves called to serve and to preach Christ in one form or another. Charles Cousar points out that "Paul's conversion and his commission to preach the gospel are not two separate events; they are one. In a single subordinate clause Paul can include God's electing him, calling him, revealing his Son to him, and sending him to the Gentiles." Cousar goes on to note that we as twenty-first century Christians can learn something "about the nature of the faith from the way Paul unites conversion and commission into a single event." In actual fact, none of us are called as Christians who are saved merely to be ministered unto. To the contrary, every Christian is simultaneously called to be saved and to serve others in some form of ministry. From the biblical perspective there are no Christians who are not also commissioned (see Cousar, pp. 33-35).

Thus the New Testament doctrine of the priesthood of the believers implies more than the fact that we have direct access to God's throne without the mediatory function of a human priest (Heb. 4:16). It also means that we have a God-given priestly function for other people. Every Christian in this sense is a minister or servant of God to other people. Every Christian, like Paul, is to preach the gospel to the nations.

5. Not a Churchly Message

Galatians 1:16b–2:1a

[16]I did not immediately consult with flesh and blood, [17]nor did I go up to Jerusalem to those who were apostles before me, but I went away into Arabia, and again I returned to Damascus.

[18]Then after three years I went up to Jerusalem to get to know Cephas and I stayed with him fifteen days. [19]But I did not see any of the other apostles except James the brother of the Lord. [20](Now in what I am writing to you, I assure you before God, I do not lie.) [21]Then I went into the regions of Syria and Cilicia. [22]But I was unknown personally by the churches of Christ in Judea. [23]They only heard that the one who persecuted us now is preaching the faith which he once ravaged. [24]And they praised God because of me.

[1]Then after fourteen years I again went up to Jerusalem.

The teachers from Judea have challenged both Paul's authority and the validity of his gospel message in Galatia. Their main line of attack was to claim "that he dealt in a secondhand gospel, one originally derived from the apostles at Jerusalem but then changed and compromised by Paul without their knowledge or approval" (George, p. 126).

Paul, as already noted, asserted that both his message (Gal. 1:11, 12) and his calling (1:1) came directly from God. But assertion is one thing and proof another. His demonstration of their divine origin follows two lines. In verses 13-16 he argues his direct commission on the basis of his radically transformed life. Then in Galatians 1:16 to 2:1 he focuses on the fact that his biography allows for no time when he could have received instruction from the other apostles.

Paul sets the foundation for his second line of argument by noting that he "did not immediately consult with flesh and blood," that is, with other people (1:16). Next he supports that assertion, as outlined in the box below.

The Logic of Paul's Argument in Galatians 1:16-2:1

1. *Premise:* he did not get his gospel from the Jerusalem apostles.
2. *First* he went to Arabia, then returned to Damascus (verse 17).
3. *Then:* after three years he traveled to Jerusalem, but only for 15 days (verses 18-20).
4. *Then:* he journeyed to Syria and Cilicia (verse 21).
5. *Then:* after 14 years he returned to Jerusalem for a second visit (2:1).
6. *Therefore:* there was no slot of time during which he could have been in Jerusalem for a long enough period for the apostles to instruct him.
7. *Therefore:* the argument of his opponents falls flat. His message came directly from God.

Acts tells us that immediately after his encounter with Christ on the road Paul preached Jesus in the synagogue in Damascus, proclaiming "He is the Son of God," to the amazement of all (9:20, 21, RSV). Thus at the very least his dramatic conversion had taught Paul about the lordship of the resurrected Jesus and something of His grace in reaching out even to such a person as he.

But that outline of a theology was far from adequate. He needed time and space to gain a better understanding of the gospel message. That is where Galatians 1:17 comes in. The natural expectation in such a situation would have been for Paul to return to Jerusalem so that he could meet with the leaders of the church. After all, they had been with Jesus throughout His earthly ministry. They obviously had information and insights that would have enriched his understanding. But he didn't take that route. Instead of conferring with "flesh and blood," he went to Arabia (verses 16, 17).

J. B. Lightfoot points out that "a veil of thick darkness hangs over St. Paul's visit to Arabia" (Lightfoot, p. 87). But we do know one thing about this episode in the apostle's life: his journey might not have been that far since the Nabatean Kingdom of Aretas IV (the Arabia of the time) extended up to Damascus itself.

We can also infer a second bit of information from Paul's cryptic comment. That is, since he reports his trip to Arabia in the context of not conferring with flesh and blood, it is only natural to conclude that he was taking time out to commune with God before he entered more fully into his preaching ministry. Ernest De Witt Burton refers to that conclusion as "almost the only possible . . . implication" (Burton, p. 55).

"The revelation of Jesus as the Son of God," Burton writes, "must at once have undermined that structure of Pharisaic thought which he had hitherto accepted, and, no doubt, furnished also the premises of an entirely new system of thought." Clearly it was not the "work of an hour or a day. The process would have been simpler had the acceptance of Jesus as the Christ been, as it was to some of his fellow Jews, the mere addition to Judaism of the belief that Jesus was the long-expected Messiah; it would have been simpler if the acceptance of Jesus had been to him what it doubtless was to many of his Gentile converts, the acceptance of a new religion with an almost total displacement of former religious views and practices." But "to Paul the revelation of Jesus as the Son of God meant neither of these, but a revolutionary revision of his former beliefs. . . . Only prolonged thought could enable him to see just how much of the old was to be abandoned, how much revised, how much retained unchanged" (*ibid.*, pp. 55, 56) as he sought to develop a form of Christianity that was both faithful to its Jewish roots and meaningful and effective in a Gentile world.

Ellen White reflects the same general opinion as Burton. During his Arabic time apart, she writes, "he calmly reviewed his past experience and made sure work of repentance. He sought God with all his heart, resting not until he knew for a certainty that his repentance was accepted and his sin pardoned. He longed for the assurance that Jesus would be with him in his coming ministry. He emptied his soul of the prejudices and traditions that had hitherto shaped his life, and received instruction from the Source of truth. Jesus communed with him and established him in the faith, bestowing upon him a rich measure of wisdom and grace" (White, *Acts of the Apostles,* pp. 125, 126).

After his Arabian experience, Paul tells us, he returned to Damascus. This may have been the time period in which he so upset the Jews there that they plotted to kill him, and friends had to let him down over the city wall at night in a basket (see Acts 9:23-25; 2 Cor. 11:32, 33).

Only after his second preaching tour in Damascus and some three years after his encounter with God, he explains, did he go to Jerusalem (Gal. 1:18). But that wasn't much of an alternative as far as his safety was concerned. On the one hand, his former Jewish friends would be out for his blood as a traitor. And, on the other, on the basis of his former reputation the Christians might not welcome him. That is certainly true of Acts 9:26's reference to this visit. "And when he had come to Jerusalem," Luke reports, "he attempted to join the disciples; and they were all afraid of him, for they did not believe that he was a disciple" (RSV).

However, his real purpose on his first post-conversion trip to Jerusalem was not evangelism but to visit Cephas (Aramaic for Peter). He probably wanted to reassure him that his persecuting days were over and that he was a true disciple of Christ. The only other leader he met was James, Jesus' brother. James, of course, had not been a follower of Jesus until after the resurrection. But, according to 1 Corinthians 15:7, Jesus had made a special resurrection appearance to James, who was apparently one of the 120 who witnessed the outpouring of the Holy Spirit on the Day of Pentecost (Acts 1:14; 2:1). He soon became a leader in the Jerusalem church (12:17; 15:13; see also Shanks, pp. 93-125). It was undoubtedly significant to Paul that James had also become an apostle, even though he had not been one of the twelve. But Paul's main reason for relating his visit to Jerusalem was to let his readers know that he had already been preaching his gospel for three years, and that, at any rate, 15 days was hardly enough time for Peter to have thoroughly instructed him. Paul saw that information to be so crucial to his argument that he swore an oath that he wasn't lying (Gal. 1:20).

After leaving Jerusalem he went to Cilicia in southeastern Asia Minor. Tarsus, Paul's hometown, was the region's capital (see map on p. 14). On the way he probably preached in Antioch and Damascus (see Acts 9:30; Gal. 1:20). The main point in mentioning that preaching tour was to inform his readers that his stay in Jerusalem had been short, that his exit had been swift due to the Jewish plot to kill him (Acts 9:29, 30), and that he was still personally unknown in Judea, except that the local churches now praised God that he had been truly converted (Gal. 1:22-24).

Paul quickly adds that he did not return to Jerusalem until 14 years later (2:1). It is probable but not certain that he means 14 years after his conversion. But he could mean 14 years after his first trip to Jerusalem. At any rate, the visit of verse 1 is undoubtedly the famine relief visit of Acts 11:29, 30, rather than the council visit of Acts 15, since "it is incredible that if this council had already taken place, Paul should omit all reference to it" in the letter to the Galatians, "where it would have been so relevant" (Morris, pp. 64, 65).

The apostle has made his point in Galatians 1:11-2:1. Not only had his radical transformation on the road to Damascus evidenced his direct apostolic commission from the risen Christ, but so did his lack of any opportunity to get his gospel from the Jerusalem leaders. Thus both his apostolic credentials and his gospel message came directly from Jesus. And, that being so, to reject him and his message was equivalent to spurning Christ Himself.

6. The Search for Unity

Galatians 2:1-10

> *¹Then after fourteen years I again went up to Jerusalem with Barnabas, taking Titus with me also. ²But I went up according to a revelation, and I laid before them the gospel that I proclaim among the Gentiles (but privately to those who seemed to be leaders) for fear that somehow I might be running or had run in vain. ³But not even Titus, who was with me, though being a Greek, was compelled to be circumcized. ⁴But because of false brothers secretly brought in, who crept in to spy out our freedom which we have in Christ Jesus that they might enslave us, ⁵to them we did not yield submission for even an hour, so that the truth of the gospel might remain with you. ⁶But from those seeming to be leaders (what they were matters nothing to me; God does not accept a person's outward characteristics)—those reputed to be leaders added nothing to me. ⁷But to the contrary, they saw that I had been entrusted with the gospel for the uncircumcized, just as Peter had been for the circumcized ⁸(for the One who worked in Peter for an apostleship to the circumcized worked also in me for the Gentiles), ⁹and realizing the grace that had been given to me, James and Cephas and John (those seeming to be pillars) gave to me and Barnabas the right hand of fellowship, that we should go to the Gentiles, but they to the circumcision, ¹⁰only they would have us remember the poor, which very thing I also was eager to do.*

These important verses not only teach us something of the biography of Paul and of his relationship with the Jerusalem apostles, but they reveal to us a great deal about the nature of the church and how those who differ can work together. Beyond that, Galatians 2:1-10 demonstrates that the gospel message is foundational for unity and that we need to evaluate all peripheral issues in terms of the gospel.

Concerning the gospel, John Stott writes that Paul "has shown in chapter 1 that his gospel came from God not man. He now shows in the first part of chapter 2 that his gospel was precisely the same as that of the other apostles; it was not different. To prove that his gospel was independent of the other apostles, he has stressed that he paid only one visit to Jerusalem in fourteen years, and that this lasted only fifteen days. To prove that his gospel was yet identical with theirs, he now stresses that when he paid a proper visit to Jerusalem, his gospel was endorsed and approved by them" (Stott, p. 40).

> **A Comparison of Apostolic Gospels**
>
> 1. Galatians 1 proves that Paul got his gospel independently of the Jerusalem apostles.
> 2. Galatians 2:1-10 demonstrates that this gospel is identical with theirs.
> 3. It is that shared gospel that provides the basis for unity.

Galatians 2:1-10 divides quite naturally into three sections. The first consists of verses 1 and 2, which provide the reason for Paul's trip to Jerusalem. We should note several things about these verses.

First, he tells us that he "went up according to a revelation" (verse 2). That thought is especially important for him to make in his letter to the Galatians. His point is that the "real apostles" did not summon him to Jerusalem so that they could scrutinize his views. No, it was God's revelation that had propelled him toward the Jewish capital.

Second, the purpose of the visit was to lay before the Jerusalem leaders the gospel he had already been preaching to the Gentiles, "for fear that somehow I might be running or had run in vain" (verse 2). It is important to realize that Paul wasn't unsure of his gospel in the sense that he needed human approval. Rather, he feared that the divisive work of the Judaizers might have a destructive impact on his work. Thus it was crucial that he overthrow their influence by demonstrating that he and the Jerusalem apostles were in agreement on the nature of the gospel.

In all of this Paul demonstrates that he is no anarchist who rejects church order—that he is not someone who has a vision of truth and is going to strike out on his own. To the contrary, the apostle believed in church order and in working with other leaders, even when serious differences stood between them.

The third thing that we should observe about Galatians 2:1, 2 is that he took Titus with him. That was no accident. Titus, being an uncircumcized Greek convert to Christianity, would serve as a test case in Paul's struggle against those in Jerusalem who were teaching that "unless you are circumcised according to the custom of Moses, you cannot be saved" (Acts 15:1, RSV).

Such a test case was of great importance to Paul, so much so that the tension within him bursts forth in Galatians 2:1-10 as a "shipwreck of grammar" (Lightfoot, p. 104) as the apostle presents his ideas in fractured sentences. Much for Paul rested on whether the Jerusalem leaders would accept Titus as a full Christian despite the fact that he wasn't circumcised.

Here Paul faced a touchy issue. After all, the Jerusalem apostles had been operating in a Jewish context in which all males were circumcised and had been aligned with the Jewish laws from their birth. The other apostles themselves undoubtedly did not see as clearly as Paul what it meant to preach Christianity in a Gentile context.

As a result, J. B. Lightfoot points out, "Paul is here distracted between the fear of saying too much and the fear of saying too little. He must maintain his own independence, and yet he must not compromise the position of the Twelve. How can he justify himself without seeming to condemn them? There is need of plain speaking and there is need of reserve" (ibid.). One tactic he used in that delicate situation was to speak "privately to those who seemed to be leaders" (verse 2).

Before moving on we should note that the rather strange phrase, "those who seemed to be leaders," surfaces again in verses 6 and 9 and is not meant as a slur on the authority and dignity of the Jerusalem apostles, but rather as a toning down device for his Galatian readers, who had been listening to Judaizers who had practically deified the Jerusalem apostles to Paul's detriment. Once again Paul asserts that his own apostolic office is on a par with the Jerusalem leaders.

Galatians 2:3-5 forms the second segment of the passage running from verses 1 to 10 and deals with the circumstances related to the struggle over the attempt of the "false brothers" (verse 4) to have Titus circumcised. Paul will finally gain the approval of the Jerusalem leaders on that point, but only after what must have been a strenuous struggle. As Paul put it, he "did not yield submission" to the Judaizing party "for even an hour" (verse 5). But circumcision wasn't the real issue for him. Rather, it was that "the truth of the gospel might remain with you" (verse 5). That was the deeper issue. As Stott observes, the "matter of fundamental importance" had to do with the "truth of the gospel, namely, of Christian freedom versus bondage. The Christian has been set free from the law in the sense that his acceptance before God depends entirely upon God's grace in the death of Jesus Christ received by faith. To introduce the works of the law and make our acceptance depend on our obedience to rules and regulations was to bring a free man into bondage again. Of this principle Titus was a test case. It is true that he was an uncircumcised Gentile, but he was a converted Christian. Having believed in Jesus, he had been accepted by God in Christ, and that, Paul said, was enough. Nothing further was necessary for his salvation, as the Council of Jerusalem was later to confirm (see Acts 15)" (Stott, p. 43).

Paul was overjoyed with the consequences of the Jerusalem meeting. The third segment of Galatians 2:1-10 finds the "pillar" apostles extending to him and Barnabas the right hand of fellowship and entrusting them with the primary responsibility of mission to the Gentiles while the Jerusalem leadership focused on the mission to the Jews (verses 6-10). The "only" of verse 10 is significant in the sense that it indicates that the Jerusalem leaders had no problem with Paul's gospel message. But as they parted they did want him to remember the poor among the Jewish believers, a task that Paul will devote much time to (see, e.g., Rom. 15:26; 2 Cor. 8:1-4; 9:1, 2). For him such caring was a natural outflowing of the law of love (Gal. 5:14).

And what can the church of the twenty-first century learn from Paul's experience in these passages? For one, we need to recognize that the unity of the international church is important. But, second, we need to understand more clearly that such unity does not have its basis in absolute agreement in every detail, but from agreement on the core essentials of the biblical message centering on the gospel and its outworking in the Christian life (as the last four chapters of Galatians will illustrate).

On that second point Richard Longenecker writes that "Christians today also need to understand that there can be differences among true believers, and that such differences—particularly when involving differing understandings of redemptive logistics or differences of culture—need not tear us apart. Indeed, where there exists a basic agreement in the essentials of the gospel, Gal 2:1-10 sets before us a prototype of mutual recognition and concern for one another, despite our differences. It teaches us, in fact, something of how to distinguish between things that really matter and things of lesser importance (the so-called *adiaphora*), where to stand firm and where to concede, and even when to defy people and pressures and when to shake hands and reciprocate with expressions of mutual concern" (Longenecker, p. 62).

And what had the meeting accomplished?

"Paul," James Montgomery Boice writes, "has done the following:

"(1) recognized the position and authority of the Jerusalem apostles without diminishing his own authority in the slightest;

"(2) indicated, in opposition to the exaggerated claims about them made by the legalizers, that the apostles were men after all and hence not always perfect in their initial reactions or conduct;

"(3) decisively separated the gospel and policies of the Twelve, for all their weaknesses, from the gospel and policies of the legalizers; and

"(4) taken note of the fact that he and the Twelve, rather than the legalizers and the Twelve, stood together" (Boice, p. 443).

Paul himself had had to learn some of those lessons. For example, when the Judaizers sought to "compel" Titus to be circumcised he resisted mightily. On the other hand, he had Timothy circumcised "because of the Jews" (Acts 16:1-3). Why the difference in his reactions between the cases of Titus and Timothy? With Titus Paul was struggling for recognition that Gentiles did not need circumcision to become justified Christians. The issue had been settled in Galatians 2:1-10 and ratified by the Acts 15 council. After those events, no one had ground anymore to "compel" anyone to be circumcised in order to be justified. That battle had been won. As Stott puts it, "once a vital principle of gospel truth had been established, Paul was willing to make policy concessions" on a voluntary basis (Stott, p. 44). That was especially true in regard to mission. Paul knew where the center of the gospel was, and he was willing to bend on those issues that did not threaten that center. He was also quite aware of the nature of the mission of the church. And he could be flexible on the non-essentials in order to accomplish that mission.

Many people in the church today need to learn from Paul the lesson of principle-based flexibility. Too many think that every hill is a hill worth dying on. And the church is too often a shambles because it's members lack the virtue of discretion that Paul so ably exemplified.

7. Refusing to Be Intimidated

Galatians 2:11-13

[11]But when Cephas came to Antioch, I opposed him to his face, because he stood condemned. [12]For before certain ones came from James he had been eating with the Gentiles. But when they came he drew back and separated himself, fearing those of the circumcision group. [13]And all the rest of the Jews joined with him in hypocrisy, so that even Barnabas was carried away by their hypocrisy.

It is easier to sing about daring to be a Daniel and "standing by a purpose true" than it is to live such a life. Such was Peter's case in Galatians 2:11-13.

The scene shifts from Jerusalem to Antioch. Verses 9 and 10 had closed with harmony established between Paul and Barnabas and the Jerusalem leadership. The latter had extended the right hand of fellowship and there seemed to be a mutual understanding.

But the trouble was not at an end. The next few verses lead to one of the most tense episodes in the New Testament as two foremost apostles face off in open conflict. Paul writes that he had to oppose Peter to "his face" in public (verse 11).

This time the trouble arose over Jews sharing a meal with Gentiles rather than over circumcision. But at bottom the two issues had one basis—the belief of some of the stricter Jews that Gentiles must first become Jews before they could be full members of the Christian church.

The immediate context for the crisis of Galatians 2:11-13 involves the fact that early Christians often shared meals together. In Acts 2, for example, we read that on a daily basis the believers were "breaking bread" together and that they "partook of food with glad and generous hearts" (verse 46, RSV). At other times they joined in the Lord's supper. Such practices offered a powerful illustration of the oneness of God's church in Christ.

But they were not without problems. After all, the Jerusalem Christians were Jewish by birth. Shared meals with a Gentile was a different issue.

That issue came into the open in the increasingly Gentile congregations in Syria and Asia Minor. The difficulty was that the Jewish people under the leadership of such groups as the Pharisees had come to see themselves as more and more exclusive, so much so that a strict Jew would not do business with Gentiles, must not eat with them, and so on. Even to touch a Gentile, they believed, made them ritually unclean.

Peter had earlier held to such rigid separationist views. But God had given him a special revelation on that very topic. In Joppa he had had a vision in which a sheet full of unclean creatures came down from heaven. He then heard a voice saying, "Rise, Peter; kill and eat." When he objected he was told that "what God has cleansed, you must not call common." The vision repeated itself three times for emphasis. Soon afterward Peter accompanied a Roman centurion's servants to his Gentile—and thus, from the rigid Jewish perspective—unclean home. Upon arriving Peter said, "You yourselves know how unlawful it is for a Jew to associate with or to visit any one of another nation; but God has shown me that I should not call any man common or unclean." After preaching to those Gentiles that "every one who believes in [Jesus] receives forgiveness of sins through his name," he baptized them (Acts 10:13, 15, 28, 29, 43, RSV).

Through that vision the disciple obtained victory over his discriminatory views. But when he got back to Jerusalem he came under fire from the "circumcision party," who "criticized him, saying 'Why did you go to uncircumcised men and eat with them?'" He successfully defended himself on the basis of the vision and the fact that the Holy Spirit had been poured out on the Gentiles the same as it had been on the Jews at Pentecost (Acts 11:1-18). That got Peter off the hook temporarily, but the powerful circumcision party remained unconvinced.

Peter, however, had been convicted on the topic. That shows up in Galatians 2:12, in which we read that he "had been eating with the

Gentiles." The imperfect tense of the Greek verb indicates that such meals had been a regular practice. He hadn't forgotten the lesson of Acts 10.

But the story takes an ugly twist when "certain ones came from James." At that point Peter reverted to his old ways and separated himself from the Gentiles (verse 12).

Why, we must ask, did a man of Peter's stature as an apostle and prophet abandon his new practice? Certainly not because he had forgotten the lesson of Acts 10. The more probable factor was fear, his special failing. "Cowardice," H. D. McDonald writes, "was Peter's besetting sin." Here, as in the Garden of Gethsemane, Peter once again "shrinks from open declaration of a truth he had already acknowledged" (McDonald, p. 52). His actions here, Oscar Cullmann suggests, "may fit the psychological picture we get from the Synoptic Gospels—the picture of the impulsive disciple Peter, over-zealous in swearing loyalty to his Lord and yet denying him in the hour of danger" (Cullmann, p. 51).

But what did he have to fear? People! Representatives of the same powerful circumcision party that had challenged him in Acts 11. The fact that they "came from James," however, doesn't mean that James agreed with them, but rather that they claimed to have his authority. Acts 15:13-21, in which he essentially sides with Paul will soon make James' own position clear.

But even the threat of trouble in his home congregation is enough to set Peter off in the wrong direction. The last thing he wants is to have people accusing him of toning down the Christian message. Those powerful spokesmen for the "straight truth" of the old ways are enough to strike fear in his heart. He is definitely intimidated.

And Peter's response stampedes the rest of the Jewish Christians at Antioch in the same direction. All break off table fellowship with their Gentile brothers and sisters in the faith. Paul could hardly believe it, but *"even Barnabas* was carried away by their hypocrisy" (Gal. 2:13). The fear of being held accountable for going against Jewish tradition had utterly intimidated everyone.

All, that is, but Paul. In a flash he saw three things clearly. First, as A. M. Hunter points out, if the church followed Peter's example "Jewish Christianity and Gentile Christianity would" go "their own separate ways, and the ideal of one Church of the living God, one Body of Christ, would have been stifled at birth!" (Hunter, p. 23). Or, as John Stott succinctly puts it, "either the whole Christian church would have drifted into a Jewish backwater and stagnated, or there would have been a permanent rift between Gentile and Jewish Christendom, 'one Lord, but two Lord's tables'" (Stott, p. 52).

A second thing that Paul recognized was that Peter's action threatened the gospel of justification by faith. In this case the disciple had not denied the gospel in his teachings but rather through his actions. At bottom the issue was the same as it was in the case of circumcision. Either justification by faith was sufficient to become a Christian or one had to become Jewish before one could be a full member of the body of Christ. Thus Paul realized that Peter's hypocrisy undermined the very heart of the gospel itself.

> ### The World Still Needs Pauls
>
> "The greatest want of the world is the want of men—men who will not be bought or sold, men who in their inmost souls are true and honest, men who do not fear to call sin by its right name, men whose conscience is as true to duty as the needle to the pole, men who will stand for the right though the heavens fall" (White, *Education,* p. 57).

The third thing that Paul realized was that immediate and forceful action was needed if crisis was to be averted. As a result, he publicly confronted Peter to his face (Gal. 2:11). As William Barclay notes, Paul "did not wait; he struck. It made no difference to him that this drift away was connected with the name and conduct of Peter. It was wrong, and that was all that mattered to Paul. A famous name can never justify an infamous action. Paul is the vivid example of the one strong man who by his steadfastness could check a drift away from the right course before it became a tidal wave" (Barclay, pp. 19, 20).

But, we find ourselves forced to ask, wouldn't a private rebuke have been wiser? Doesn't open conflict between leaders damage the church unnecessarily? "Perhaps," suggests Hunter, "but in this case the wrong had been public and was notorious, and the only remedy was a public remonstrance" (Hunter, p. 23).

In closing, we should note three reasons why Paul included his public confrontation in his letter to the Galatians. First, the incident further clarifies that Paul was not a lesser apostle than those from Jerusalem. None of them had the authority to change the gospel. And anybody who did could be challenged. Second, the report of the incident reinforces the message of Galatians 2:1-10 that only the gospel provides the foundation for Christian unity. And third, the account paves the way for Paul's transition to "the themes of justification by faith and dying with Christ" that will dominate the heart of the epistle (Cousar, pp. 49, 50).

8. One Gospel for All

Galatians 2:14-21

[14]But when I saw that they were not walking a straight path with respect to the truth of the gospel, I said to Cephas before all, "If you, being a Jew, live like a Gentile and not like a Jew, how is it that you compel the Gentiles to live like Jews? [15]We are Jews by nature and not Gentile sinners, [16]yet knowing that a person is not justified [i.e., made right with God] by works of law but through faith in Jesus Christ, even we have believed in Christ Jesus so that we might be justified by faith in Christ and not by works of law, since by works of law no flesh will be justified. [17]But if in seeking to be justified in Christ we ourselves have been found to be sinners, is Christ then a minister of sin? Certainly not! [18]For if I build again what I had destroyed, then I prove myself to be a transgressor. [19]For I through law died to law that I might live to God. I have been crucified with Christ; [20]it is no longer I who lives but Christ who lives in me. And that life which I now live in the flesh, I live by faith in the Son of God, who loved me and gave Himself for me. [21]I do not reject the grace of God; for if justification is through law, then Christ died for no purpose."

This passage is not the easiest to understand. It is even "difficult to decide at what point Paul's quotation of his rebuke to Peter comes to an end and passes into his general exposition of the principle at stake" (Bruce, p. 136). Some conclude the quotation at the end of verse 14, others at the end of verse 16, and yet others at the end of verse 21. That latter option seems best, since it takes into account that Paul has a well-crafted argument that extends from verse 14 up to the end of the chapter.

The reason that most people find verses 14-21 to be so difficult is that they fail to see their purpose in their context. Most of us are tempted to approach them as a discussion of how a person is justified—by faith rather than works.

But that is *not* what Paul is doing. He is *not* speaking to how an individual is saved even though what he says certainly informs our understanding of salvation by faith. Rather, he is addressing a *social issue* between Jews and Gentiles. As Charles Cousar observes, "Paul's statements on justification arise out of his reflection on and defense of the Gentiles' entrance into the church, not out of his reflection on the question of how personal guilt is alleviated. . . . The context is a social setting. The specific point Paul wants to make in that context is that God's favorable judgment in Christ means by its very nature that Gentiles are included in the Christian community on no different level or no different terms than Jews. Both belong at the same table. To put it in negative terms, treating Gentiles as second-class citizens by withdrawing from the common meals" rests upon a form of justification by works (i.e., circumcision and the keeping of other Jewish customs) and is thusly a "form of justification by works and thus a denial of the gospel. What Peter fails to recognize at Antioch is that Jews can be justified only together with Gentiles" (Cousar, pp. 56-58). If anything more than faith is required then Christ died in vain (Gal. 2:21).

The issue raised is a serious one. The roots for it go back to the meeting between Paul and the Jerusalem apostles in Galatians 2:1-10, which in effect had implied that "the Jews would go on living like Jews, observing circumcision and the law, but that the Gentiles were free from these observances" (Barclay, p. 20). Obviously, the matter couldn't continue on like that, since it would eventuate in two quite different and mutually exclusive forms of Christianity. The issue came to a head when Peter removed himself from table fellowship with the Gentiles in Galatians 2:11-13. With that all-important context in mind we can begin to unpack the logic of verses 14-21 step by step.

1. Verse 14 begins Paul's message to Peter. In effect, he is saying, Peter, "you shared the table with the Gentiles; you ate and lived as they ate; therefore you approved in principle that there is one way for Jew and Gentile alike. How can you now reverse your whole decision? You were quite willing to live like a Gentile; and now you have swung round, and you want the Gentiles to be circumcised and take the law upon them and

become Jews" before you eat at the same table with them (Barclay, p. 21). That made no sense to Paul.

2. In verses 15 and 16 he is saying to Peter that even though they were both born as Jews (verse 15), they had both come to agree on two points. First, that no person (Jew or Gentile) could be justified or made right with God through human effort or works of law. Second, they had shared the conviction that the only way to be justified was by faith in Jesus Christ (verse 16).

If that is so, the argument implies, then what role does circumcision and other Jewish observances play? The obvious answer is none. The plain fact is that all people, both Jews or Gentiles, receive justification in exactly the same way. On what grounds, therefore, is there a need to separate at meals? None, is once again the only conclusion.

3. Verse 17 shifts Paul's argument away from his exposition of how both Jews and Gentiles are justified by faith and into a defense against one of the major arguments leveled at him by those who focused on the law. His firm rejection of salvation by works of any kind raised the fear among some that he had no concern for upright living. Or, put somewhat differently, "since Christ does not insist on good works as a condition of salvation, does that not mean that he encourages sin?" (Morris, p. 87). Paul rejects that suggestion with an explosive "certainly not!"

4. As verse 18 teaches, it won't do to go back to a belief in some sort of salvation by works, which he and Peter had both rejected. That position had been destroyed, since the law can point out sin, but it cannot save (see Rom. 3:20-25). All the law did for Paul was prove him to be a transgressor. But it also, he will later explicitly note, pointed him to Christ and the true way of salvation (see Gal. 3:23-25).

5. That thought brings Paul to an absolutely crucial point in his argument in Galatians 2:19, 20: His union with Christ did not lead to disobedience, but of Christ living out His principles in Paul's life.

In short, Paul had gone through a total transformation. He had died to law keeping as the way to justification. That temptation had been crucified (verse 19). But, as in Romans 6:1-8, there had also been a resurrection to a new way of life. It was Christ who was now living out His life and His principles through the apostle. Thus the life Paul now lived was one embedded in faith "in the Son of God, who loved me and gave Himself for me" (Gal. 2:20, RSV).

In order to understand fully Paul's teaching in verses 16-20, we need to have a fuller grasp of his view of justification. Too often people have described it merely in terms of a law court that condemns people or declares them guilty, but then justifies or declares them not guilty or righteous.

That solution is true as far as it goes, but it does not take in Paul's full usage of the word. Justification or righteousness (they are the same word in Greek) in Jewish thought is a covenant concept. Thus to be righteous means that a person is in a right relationship with God. In the Old Testament, Alister McGrath notes, righteousness or justification is much more than an impersonal standard of justice; it is a *personal concept:* "it is essentially the *fulfillment of the demands and obligations of a relationship between two persons.* . . . To be 'right with God,'" therefore "is to trust in his gracious promises and to act accordingly" (McGrath, pp. 24, 28; cf. Knight, *Pharisee's Guide,* p. 94). That relationship aspect underlies one of Paul's key phrases in Romans: "the obedience of faith" (Rom. 1:5; 16:26, RSV). In short, obedience does not lead to a saving relationship with Christ, but it does *flow out of it* as Christ lives out His life in us (Gal. 2:20). Justification, for Paul, always leads to ethical living. He has set up the entire book of Galatians on that basis with chapters 3 and 4 highlighting justification by faith and chapters 5 and 6 focusing on the ethical outcome of saving faith. For too long have theologians concentrated on the distance between justification and sanctification in Paul's writings. A careful reading of his works demonstrates their connection rather than their separation (see Cousar, p. 60; Knight, *I Used to Be Perfect,* pp. 41-56).

6. But Galatians 2:21 demonstrates that just because a close connection exists between justification by faith and ethical living by faith does not mean that we should confuse them or lump them together. On that point Paul is quite clear in his final assertion to Peter in Galatians 2:21. Grace is the only way for Paul, "for if justification is through law, then Christ died for no purpose." The only reason He died is because humans could not attain to righteousness by their own efforts. His substitutionary death, as Paul sees it, was an absolutely essential part of the plan of salvation. That being so, all people—both Jew and Gentile—are justified through faith. No other way exists. As a result, there is only one fellowship table, and Peter and his associates were dead wrong in separating themselves. Doing so undercut not only equality before God in justification but the very nature of the church itself.

Part III

Theology: Justification by Faith as the Basis of Christian Liberty

Galatians 3:1–4:31

9. Bewitched Believers
and the Sin of Goodness

Galatians 3:1-5

¹O foolish Galatians, who has bewitched you, before whose eyes Jesus Christ was publicly portrayed as crucified? ²This is only what I want to learn from you: Did you receive the Spirit by works of law or by hearing with faith? ³Are you so foolish? Having begun by the Spirit, are you now ending in the flesh? ⁴Did you experience so many things in vain?—if it was really in vain. ⁵Therefore, does He who provides you the Spirit and works miracles among you do so by works of law or by hearing with faith?

You crazy Galatians! Did someone put a hex on you? Have you taken leave of your senses? Something crazy has happened, for it's obvious that you no longer have the crucified Jesus in clear focus in your lives. His sacrifice on the Cross was certainly set before you clearly enough" (Gal. 3:1, Message).

No matter how you translate it, Paul's cry to the Galatians in chapter 3 is anything but pleasant. This is the first time since Galatians 1:11 that he has personally addressed them. But in chapter 1 he used "brothers." Here his approach to them is much less endearing, a symbolism that sets the tone for what is to follow.

To put it bluntly, the apostle is deeply discouraged with his Galatian converts. And the reason is not difficult to discover. They were in danger of doing the very thing that he had seen as the ultimate heresy in his closing words to Peter. By even thinking of adding circumcision and other Jewish requirements to faith as the way of becoming right with God (justified) they were nullifying the grace of God and making the death of Jesus meaningless (Gal. 2:21).

In Galatians 3:1-5 Paul appeals to the Galatians' own experience to substantiate his point that justification is by faith alone. Without the slightest doubt he believed that they had had a genuine conversion experience in which they had grasped both the significance of the cross and had received the Holy Spirit. He now urges them to remember *how* they had become Christians.

His forceful greeting in which he called them "foolish" undoubtedly got their attention. The Greek word used here is *anoētos* and not *mōros*. If he would have employed *mōros* (from which we get moron) he would have been claiming that the Galatians were mentally deficient. By way of contrast, *anoētos* "puts the emphasis not on natural stupidity but on failure to use one's mental and spiritual powers" (Arichea, p. 53). As Timothy George reminds us, "no one can read the Letter to the Galatians without realizing that Paul presupposed a high level of intellectual ability on the part of his readers. The Galatians were not lacking in IQ but in spiritual discernment. They were like the disciples on the road to Emmaus whom the risen Christ characterized as 'foolish *[anoētos]* . . . and . . . slow of heart to believe all that the prophets have spoken' (Luke 24:25)" (George, p. 206).

The word "foolishness" was a wake up call for the Galatians. In contemporary parlance he was telling them to get their act together. Unfortunately, that call has continued to be needed throughout Christian history. Paul would have the same startling address for many church members in the twenty-first century. Many still don't see clearly the true center of their faith and they still teach that we must add works to faith to find acceptance with God. All such in Paul's terminology are "foolish."

And why are they foolish? Because they recognize neither the depth of human weakness nor the meaning of Christ's sacrifice on the cross. But the Galatians should have had no problem on those points. After all, in the apostle's preaching he had "publicly portrayed" the crucified Christ (Gal. 3:1). The Greek word translated as "publicly portrayed" indicated the posting of important notices on a placard in a public location for all citizens to read. To Paul "the conduct of the Galatians is inexplicable because the true gospel has been so clearly preached to them" (Boice, p. 453). "The phrase 'Jesus Christ crucified,'" Ronald Fung points out, "concisely summarizes the decisive event in salvation history and, as such, the fundamental content of the Pauline [message]. If only the Galatians had fixed their eyes on that placard, it would have enabled them to escape the fascination of the false teachers" (Fung, p. 129).

One of my most memorable mental images is that of a painting I saw in Luther's church in Wittenburg, the home of the Protestant Reformation. It depicts the Reformer preaching. But he is not facing the congregation. The congregation, meanwhile, listens intently but its members are not looking at Luther. Both Luther and his parishioners have their eyes focused on Christ on the cross. The painting reminds me of Paul's preaching to the Galatians. Christ was the focal point. So He needs to be in our preaching today. And when we truly see what the cross of the crucified Christ means in our lives it will shield us from the false teachers in the church of our day just as it would have protected the Galatians from the Judaizers 2,000 years ago. A correct vision of the cross is still the only antidote for the problem of bewitchment.

In Galatians 3:2 Paul moves from appealing to the Galatians to focus on their experience with the crucified Christ, to their experience with the Holy Spirit. In the process he makes it plain that Christians receive the Spirit at the beginning of their experience. As Leon Morris puts it, "the gift of the Holy Spirit is not reserved for those who have made great progress in the Christian faith, but is a gift conferred on every true beginner" (Morris, p. 96). John 3:5, which teaches that true believers are born both "of water and the Spirit" (RSV), reinforces that truth. Paul doesn't question whether the Galatians had received the Spirit. That God had bestowed it on them at conversion was a given for him. But he does question them as to whether they received the Spirit by works or by faith. Their own experience, he argues, should have taught them that God had granted the Spirit to them as a gift through faith and not as a result of something that they had personally done.

Again in Galatians 3:3 Paul suggests that the Galatians were foolish. Or as the *Revised English Bible* puts it, "Can you really be so stupid?" He implies that they had probably not thought through the position that they were in danger of accepting. To prod their thinking on the topic he asks another rhetorical question: "Having begun by the Spirit, are you now ending in the flesh?" "Evidently," writes Charles Cousar, "part of the appeal of the agitators to the Gentile Christians in Galatia was the notion that circumcision with all it symbolized was like icing on the cake. It completed and even perfected the freedom of the gospel. Paul, however, declares such a move to be a fatal step backwards" (Cousar, p. 67). The flesh can add nothing to God's gift. In fact, works of the flesh actually negate the divine gift itself. To Paul the Galatians were indeed foolish on this topic.

We should note in passing that verse 3 is the first time in Galatians that the apostle contrasts the works of the flesh and the gift of the Spirit. He will do the same in Galatians 5:18-23, but there the works of the flesh are such things as idolatry, strife, and drunkenness. In Galatians 3:3, by contrast, the works of the flesh are such things as circumcision. Circumcision is hardly the same type of sin as licentiousness or drunkenness, but for Paul all of them constitute works of the flesh. What we need to realize is that "the more sinister enemies of the faith are not always the obviously irreligious practices of the world but often the potent forces of morality and religion which operate within" the church (ibid.). In fact, the sin of goodness is probably more destructive of true Christianity than those evil acts that we usually regard as sin. Why? Because a person who does an evil thing feels the need to repent, but those who commit vegetarian sins merely assume that they are better than other people. But from Paul's perspective in Galatians 3 there is no more deadly sin than adding good actions to God's saving grace, since such actions "nullify the grace of God" and make a mockery of Christ's sacrifice (Gal. 2:21, RSV).

A Lesson on the Works of the Flesh

Evil Works of the Flesh "	_Good" Works of the Flesh_
"Sexual immorality, impurity sensuality, idolatry, sorcery, enmity, strife, jealousy, fits of anger, rivalries, dissensions, divisions, envy, drunkenness, orgies, and things like these" (Gal. 5:18-21, ESV).	Circumcision, and other _good religious practices_ that seek to add human merit to God's grace in justification (Gal. 2:21–3:3).

The lesson that the Galatians (along with most contemporary church members) need to learn is that the good churchly sins are more deadly to Christianity than the evil ones, because they erode its very heart.

The good news of Galatians 3:1–5 appears in verse 4, in which Paul suggests that perhaps their past experience hadn't been in vain. It isn't too late. They can still wake up and exchange their foolishness for God's wisdom.

10. The Abraham Lesson

Galatians 3:6-9

> *⁶Just as Abraham "believed God and it was accounted to him as righteousness," ⁷even so understand that those of faith are descendants of Abraham. ⁸The Scripture, foreseeing that God would justify the Gentiles [or nations] by faith, preached the gospel beforehand to Abraham, saying, "All the nations will be blessed in you." ⁹So those of faith are blessed with the believing Abraham.*

The lesson of Abraham is central to Paul's argument in his epistle. For one thing, all Jews regarded him as the father of their people. If Paul's Judaizing opponents looked toward Moses as their teacher in the Galatian controversy, then Paul would go several centuries back to Abraham. A second important thing about Abraham is that he received circumcision as the sign of God's covenant with his descendants (Gen. 17:9-14). Thus the Jews saw themselves as his heirs in both a religious and an ethnic sense. No one in Jewish thinking was more important than "Father Abraham." Thus he makes an excellent example for Paul to use in his argument.

The Judaizers, following the Jewish understanding of Abraham, also saw the patriarch as a crucial element in their argument. John Ziesler writes that the fact that both here and in Romans 4 Paul concentrates so heavily on Abraham may suggest that his opponents customarily made use of his example. In effect, Ziesler pictures the Judaizers as saying, "'Abraham is the father of the people of God, and if you Gentiles wish to be within that people you must not only have faith in Christ but also follow the example of Abraham and accept circumcision and what is implied in it, the observance of the will of God as conveyed by the Torah. If it was good enough for Abraham it is certainly good enough for you'" (Ziesler, p. 34).

The problem between Paul and the Judaizers centered on two divergent understandings of Abraham's acceptance with God. To grasp the impact of the apostle's use of Abraham we need to remember that the Jews firmly held that the patriarch had been justified (accounted righteous) by works. Basing their thoughts upon Genesis 26:5 (that God blessed Abraham because "Abraham obeyed my voice and kept my charge, my commandments, my statutes, and my laws," RSV) the Jews reasoned that he "kept the entire Torah [law] even before it was revealed"(m. Qiddushin 4:14). Again, in the Jewish book of Jubliees we read that "Abraham was perfect in all of his actions with the Lord and was pleasing through righteousness all of the days of his life" (Jubilees 23:10). The Prayer of Manasseh mentions that Abraham, Isaac, and Jacob didn't need to repent to God because they were righteous and "did not sin against you" (Prayer of Manasseh 8). Again, the Wisdom of Sirach states that "Abraham was the great father of a host of nations; no one has ever been found to equal him in fame. He kept the law of the Most High; he entered into a covenant with him, setting the mark of it on his body. When put to the test he proved steadfast" (Wisdom of Sirach 44:19, 20). In short, in traditional Jewish thought Abraham's justification had resulted from works.

In response to that line of thinking, Paul quotes from Genesis 15:6. Abraham "'believed God and it was accounted as righteousness'" (Gal. 3:6). Here we need to recall the circumstances of that verse. Abraham and Sarah were old and childless, but God had promised that he would have a son, and the Lord assured him that his descendants would be as many as the stars in the sky (Gen. 15:4, 5). Against all odds, Abraham "believed the Lord; and he reckoned it to him as righteousness" (verse 6, RSV).

Clearly Paul is using Genesis 15:6 to prove that Abraham was counted righteous by faith rather than works. But, Dieter Lührmann points out, the understanding of the text "looks different . . . when one reads the text for itself and then inquires into its transmission through Jewish tradition" (Lührmann, p. 56). In 1 Maccabees 2:52, for example, we find the following quotation: "Did not Abraham prove faithful under trial, and so win credit as a righteous man?" That passage changes the idea of faith into faithfulness or a meritoriousness that deserved a reward. Again Rabbi Shemaiah, who lived about 50 B.C., represents God as saying: "The faith with which their father Abraham believed in me merits that I should divide the [Red] sea for them, as it is written: 'And he believed in the Lord, and he counted it to him for righteousness'" (see Knight, *Walking With Paul*, p. 98).

Thus the Jews by the time of Paul had consistently interpreted Abraham's faith as a type of merit-earning faithfulness. In short, they saw it in terms of good works.

Paul was aware of that line of thought. He also knew that it was wrong and needed to be overturned, a task that he would later devote himself to undertaking in greater detail in Romans 4:4-8. But in Galatians 3 he merely asserts the fact that it was faith as belief in God rather than faith as action for which God counted Abraham as righteous. Thus "to his opponents . . . Paul in effect replies, 'If faith and faith alone was good enough for Abraham, it certainly ought to be good enough for the Gentiles'" (Ziesler, p. 35). Therefore, he sums up in Galatians 3:7, it is "those of faith" who are the true "descendants of Abraham." Here the apostle has reached an important conclusion, since in Galatians 2 the core struggle was really over who constituted the people of God and were thus worthy of table fellowship and, by extension, full membership in the Christian community. Paul has been asserting that it is those who have faith in Christ even though they have not become Jews, while his opponents have been arguing that the children of Abraham are only those who have been circumcised as he was and who hold to the Jewish customs.

Having established the point from Genesis 15:6 that those who constituted Abraham's true children were those who had righteousness by faith, Paul in Galatians 3:8 cites Genesis 12:3 to prove that the Gentiles were to be blessed through Abraham: "'All the nations will be blessed in you.'" It is important in understanding this second Genesis quotation to realize that the word translated as nations is also the Greek word for Gentiles. Thus Paul has demonstrated from the Jewish Scripture that Abraham is not only the father of those who have faith within the covenant, but also of those of every nation who have faith. That is, he is the spiritual father of both Jews and Gentiles, who have both been justified or counted righteous on the basis of faith alone. In God's eyes they are not two groups or two diverse varieties of Christians, but one body unified in their justification through faith. There is only one way to get right with God. And that one way is the basis for defining who is in Christ and what the church is.

There are at least three things that we can learn from Galatians 3:1-9. First, the nature of the gospel. "The Pentateuch [five books of Moses]," Charles Cousar summarizes, "does not offer two ways of salvation—one based on human performance in keeping the commandments and another based on a divine activity to which humans respond by faith. The law from the beginning has indicated only one way of salvation, and that is something done by God and not by humans. The person who *really* keeps the law realizes that the law can never justify and so puts his trust in the faithfulness of God. Paul's complaint with the agitators in Galatia is not that they devote too much attention to the law, but that they read it wrongly and distort its meaning. . . . They fail to hear that the law [the writings of Moses] contains a promise of the gospel" (Cousar, pp. 74, 75).

The second thing that the first part of Galatians 3 teaches us is what the gospel offers. Verse 8 sums up that topic with the word blessing. "It is," John Stott points out, "a double blessing. The first part is justification (verse 8) and the second is the gift of the Spirit (verses 2-5). It is with these two gifts that God blesses all who are in Christ. He both justifies us, accepting us as righteous in His sight, and puts His Spirit within us" (Stott, p. 74).

Finally, we discover from our passage what we have to do to receive the blessing of the gospel. "The proper answer is 'nothing'! We do not have to do anything. We have only to believe. Our response is not 'the works of the law' but 'hearing with faith,' . . . believing the gospel" (*ibid.,* p. 75).

11. The Way of Law
Versus the Way of the Cross

Galatians 3:10-14

[10]For all those who rely on works of law are under a curse. For it is written, "Cursed is everyone who does not abide by all things written in the book of the law, to do them." [11]Now it is evident that no one is justified before God by law, because "The righteous will live by faith." [12]But the law is not of faith. To the contrary, "The one who does these things will live by them." [13]Christ redeemed us from the curse of the law, becoming a curse for us—because it is written, "Cursed is everyone who hangs on a tree"—[14]that in Christ Jesus the blessing of Abraham might come to the Gentiles, that we might receive the promise of the Spirit through faith.

Galatians 3:10-14 finds Paul in the midst of the most intense argument from the Jewish Bible in all of his writings. In verses 6-9 he cited the Old Testament two times, and he will quote it four more times in verses 10-14. From his perspective he is in a death struggle with an aggressive body of Jewish Christians thoroughly rooted in Old Testament teachings. Paul knows that the only way he can win his case and demonstrate the correctness of his position to his Galatian converts is to beat the Judaizers on their own ground. As a result, he permeates his response with Old Testament quotations.

Paul forms his argument around two Old Testament passages that contain the word "will live by" (Gal. 3:11, 12). The first, "'The righteous will live by faith,'" appears in verse 11 and cites Habakkuk 2:4, while the second, "'The one who does these things will live by them,'" is found in verse 12 and is taken from Leviticus 18:5.

The apostle skillfully weaves his argument around each of those passages and comes up with what we might call *the two ways to life*. In the process, as William Barclay points out, Paul seeks "to drive his opponents into a corner from which there is no escape" (Barclay, p. 27).

Galatians 3:10-14 begins with the path of getting right with God through law keeping. He is speaking to "all those who rely on works of law." In his discussion Paul sets up a chain of reasoning built on Old Testament quotations. "'Suppose,'" suggests Barclay as he leads us into Paul's argument, "'you do decide that you are going to take the course of trying to win God's favour and approval by means of accepting and obeying the law, suppose you do try to get into a right relationship with God that way, what, then, is the logical inevitable consequence?'" *(ibid.)*.

First, the premise runs, you must stand by your decision. You can not straddle the fence here. If you choose the way of law, you will have to live by the law (Gal. 3:12). And not just part of it—you will have to "abide by all things written in the book of the law, to do them" (verse 10).

The Inescapable Logic of Paul on the Inadequacy of the Law

1. A person who seeks righteousness by the law must keep all of it (Gal. 3:10, 12).
2. No human has successfully kept all of it (implied in Galatians, but demonstrated in Rom. 3:1-18, 23).
3. Thus all are under the curse of the broken law (Gal. 3:10).
4. Therefore, the way of the law is the way of the curse.

Second, it is impossible to keep all of the law. No one has ever done it. People have tried, but all have failed. Paul doesn't dwell on this point in Galatians—rather, he merely assumes it. But he does so on excellent Old Testament grounds. In Romans, in which he does develop the argument, he quotes six passages from the Jewish Bible that demonstrate that none have attained righteousness through the law (Rom. 3:11-18), that "all have sinned and fall short of the glory of God" (verse 23), and that no one will be justified by law keeping because the very purpose of the law is to point out sin rather than to save people from it (verse 20). Thus, even though Paul doesn't argue the universality of failure to keep the law in

Galatians 3, he doesn't fear any contradiction, given its strong Old Testament support.

That assumption leads the apostle to his third point: If all have failed in observing the law, then all are under condemnation. After all, doesn't Deuteronomy 27:26 teach that everyone who fails to keep *everything* that the law teaches is cursed? (see Gal. 3:10).

The conclusion is plain enough for all to see: "The logical and inevitable end of trying to get right with God by making law the principle of life is a curse" (Barclay, pp. 27, 28). Paul wanted that conclusion to stand out clear and plain in the minds of his Galatian converts.

Having exhausted the keeping the law leads to being right with God logic, Paul sets forth the alternative from Habakkuk 2:4: " 'The righteous will live by faith' " (Gal. 3:11). The passage's original context is of interest. The prophet Habakkuk had complained that God was using the ruthless Babylonians to punish Israel for their sinful ways. How could that be? How could God use the wicked to punish the wicked? God then told Habakkuk that the proud Babylonians would eventually fall, but that the righteous among the Israelites would live by their faith through their humble and consistent trust in His power and mercy.

Paul's Argument on the Way of Faith

1. The alternative to the way of law is the way of faith (Gal. 3:11).
2. But faith in what? The objective basis of faith is the substitutionary atonement of Christ who became a curse for us (3:13).
3. For Paul the curse of sin has no other solution.

Paul took Habakkuk's passage and applied it to salvation from sin. In short, though it is impossible to gain righteousness through obedience, it is possible to do so by simple trust in God: " 'The righteous will live by faith.' "

Just as the way of law approach to getting right with God has an inherent chain of logic, so also does the way of faith approach. If point one in the chain of faith approach is that "the righteous will live by faith," the second point in the logic chain is the question, Faith in what?

The apostle is more than happy to answer that question—it is nothing short of the gospel itself. But before we go to his solution, we need to recall the problem.

1. All people have failed in keeping the law.
2. Therefore all people have fallen under the curse of the penalty of the broken law. All deserve death (cf. Rom. 6:23). There appears to be no way out.

But, Paul retorts, there is an escape: "Christ redeemed us from the curse of the law" by "becoming a curse for us" (Gal. 3:13). In short, Christ died in our place. As Ellen White so nicely put it, "Christ was treated as we deserve, that we might be treated as He deserves. He was condemned for our sins, in which He had no share, that we might be justified by His righteousness, in which we had no share. He suffered the death which was ours, that we might receive the life which was His. 'With His stripes we are healed'" (White, *The Desire of Ages*, p. 25). Martin Luther would refer to that transaction as the "great exchange." And Paul would speak of it to the Corinthian church when he wrote that "for our sake he made him to be sin who knew no sin, so that in him we might become the righteousness of God" (2 Cor. 5:21, RSV).

Martin Luther on the "Great Exchange"

Writing to a monk in distress about his sins, Luther admonished: "Learn Christ and him crucified. Learn to pray to him and, despairing of yourself, say: 'Thou, Lord Jesus, art my righteousness, but I am thy sin. Thou hast taken upon thyself what is mine and hast given to me what is thine. Thou has taken upon thyself what thou wast not and hast given to me what I was not'" (Luther, *Letters*, p. 110).

To Paul the substitutionary atonement was the very heart of the gospel. For him Jesus was truly "the Lamb of God, who takes away the sin of the world" (John 1:29, RSV). Jesus as the Lamb of God was to Paul the only valid object of the faith that makes men and women right with God. Benjamin Warfield caught that vision when he wrote that the vicarious, substitutionary sacrifice of Christ provides the fundamental distinctiveness of Christianity. "Christianity did not come into the world to proclaim a new morality," but to present the Christ who died for our sin. "It is this which differentiates Christianity from other religions" (Warfield, p. 425).

It is in the cross of Christ that Paul finds the remedy to the curse of the penalty of the broken law: "Christ redeemed us from the curse of the law" by "becoming a curse for us" (Gal. 3:13). Christians enter into their redeemed state through faith and faith alone (3:11; 2:16). Through faith in the crucified Christ they receive "the blessing of Abraham" which not only includes being made right with God but "the promise of the Spirit" (3:14).

12. The Abraham Covenant

Galatians 3:15-18

> [15]*Brethren, I speak in terms of a human example; even with a human will [or covenant], no one can annul it or add to it once it has been ratified. [16]Now the promises were spoken to Abraham and to his offspring. He does not say, "And to offsprings," referring to many, but concerning one, "And to your offspring," which is Christ. [17]I mean this: the law, which came 430 years later, does not invalidate a covenant that had previously been ratified by God, so as to nullify the promise. [18]For if the inheritance is by law, it is no longer by promise. But God had given it to Abraham by promise.*

Not all biblical passages are equally easy to understand, and Galatians 3:15-18 is one of the more challenging ones. Part of the reason for its difficulty is that it uses rabbinic forms of argumentation rather than the kind of reasoning that makes sense in our culture.

But we can grasp the meaning of verses 15-18 more easily if we remember where the apostle has been in his argument. Verses 6-9 make it absolutely clear that Abraham was justified by faith and that the promise that came through Abraham to the Gentiles was based on faith. "So then," Paul concludes, "those who are men of faith are blessed with Abraham who had faith" (Gal. 3:9, RSV).

If that is so, what about the way of law that the Judaizers have taught as a method to get right with God? In verses 10-14 Paul argued that the way of the law brought nothing but a curse. But that is where the gospel of Christ enters. Christ took the curse of the broken law on Calvary's tree so that the promise of Abraham might come to the Gentiles through faith.

But, some might be asking, what is the place of the law? Where does it fit into God's plan? Paul will dedicate Galatians 3:15-25 to answering such questions.

The first segment of his response appears in verses 15-18. Undergirding the passage in his mind is the relationship of Abraham, through whom came the promise, and Moses, through whom came the law. Paul is arguing for the superiority of the way of Abraham (the path of faith) over the way of Moses (the path of the law).

But all such dialogues have an inherent problem. "After all, the God who gave the promise to Abraham and the God who gave the law to Moses are the same God! . . . We cannot set Abraham and Moses, the promise and the law, against each other, accepting the one and rejecting the other. . . . If God is the author of both, He must have had some purpose for both. What, then, is the relation between them?" (Stott, p. 87).

Galatians 3:15-18 argues the negative aspect of the relationship between promise and law—namely, that the coming of the law did not annul the promise of God. Verses 19-25 (see sections 13, 14) will treat the positive side of the topic.

The general aim of verses 15-18 is quite clear, even if the argumentation does not reflect modern reasoning. Paul's purpose is to demonstrate the superiority of the way of faith and grace over the way of law as a means of getting right with God.

His first line of attack is to point out the fact that the way of faith is older than the way of law. That is not difficult to demonstrate since Abraham preceded Moses by some 430 years. While some students get sidetracked by the exact referents of the 430 years, his point is crystal clear: that the promise through faith preceded the formal giving of the law at Sinai by a long period of time.

So what? That's obvious, you may be thinking. That is where Paul's argument regarding human wills comes in. He recognizes that it is merely a human example (verse 15) and thus not an exact parallel with God's acts, yet he believes that it throws light on the topic. His argument builds in the following way:

- A human will cannot be annulled or added to once ratified. The only person who can add to it or change it is the testator, the one who drew up the stipulations of the will in the first place.

- The law, which arrived 430 years after the promise, did not alter the previous agreement or covenant in any way (3:17). It couldn't. That was not its purpose.
- Therefore, the inheritance is still by promise and not by law.

It is the promise to Abraham—the covenant with him—that is absolutely central to Paul in Galatians 3. He first raised the topic in verse 8: "In you shall all the nations of the earth be blessed" (RSV), citing Genesis 12:2, 3. Then in Galatians 3:16 he referred to the promise of Genesis 13:15 and 17:7, 8, on which he bases his (to us) rather strange argument of offspring (seed) rather than offsprings (seeds). "And," we read, "I will establish my covenant between me and thee and thy seed after thee in their generations for an everlasting covenant, to be a God unto thee, and to thy seed after thee" (Gen. 17:7, KJV). After making the point, in good rabbinic style, that Genesis uses the singular rather than the plural, Paul goes on to claim that that singular descendant is Christ (Gal. 3:16).

Paul knew, of course, that the literal reference of the promises in Genesis was to Abraham's physical

> ## Some Thoughts on the Law and the Promise
>
> "God's promise to Abraham was a serious undertaking. It is not to be set aside by the fact that hundreds of years later God gave Israel a law which would be their guide as they sought to serve him. Paul is not denying the validity of the law. He is not saying that Jews ought not to take it as their guide and seek to keep its many provisions. Those God-given provisions showed them the way they ought to live. But he is saying quite firmly that those provisions did not provide a path by which they could merit salvation" (Morris, pp. 111, 112).

descendants, who were to receive the land of Canaan. Thus most translations render the Hebrew word in Genesis 17:7 as "descendants" (so RSV), even though the original word is a singular. But it is a "collective singular" (Dunn, p. 183) that could be translated as either a plural or a singular. Thus even though the promise was for Abraham's many physical descendants (as many as "the dust of the earth" [Gen. 13:16, RSV]) the apostle "knew that this did not exhaust its meaning; nor was it the ultimate reference in God's mind. Indeed, it could not have been, for God said that in

Abraham's seed all the families of the earth would be blessed. . . . Paul realized that both the 'land' which was promised and the 'seed' to whom it was promised were ultimately spiritual. God's purpose was not just to give the land of Canaan to the Jews, but to give salvation (a spiritual inheritance) to believers who are in Christ" (Stott, p. 88).

G. Walter Hansen helps us grasp the wider implications of the use of the singular of descendant or seed when he writes that "we have to realize that Paul's definition of *seed* contradicts the Jewish nationalistic interpretation of this term. Jews were convinced that the term seed referred to the physical descendants of Abraham, the Jewish people. Therefore they believed it was absolutely necessary to belong to the Jewish nation in order to receive the blessings promised to Abraham" (Hansen, pp. 97, 98). That logic, of course, formed the rationale as to why Gentile Christians needed to be circumcised and observe the law of Moses in order to be right with God.

But the way Paul employed seed in Galatians 3 is a bit more complex than just the fact that its use in the singular referred to Christ. In verse 29 we read that "if ye be Christ's, then are ye Abraham's seed, and heirs according to the promise" (KJV). Thus, Hansen points out, "Christ, the one seed of Abraham, includes within himself a new community of all believers where there are no racial, social or gender divisions." The promised seed of Abraham becomes "the center of a new unity" (*ibid.,* p. 98).

As a result, the qualifying factor for belonging to God's community is not circumcision but faith in Christ. That faith alone puts people into a right relationship with Him.

Paul binds off his argument in verse 18 by writing, "for if the inheritance is by law, it is no longer by promise. But God had given it to Abraham by promise." The apostle's argument has no middle ground. The inheritance comes either through law or through promise rather than through some combination of the two. In the end "Paul stakes his case on the theological axiom that salvation is always, first to last, a matter of divine initiative and grace. The point is strengthened by the idea of inheritance . . . , since the disposition of an inheritance is wholly in the hands of the testator" (Dunn, p. 186). The means of getting right with God is always His gift (Gal. 3:18).

And that is good news for not only the Galatians of old but to us in the twenty-first century. Not endless deeds but faith in Christ who became a curse in our place on the cross of Calvary (verse 13) will alone put us in right relationship with God. To have faith is to be in the path of Abraham with whom God established His covenant of faith.

13. Another Look at Law

Galatians 3:19-22

> *[19]Why then the law? It was added because of transgressions, until the descendant should come to whom the promise had been made; having been ordained by angels through the agency of a mediator. [20]Now a mediator is not needed if there is only one, and God is one.*
>
> *[21]Is the law then against the promises of God? Certainly not; for if a law had been given that was able to give life, then righteousness would indeed be by law. [22]But the scripture imprisoned everyone under sin, so that the promise by faith in Jesus Christ might be given to those who believe.*

Galatians 3:6-9 has made it clear that faith justified Abraham and that God's promise to Abraham was grounded in faith. Next, in verses 10-14 Paul argued that the broken law leads to a curse but that Christ absorbed it on the cross for those who have faith in Him.

Those points are clear. But they also raise a question. If faith is everything in getting right with God, then what is the point of the law? Paul treats that question in verses 15-25. In the first segment of his answer the apostle contrasts promise and law chronologically and demonstrates the superiority of the way of faith and grace over the way of law as a method of getting right with God.

The significance of Paul's main point appears to be clear enough for all his readers to grasp. But that very point has left them with some important questions that need answering. The first question surfaces in verse 19: "Why then the law?" In that verse Paul seems to put words into the mouths of his detractors. Their thought process runs something like the following. If, as he argues, faith is the only way to get right with God, where does the law come in? What is its function? The implied answer of the Judaizers is "nowhere," that Paul's emphasis on faith has left no room for the law, and that his gospel has totally eclipsed the law. That very accusation would later surface in Jerusalem where certain Jews from Asia Minor pointed Paul out as "the man who is teaching men everywhere against the people and the law" (Acts 21:28, RSV).

But, Paul is quick to point out, that is far from his position. Rather, it is a caricature of it. The law, he notes, "was added because of transgressions" (Gal. 3:19). Here for Paul is a major purpose of the law, though he doesn't make his point in Galatians as clearly as he does in Romans. In Romans 3:20, for example, we read that "through the law comes knowledge of sin" (RSV). Again, he writes that "if it had not been for the law, I should not have known sin" (7:7, RSV). And in Romans 4:15 he adds that "the law brings wrath, but where there is no law there is no transgression" (RSV). George Duncan sharpens the point of Paul's argument a bit when he observes that "'transgression' *[parabasis]* and 'sin' *[hamartia]* are in Paul always to be distinguished. . . : men may *sin* in ignorance, but they *transgress* only when they have a recognized standard of what is right, and it was to provide such a standard that the Law was brought in" (Duncan, p. 112). Thus the law not only identifies sin in a general sense but also the more precise category of transgression.

That truth, however, does not exhaust Paul's teaching in Galatians 3:19. He goes on to say, "until the descendant should come to whom the promise had been made." Here we find the apostle tying the purpose of the law to the role of Christ in a way that he will not clarify until verses 22 to 25. But even in verse 19 it is clear that the law and its exposure of transgressions in some way leads us to Christ.

Martin Luther caught that idea when he wrote that "the law then can do nothing, saving that by his light it lighteneth the conscience that it may know sin, death, the judgment and the wrath of God. Before the law come [sic], I am secure: I feel no sin: but when the law cometh, sin, death and hell are revealed to me. This is not to be made righteous, but guilty and the enemy of God, to be condemned to death. . . . The principal point therefore of the law" is to "sheweth unto them their sin, that by the knowledge thereof they may be humbled, terrified, bruised and broken, and by this means may be driven to seek grace, and so to come to that blessed Seed" (Luther, *Commentary,* p. 316).

Thus the Judaizers are dead wrong in their evaluation of Paul's theology. Just because a person is saved by grace through faith does not mean that the law is unnecessary, "for he was quite clear that it had an essential part to play in the purpose of God. The function of the law was not to bestow salvation, however, but to convince men of their need of it. To quote Andrew Jukes, 'Satan would have us to prove ourselves holy by the law, which God gave to prove us sinners'" (Stott, pp. 89, 90).

Paul's point in the first part of Galatians 3:19 is clear enough even though the last part of that verse and all of verse 20 remains obscure. Of verse 20 J. B. Lightfoot in the nineteenth century remarked that the number of interpretations ranged somewhere between 250 and 300 (Lightfoot, p. 146). By 1953 that estimate, in a play on verse 17, had grown to 430 (Ridderbos, p. 139). In spite of that ambiguity, however, Paul's point in verse 19 is clear.

Galatians 3:21 raises a second question that Paul anticipates from the Judaizing party: "Is the law then against the promises of God?" His reply is a resounding "certainly not." As he saw it, law and promise had complimentary functions—they worked together. The law pointed out sin and drove sinners to the promise in Christ for forgiveness from the curse of the broken law (3:10-14).

It is impossible for the law to be against the promise, because God gave both to His people. Law and promise have *different functions,* but that does not make them contradictory. The purpose of law is to point out sin, while that of promise is to provide the solution to the sin problem. The two have a complementary relationship.

Interestingly enough, Paul implies in verse 21 that it was the Judaizers who pit the law over against the promise in their claim that salvation comes through law. His answer to that proposition he sets forth in the second half of verse 21, in which he writes that "if a law had been given that was able to give life, then righteousness would indeed be by law."

That is a crucial point for us to understand, especially since so many in our day teach that in the Jewish dispensation people were justified through law keeping, but that since Christ came humanity is saved by grace. Paul will have none of such arguments. For him it has always been impossible to be justified before God by obeying the law. That was never its proper function. As Lewis H. Hartin put it, "whatever Paul is teaching in Gal. 3:19-25 he is not teaching the doctrine of a pre-Christian era of salvation by law versus a Christian Era [sic] of salvation by grace" (Nichol, vol. 6, p. 958).

Paul caps off his argument of verses 19-22 in verse 22 in which he writes that "the scripture imprisoned everyone under sin, so that the promise by faith in Jesus Christ might be given to those who believe." The verse presents two key ideas. The first is that everyone is imprisoned under sin. Here the apostle probably has Deuteronomy 27:26 in mind, which he had quoted earlier in Galatians 3:10: "'Cursed is everyone who does not abide by all things written in the book of the law, to do them.'" Two of Paul's clearest teachings in Romans are that "all have sinned and fall short of the glory of God" (3:23, RSV) and that "the wages of sin is death" (6:23, RSV). Here in Galatians 3 he merely phrases the same thoughts in a different manner when he claims that everyone is imprisoned under sin.

> ## Law and Gospel Are Complementary Rather Than Contradictory
>
> "The law should not be viewed as contradictory to the gospel. By reducing all to the level of sinners, the law prepares the way for the gospel. But neither should law be viewed as if it were the same as the gospel. The law has a negative purpose: it makes us aware of our sin. But it does not, indeed it cannot, set us free from bondage to sin. The promise of blessing comes only through faith in Christ" (Hansen, p. 106).

Fortunately, he also sets forth the solution to that predicament—faith in Christ. To Paul that was the only way that anyone throughout history could ever be saved from sin. It was true in his day, and it's true in ours. Sin has always been a jailer, and Christ has always been the one to set us free. It is not the acquiring of merit by doing good things that releases us from the jailhouse of sin, but our expression of faith in Christ and what He did for us on the cross (Gal. 3:13).

14. Salvation's Social Results

Galatians 3:23-29

23But before the faith came, we were kept under law, being imprisoned in regard to the faith about to be revealed. 24So then the law was our guardian to lead us to Christ, so that we might be justified by faith. 25But the faith having come, we are no longer under a guardian. 26For all of you are sons of God through faith in Christ Jesus. 27For all who were baptized into Christ have put on Christ. 28There is neither Jew nor Greek, there is neither slave nor free, there is neither male nor female, for all of you are one in Christ Jesus. 29And if you are Christ's, then you are Abraham's descendant, heirs according to promise.

Galatians 3:23-29 in one sense brings to a climax an argument that started with Peter's breaking off table fellowship with Gentile believers back in Galatians 2:12. Part of Paul's response to Peter was his argument that faith rather than law justified both Jews and Gentiles. Thus they belonged to the same community of faith and should eat from the same table despite the historical distinctions that had separated them one from another (see 2:16-21 and section 8). In chapter 3 Paul has expanded upon that theme. His argument will reach its climax in verses 26 to 29 in which he concludes that for Christians there are no racial or social distinctions since God has rescued all from sin in the same manner—through faith in Christ.

But before coming to the apex of his argument Paul will visit the proper function of the law once more in verses 23 to 25. In verse 23 he again pictures the law as a jailer (cf. verse 22). But in verse 24 he puts forth a new image. There he suggests that the law is a "guardian to lead us to Christ, so that we might be justified by faith."

In the guardian metaphor we have a more positive image of the law's task than that of jailer. The guardian was not the teacher or schoolmaster as suggested by the King James Version. Rather the *"paidagōgos* [guardian] was a slave employed in Greek and Roman families to have general charge of a boy in the years from about six to sixteen, watching over his outward behaviour and attending him whenever he went from home" (Burton, p. 200). The *paidagōgos* was not the teacher but one who led the young person to the teacher in order to get the proper instruction.

Thus "Paul is saying that the law was not the teacher that makes clear the way of salvation." Rather "it was the leader, which, properly followed, . . . could do no more than show them that they had need of salvation and it pointed to the One who would bring salvation" (Morris, p. 119). The law, therefore, had a quite restricted function.

But the central element in Paul's discussion of the law in verses 23 through 25 is that the law had a preliminary function. Verse 23 has a phrase indicating that it had the jailer function until the faith was revealed, while verse 25 explicitly states that "the faith having come, we are no longer under a guardian." The emergence of "the faith" in both verses in their overall context is a reference to the coming of faith in Jesus or the gospel (see verse 22).

F. F. Bruce appears to be correct when he notes that "the 'coming of faith' . . . may be understood both on the plane of salvation-history and in the personal experience of believers" (Bruce, p. 181). On the level of salvation-history the reference to the coming of faith equates with the incarnation of Christ, who died to remove the curse of the broken law (Gal. 3:13). But that does not mean that no one before that time had faith (see Hebrews 11). Rather it means that the appearance of Christ finally revealed the object of saving faith.

On the personal level the coming of faith in the lives of believers "coincides with their abandonment of the attempt to establish a righteous standing of their own, based on legal works, and their acceptance of the righteousness which comes by faith in Christ" (Bruce, p. 181).

On both the salvation-history and personal levels the law loses its guardian function when faith arrives (Gal. 3:25). That was true once for all for the Jewish nation when Christ died for the world's sins. But on the personal level the loss of the guardian function may take place repeatedly. When one accepts Christ's grace by faith that role ceases *until* a person steps out of a relationship with Him. At that very point the law again resumes its guardianship responsibility, points out the person's fault, and seeks to lead him or her back to a faith relationship with Christ.

Verse 26 begins to take Paul's argument a giant step forward when it claims that all become "sons of God through faith in Christ Jesus." Here is truly a radical idea for the Jewish mind. In Jewish thinking the children of God were the literal descendants of Abraham, those who both had the promise and who kept the law. Circumcision was the outward sign of being a son of God. But now Gentiles, Paul claims, are sons of God through faith.

Paul's position in verse 26 also contradicts much modern teaching, which asserts that all human beings are God's children. The Bible declares that He created everybody but it does not apply the universal fatherhood of God to all humanity. To the contrary, His children are those who have faith in Christ. In that teaching Paul agrees with John who claimed that "to all who received him, who believed in his name, he gave power to become children of God; who were born, not of blood nor of the will of the flesh nor of the will of man, but of God" (John 1:12, 13, RSV; cf. John 3:5, 7; Rom. 8:14-17).

Galatians 3:27 ties the rite of baptism to coming to faith in Christ when it claims that "all who were baptized into Christ have put on Christ." It is important to recognize that the apostle is not arguing that we become children of God through baptism. After all, John Stott asserts, "it is inconceivable that Paul should now substitute baptism for circumcision and teach that we are in Christ by baptism! The apostle clearly makes *faith* the means of our union with Christ. . . . Faith secures the union; baptism signifies it outwardly and visibly" (Stott, p. 99).

In verses 28 and 29 Paul leads his readers to the apex of the argument that began with the breakdown of table fellowship between Jews and Gentiles in Galatians 2:12. On the basis of the fact that all—both Jews and Gentiles—are justified by faith alone without works of law (see 2:16), Paul asserts that "there is neither Jew nor Greek, there is neither slave nor free, there is neither male nor female, for all of you are one in Christ Jesus. And if you are Christ's, then you are Abraham's descendant, heirs according to promise."

Here is the point that Paul has been driving toward. In effect he is claiming that "the new vertical relationship with God results in a new horizontal relationship with one another" (Hansen, p. 112).

In one fell swoop Paul erases for believers the great social divisions of race, rank, and sex in the church. He does not mean that distinctions no longer exist, but rather that they no longer matter in the sense that they no longer create barriers to fellowship among believers. For Jews Paul's teaching was particularly revolutionary because it reversed the sentiments of the prayer offered daily by Jewish males in which they thanked God that He had not made them a Gentile, a slave, or a woman. "Paul's argument," G. Walter Hansen reminds us, "is that Gentiles do not have to become Jews to participate fully in the life of the church. Neither do blacks have to become white or females become male for full participation in the life and ministry of the church" *(ibid., p. 113)*.

Many in the twenty-first century church will find Paul's teaching just as threatening as the Judaizers of old. After all, Bruce notes, "no more restriction is implied in Paul's equalizing of the status of male and female in Christ than in his equalizing of the status of Jew and Gentile, or of slave and free person. If in ordinary life existence in Christ is manifested openly in church fellowship, then, if a Gentile may exercise spiritual leadership in church as freely as a Jew, or a slave as freely as a citizen, why not a woman as freely as a man?" (Bruce, p. 190). The implications for the church of Paul's logic are extensive indeed. The social ramifications of salvation by grace do not stop at the frontier between Jew and Gentile.

In Galatians 3:29 Paul returns to the theme of promise that had occupied him in verses 6-9 and 15-18. It was never far from his mind that God promised Abraham that the Gentiles (i.e., nations) would be blessed through the patriarch (verse 8; Gen. 12:3) and that he was counted righteous because of his faith rather than his works (verse 6; Gen. 15:6; cf. Rom. 4). The true heirs of God's promise to Abraham, his true descendants, are those who have faith in Christ rather than those who just have a blood relationship. With that conclusion Paul toppled the argumentative structure of the Judaizers. But he isn't finished with the implications of Abraham for Christians yet. He will continue to flesh out the topic in Galatians 4.

15. The Gift of Adoption

Galatians 4:1-7

> *¹Now I say, for as long as the heir is a minor, he differs nothing from a slave, even though he is owner of everything. ²But he is under guardians and administrators until the date set by the father. ³So we also, when we were minors, had been enslaved under the elemental things of the universe. ⁴But when the fullness of time came, God sent forth His Son, born of a woman, born under law, ⁵so that He might redeem those under law, that we might receive adoption. ⁶And because you are sons, God has sent forth the Spirit of His Son into our hearts, crying, "Abba! Father!" ⁷So you are no longer a slave but a son; and if a son also an heir through God.*

Galatians 4:1 is in one sense a continuation of the last verse of chapter 3 with its conclusion that "if you are Christ's, then you are Abraham's descendant, heirs according to the promise." The word that joins the two passages together is "heirs."

The apostle has a special purpose in that linkage. Chapter 3 ended with the high status of those who had accepted Christ by faith. They were no longer under bondage to earning their own way through the law. Having accepted God's gift, they had become members of God's family.

But a threat lurked here—one that was then affecting the Christians in Galatia. In a word, they were in danger of falling away from their experience of faith and returning to some form of seeking to earn their justification—the very thing that the Judaizers were pressing on them.

In the face of that peril, Paul in Galatians 4:1-11 follows a line of logic which argues that "to submit now [after having accepted Christ's justification by faith] to the rule of the law was to turn the clock back . . . , and so to return to a more limited and unnecessarily restricted status before God" (Dunn, p. 209).

In order to achieve his purpose, the apostle presents his argument in two stages:

1. A recapitulation in Galatians 4:1-7 of the final section of Galatians 3:23-29, in which individuals moved from being under the custody of the law to being full children of God and heirs of God's promise.
2. A warning in verses 8-11 not to turn back to the "weak and impoverished elemental things" by which they had lived prior to their conversion.

We will treat the first stage (verses 1-7) in the current section and verses 8-11 below in section 16.

Verses 1-7 employs an approach that Paul uses more than once (see, e.g., Eph. 2:1-10). It begins with his readers' discouraging previous condition and concludes with their privileges now as people in Christ. He joins the two parts by an all-important transitional "but" that highlights the contrast.

Galatians 4:1-3 describes believers in terms of their minority. Paul notes that they are truly heirs to the promise but that they do not yet have full rights. In fact, their condition is no better than that of a slave, even though they potentially own everything (verse 1). The apostle, of course, knows that they are not really in the same state as slaves. After all, heirs have a hope when they reach maturity that slaves don't have. But Paul's point is that "both, the minor and the slave, lack the capacity of self-determination" (Betz, p. 203).

Verses 1 and 2 paint a picture of a man who had died but who had left a will leaving his property to his minor son with the provision that the boy would be under guardianship until he reached a predetermined age. Until that time his guardians would have charge of his overall life and adminis-

> **Paul's Line of Thought in Galatians 4:1-7**
>
> 1. Before accepting Christ by faith you were like minors "enslaved under the elemental things of the universe" (verses 1-3)
>
> BUT
>
> 2. Now through Christ you have been set free and are children of God with the full rights of those who have come to maturity (verses 4-7).

trators would have the narrower responsibility of overseeing his business matters (see Ramsay, pp. 391, 392).

It is just such a condition, Paul argues, that people were in before they found Christ: "We were minors, . . . enslaved under the elemental things of the universe" (Gal. 4:3). The Greek word translated as "elemental things" is an important one that shows up again in verse 9, in which it plays a key role in Paul's appeal to his Galatian readers. Unfortunately, its exact meaning is unclear. It can signify either rules or regulations (Rogers, p. 428) or "the widespread belief in the Hellenistic world that human destiny was controlled by nonhuman forces" (Cousar, p. 92), such as the stars and other heavenly bodies. Both interpretations have linguistic evidence for them and both even find support in the context of Galatians 4. But the decisive factor in favor of interpreting the word as the spiritual forces behind the world appears in verse 8, which speaks of the Galatians having served "those things that by nature are not Gods."

The surprising fact of the passage, Charles Cousar points out, is that "Paul equates life under the law with bondage 'to the elemental spirits of the universe'" (Cousar, p. 93). The apostle apparently held that going back to the old Jewish system with its circumcision and cultic calendar (see verse 10) was equivalent to returning to paganism in terms of its enslaving results. Both systems were false since they both fell short of the way of faith, the only way to get right with God.

Galatians 4:4 begins with what H. D. McDonald calls "one of the decisive 'buts' of scripture" (McDonald, p. 93). That "but" marks a new beginning with the arrival of Jesus,

- sent forth by God at the right time,
- "born of a woman,
- "born under law,
- "so that He might redeem those under law,
- "that we might receive adoption" (verses 4, 5).

Verses 4 and 5 are bursting with meaning. First, the coming of Jesus was no accident. God was working out His purpose in world history. It was at the "fullness of time" that "God sent forth His Son." "The fullness of time" phrase occurs nowhere else in the New Testament, but we do find a close parallel in Mark 1:14, 15, which reports that "Jesus came into Galilee, preaching the gospel of God, and saying 'The time is fulfilled, and the kingdom of God is at hand; repent, and believe in the gospel" (RSV). Daniel 9:24-27 has preserved time prophecies that help us grasp the meaning of "the fullness of time." Discussing the 70 weeks of years, the passage indicates the moment for the coming of "the Messiah the Prince," who would "make reconciliation for iniquity," and "bring in everlasting righteousness" (KJV). The Babylonian Talmud (see b. Sanhedrin 97a, b) has preserved some discussion on the topic.

Galatians 4:4 not only tells us that Jesus was sent at the right time, but also that He became fully human ("born of a woman") at the incarnation, and that He was born Jewish ("born under law") in line with the Old Testament prophecies related to the fact that the Messiah would come through the line of both Abraham and David (see Matt. 1:1). Only by being part of that line could He be the "offspring" who would bring the blessing of Abraham to the Gentiles (Gal. 3:14-18).

Galatians 4:5 goes on to tell us that Christ will do two things for those who accept Him. First, he will "redeem those under law." Redeem is a term from the marketplace. It means to purchase or to buy. Paul uses the word when he speaks of Christ paying the price to free individuals from their enslavement to sin. The price of course was His sacrifice on Calvary, where "Christ redeemed us from the curse of the law," becoming a curse for us on the cross (3:13, RSV).

The second thing that Christ did was to adopt those who had been redeemed from the curse of the broken law (4:5). We noted in section 14 that people get adopted into the family of God when they accept Christ's gift to them by faith (see 3:26; John 1:12, 13; Rom. 8:14-17).

Even though Paul has changed his metaphor from being a child coming of age (Gal. 4:1-3) to that of a person being adopted in verses 5-7, his meaning is clear and consistent. Through Christ we are set free, we enter our full rights, and we become in the fullest sense a part of the family of God. And, wonder of wonders, it's all a gift that we receive by faith. At the very moment we accept Christ's sacrifice we find ourselves adopted into God's family. And with that adoption comes the gift of the Holy Spirit who inspires us to call God "Abba! Father!" (verse 6). Abba is the Aramaic term for father. J. M. Boice notes that "it is not always recognized how unusual the addressing of God as 'Father' was in antiquity nor what an unforgettable impression Jesus' habitual mode of praying made on his followers." Boice points out "that in Jesus' day (1) no one ever addressed God directly as 'My Father,' because it would have been thought disrespectful; (2) Jesus always used this form of address in praying, much to the amazement of his disciples; and (3) Jesus authorized his disciples to use this form of address after him, and they did" (Boice, p. 474). And we can too because we have been adopted by grace through faith into the family of God. So we are no longer slaves but God's children and heirs of the Abrahamic promise through God's gift (Gal. 4:7; 3:28, 29).

16. Progress in Reverse

Galatians 4:8-11

> *⁸Formerly, not knowing God, you served as slaves those things that by nature are not gods. ⁹But now after you have come to know God, or rather have come to be known by God, how is it that you are turning again to the weak and impoverished elemental things? Do you desire to become enslaved again? ¹⁰You observe days and months and seasons and years. ¹¹I fear for you, that somehow I have labored in vain for you.*

Paul in Galatians 4:4-7 highlighted the dignity of the Galatian converts as children of God and heirs of the Abrahamic promise. Now in verses 8-11 he moves on to their failure to live up to their heavenly status.

In verse 8 and the first part of verse 9, however, the apostle once again contrasts their former life with their present one. Formerly, he points out, they had served as slaves to false gods, but now they had come to know the true God. That is good and what Paul's mission was all about—to rescue people from delusion and spiritual ignorance and slavery, and to enable them to become acquainted with God as Father rather than as someone or something to fear.

He frames both verses 8 and 9 in terms of knowledge. The Galatians had advanced from not knowing God to knowing Him. But Paul adds a strange twist with the words, "or rather have come to be known by God" (verse 9). The implication is that the initiative in salvation is God's. We as humans do not gain salvation by becoming more knowledgeable. Rather, it is the God who knows us who also seeks us and sends the Son to rescue us in our enslaved plight (verses 9, 4). The fact that the Lord takes the initiative in the plan of salvation is a theme all through the Bible (see, e.g., Gen. 3:9; Luke 15:4, 8; 19:10). In the context of Galatians 4, we did not begin to know God until after He had already come to know us and developed a plan to rescue us from the grasp of sin and hopeless enslavement to an ever-condemning broken law.

That is good news. And, as noted above, it was also good that the Galatian converts had responded positively to divine initiative and had turned away from false religion. Paul had been gratified with the results of his preaching. They had accepted Christ by faith and had begun to move in the right direction under the guidance of the Holy Spirit (Gal. 3:2-5).

That brings us to the assertive "but" in Galatians 4:9. They had started on the right course, *but* now they were beginning to drift in the wrong direction. As a result, Paul asks them how it is that they "are turning again to the weak and impoverished elemental things?" He further inquires whether they want to become enslaved again. In section 15 in our discussion of Galatians 4:3 we noted that the "elemental things" referred to false religion, both pagan and faulty Judean/Christian presuppositions. More specifically, we observed that going back to the old Jewish system as advocated by the Judaizers with its circumcision and cultic calendar was equivalent to Paul to returning to paganism in terms of its enslaving results.

The weakness and impoverished nature of the pagan approach to religion was probably not difficult for the apostle's Galatian converts to see. But they may have had a hard time seeing the Jewish laws as having the same characteristics, especially since the law-pushing Judaizers seemed so sincere as they came preaching "another gospel" (Gal. 1:6) with Bibles in hand.

But Paul would not compromise here. To him any reliance on Jewish ceremonies and law for getting right with God was just as faulty as worshiping false gods (4:8). Neither held any real hope, because both routes were "weak and impoverished" (verse 9).

And why, we need to ask, was even the law weak and poverty-stricken? "It is *weak*," suggests William Barclay, "because it is helpless. It can define sin; it can show a man when he is sinning; it can convict him of sin; but it can neither find for him forgiveness for past sin nor strength to conquer future sin. The law's basic and inherent weakness always was, and is, that it can diagnose the disease but it cannot produce a cure" (Barclay, p. 39).

Yet it is toward the impotent Jewish law that the Judaizers sought to lead Paul's Galatian converts. They needed, the Judaizers sincerely and persuasively argued, to be circumcised and keep the law if they desired the full privileges of church membership. If they wanted to get right with God they must add observance of the law to their faith. Having taken the first step, the step of faith, now they should take the second step and come into harmony with the Jewish ways so that they could be genuine children of Abraham. Such a route, the Judaizers urged, was the way of progress.

Not so! Paul exclaimed. Turning to the "weak and impoverished elemental things" would only lead them back to slavery (4:9). They would be progressing in reverse. Or, as Leon Morris puts it, "the Galatians thought they were making progress in the Christian faith when they embraced the teaching of the Judaizers. Paul saw them as essentially reverting to the lives they had led before they became Christians" (Morris, p. 134).

Galatians 4:10 sheds light on some of the concrete practices the Galatians were becoming involved in when it tells them "you observe days and months and seasons and years." Sam Williams notes that Paul's "reference, presumably, is to special times of worship and celebration according to the cultic calendar of Judaism. Coming as it does immediately after the question of verse 9, this exclamation implies that the religious observances pegged to a cultic calendar are among the 'elemental principles' the Galatians wish to return to. Exactly which cultic occasions he refers to is impossible for later readers to know . . . , but Paul apparently feared that these practices would lead to the final step of circumcision" (Williams, p. 114).

Even if we cannot know with absolute certainty what the apostle meant by "days and months and seasons and years," it is probable that by "days" he meant the seven annual ceremonial Sabbaths (such as Passover and the Day of Atonement) outlined in Leviticus 23, that "months" refers to cultic celebrations tied to cultic events in the recurring monthly cycle, that "seasons" alludes to cultic seasonal events of more than one day's duration, and that "years" involves in some way the recurring sabbatical years and the years of Jubilee.

Some would go beyond the ceremonial time periods to include the weekly Sabbath in Paul's list. But that is not evident from the passage itself or from parallel texts in Paul's other letters, such as Colossians 2:16, 17. In fact, that text provides a major argument against the inclusion of the weekly Sabbath, since it claims that the new moons and sabbaths in question were "a shadow of things to come" (KJV). All of the ceremonial time periods in the Jewish calendar pointed to the advent of Jesus (they were "a shadow of things *to come")*, but the weekly Sabbath pointed back to God's work at creation (Gen. 2:1-3; Ex. 20:8-11). Thus the weekly Sabbath not only existed long before the Jewish laws given through Moses, it also had a different purpose. The ceremonial time periods anticipated the arrival of Jesus (Col. 2:17), whereas the weekly Sabbath was a remembrance of God's past work as Creator and Savior (Ex. 20:11). The weekly Sabbath is a part of God's eternal and universally valid moral law made explicit in the Ten Commandments, whereas the ceremonial sabbaths and other cultic calendric events were a part of the strictly Jewish economy that met their fulfillment or antitype in Christ.

But to argue over days is to miss Paul's point. While it is true that Paul consistently protested against returning to the ceremonial calendar of the Jews, even the observance of a valid Lord's Day or Sabbath would be wrong if a person expected to gain some merit toward salvation. Paul has made himself perfectly clear that "a man is not justified by works of the law but through faith in Jesus Christ" (Gal. 2:16, RSV). Keeping the Sabbath and the other nine commandments is a response to salvation—not a way to achieve it. His understanding of justification will not allow anything to be added to faith—not meritorious weekly Sabbath observance and most certainly not the ceremonial holidays of the Jewish cultic year.

One of the main lessons of Galatians 4:1-11 for modern Christians is that we need to remember who we were and who we have become as Christians. Before we met Christ we were enslaved to false ideas and inadequate ways of getting right with God and condemned by the penalty of the broken law. But through faith in Christ and His solution on Calvary to the curse of the broken law we have become a part of the family of God and heirs of the kingdom promises made to Abraham. If we are to make true progress in our walk with God we need to avoid the "weak and impoverished things" as a way of getting right and staying right with God. The only thing that we can truly rely on is God's amazing grace. And that we can receive only through faith.

17. A Pastor's Heart

Galatians 4:12-20

[12]Brothers, I beg you, become as I am, because I also became as you are. You did me no wrong. [13]Now you know that it was because of an illness of the flesh that I preached the good news to you at the first. [14]And even though my bodily condition was a trial to you, you did not despise or scorn me, but you received me as an angel of God, as Christ Jesus. [15]Where then is your joy? For I testify to you that if possible you would have torn out your eyes and given them to me. [16]So then, have I become your enemy because I told you the truth? [17]They take an interest in you, but not in an honorable way, but to exclude you, that you may take an interest in them. [18]Now it is always good to take an interest in a good thing and not only during my presence with you. [19]My children, for whom I again suffer birth pains until Christ is formed in you, [20]I desire to be present with you just now and to change my tone of voice, because I am perplexed about you.

Throughout much of Galatians we have been hearing Paul the theologian, a man who could split theological hairs to make his point. But in Galatians 4:12-20 we meet him as pastor. In these verses the apostle moves beyond the intellect to an appeal to the heart. In previous passages Paul may have referred to his readers as "foolish" and "bewitched" (3:1, RSV) or as traitors to the gospel (1:6), but now Paul calls them "children" while picturing himself as their parent in the faith (4:19). As John R. W. Stott puts it, "in Galatians 1-3 we have been listening to Paul the apostle, Paul the theologian, Paul the defender of the faith; but now we are hearing Paul the man, Paul the pastor, Paul the passionate lover of souls" (Stott, p. 111).

He begins by begging them to become as he was because he had become like them (verse 12). The meaning of his statement is not altogether clear on the surface. It is only in the overall context of Galatians that we can understand it. We find one key to unpacking it in Paul's confrontation with Peter in Galatians 2:14: "If you, though a Jew, live like a Gentile and not like a Jew, how can you compel the Gentiles to live like Jews?" (RSV). In what ways, we need to ask in the context of Galatians, had Paul and Peter become like Gentiles? To begin with, they both had grasped the fact that their justification had come through faith, rather than through works of the law (2:16). As a result, they had given up ideas of gaining merit from circumcision or other aspects of the Jewish law. They were clear on that point. As Ronald Fung points out, "in exchanging adherence to the law for faith in Christ, Paul became a 'Gentile sinner,' as the Galatians were" (Fung, p. 195).

It is on that basis that "he now beseeches them to become as he is, to be free from legal bondage and to know the liberty that is in Christ" *(ibid.)*. In short, Paul had come to realize that the legal ceremonialism of Judaism did not contribute to his standing before God. The Galatians, in like manner, needed to keep themselves free from bondage to circumcision and Jewish ceremonies as something that contributed to their position before God. Beyond that, they must reorient themselves to the fact that justification is a gift from God that they could receive only through faith. That is what Paul is *begging* them to do in verse 12. The apostle could threaten but he could also plead in love when necessary. He was a pastor who above all things desired the salvation of his flock.

Beginning with the last part of Galatians 4:12 and up through verse 16 Paul sets forth the Galatians' attitude toward him. "You did me no wrong," he exclaims in verse 12. That is, Paul has no complaints regarding how they treated him during his first missionary visit to Galatia. *And why,* you may be thinking, *would they want to do him wrong?* The answer surfaces in verses 13 and 14.

Paul apparently had contracted some disgusting disease or condition that could easily have predisposed strangers to despise and reject both him and his message. According to Galatians 4:13, he had apparently not planned to spend much time in Galatia. It was only "because of an illness of the flesh" that he had first preached to them. As G. G. Findlay remarks, "if he had been able to proceed, he would not have lingered in their country." However, he was not only unfit to continue his travels immediately, but "the Apostle's state of health made it at that time a trial for any one to listen to him" (Findlay, p. 276). Yet the Galatians not only did him no wrong, they accepted his message with joy (Gal. 4:12, 15). They listened to him as if he were an angel or even Christ Himself (verse 14). Beyond that, Paul reports that if they had been able they would have torn out their eyes and given them to him (verse 15).

That last comment has led some students of Galatians to conclude that Paul's malady must have involved his eyes. Some have conjectured that for some reason he never recovered from the blinding flash on the Damascus road (see Acts 9:3)—that God had allowed him to have an ongoing thorn in the flesh to keep him humble and always recognizing that he had been saved by grace (see 2 Cor. 12:7-9). Others have taken the words in the closing section of the Galatians' epistle ("see with what large letters I am writing to you with my own hand," Gal. 6:11, RSV) as additional evidence that Paul's problem had to do with his eyes.

His problem may have involved his eyes, but that is not altogether clear from the Bible itself. After all, the fact that the Galatians were willing to tear out their eyes for him may simply mean that they would have done anything for this man who had brought the gospel to them. And that is the essential point. We don't need to know the exact nature of Paul's illness to understand his meaning. The point that he is making is that the Galatians accepted him and his gospel message without reservation. They received it with joy (4:15).

So far so good. But then comes verse 16 and the negative refrain we have seen repeated again and again in Galatians. You accepted me and my message, Paul has repeatedly asserted, but! Something has happened. Their response to both him and his message has reversed.

That brings us to verses 17 to 20 and Paul's attitude to the Galatians. If their reaction to him has changed, his toward them has not. But that does not mean that there is no problem. The current difficulty is not primarily with the Galatians but with those false preachers who have flattered them with attention in order to lead them away from Paul and his gospel and thus "exclude" them from Christ (verse 17). He does not aim his anger at his Galatian converts, but at those who had come from Jerusalem to teach them that he wasn't a real apostle (see comments on Gal. 1:1 in section 1) and that his message of justification by faith alone was insufficient for their salvation. They may have come in the garb of friends, but they were really enemies who did not have the best interests of the Galatians in mind.

It is at that very point in his argument that Pastor Paul's love and concern for his children in Christ comes to the fore. He tells them that he had suffered the pains of childbirth once already for them when they became Christians. While that was difficult, he is willing to endure it again in order that Christ might be formed in them (Gal. 4:19). Here, suggests John Calvin, is the pastor's true work—not to form others to be like himself, but to be like Christ (Calvin, p. 83). Genuine Christian preaching and teaching must always help people become more and more like Jesus. It enables them to find joy in Christ and to live a life of joy in spite of their earthly problems.

> ### The Problem of Lost Joy
>
> "Legalism can steal joy because
>
> • it makes people feel guilty rather than loved; . . .
> • it stresses performance rather than relationship; and
> • it points out how far short we fall rather than how far we've come because of what Christ did for us.
>
> "If you feel guilty and inadequate and your joy is gone, check your focus. Are you living by faith in Christ or by trying to live up to the demands and expectations of others?" (Barton, p. 141)

From Paul's perspective, it is the enemy of Christ that takes the joy out of Christianity (Gal. 4:15) and leads people to see religion as a constant round of legalistic behaviors in an attempt to gain assurance that they are finally good enough for God to accept them.

It is such teachings that the Pauls of every generation must fight. But there is nothing worse than pastors and church members who get confused about the identity of the enemy. The apostle is clear that it is not the stumbling Galatian members who are the threat, but those from Jerusalem who were misleading them. It is unfortunate that the church down through history has always had emissaries "from Jerusalem" who are out to pervert the gospel of justification by grace through faith alone. Fortunately, the church has always had its Pauls who have had to thunder at the law faction but are also able to change their tone (verse 20) in appealing to struggling saints within the church. The apostle would want each of us to spread God's joy by having a true pastor's heart.

18. A Tale of Two Sons

Galatians 4:21-31

[21]*Tell me, you who desire to be under law, do you not understand the law?* [22]*For it is written that Abraham had two sons, one by the maidservant and one by the free woman.* [23]*But the one by the maidservant was born according to flesh, and the one by the free woman through promise.* [24]*This is an allegory, for these women represent two covenants; one from Mount Sinai bearing children to slavery, she is Hagar.* [25]*Now this Hagar is Mount Sinai in Arabia, who corresponds to the present Jerusalem, for she is in slavery with her children.* [26]*But the Jerusalem above is free; she is our mother.* [27]*For it has been written,*

> *"Rejoice, Barren woman who does not give birth, break forth and shout, you who are not having birth pains; Because the children of the desolate one are many more than of the one having the husband."*

[28]*Now you, brothers, are children of promise like Isaac.* [29]*But just as the one born according to flesh persecuted the one born according to spirit, so it is now.* [30]*But what does the Scripture say? "Throw out the maidservant and her son, for the son of the maidservant will never inherit with the son of the free woman."* [31]*Therefore, brothers, we are not children of a maidservant but of the free woman.*

Some people find Galatians 4:21-31 to be the most difficult section of the letter. But at least two keys will help us to unlock its meaning. "One," Richard Longenecker points out, "is that the central question dealt with by Paul in his use of both the example of Abraham in 3:6-9 and the Hagar-Sarah story in 4:21-31 is one of self-identification: Who are Abraham's true children? On this matter the Judaizers and Paul were diametrically opposed" (Longenecker, p. 219).

The Judaizers of Galatia, of course, had their solution to that identity. "The true descendants of Abraham" for them, notes C. K. Barrett, "are the Jews, who inhabit Jerusalem. Here are the true people of God; and it will follow that Jerusalem is the authoritative centre of the renewed people of God, now called the church. Those who are not prepared to attach themselves to this community by the approved means (circumcision) must be cast out; they cannot hope to inherit promises made to Abraham and his seed" (cited in *ibid.*, p. 218).

Paul, of course, has quite a different opinion. In Galatians 4:21-31 he uses the Hagar-Sarah story to turn the Judaizers' logic on its head. To do so he will employ a particularly Jewish form of argumentation that some modern Christians may find difficult to follow. We need to remember that Paul was a trained rabbi and was quite skillful in utilizing rabbinic methods. First, we must realize that for the rabbis any passage of Scripture had four meanings. William Barclay lists them as

1. the literal meaning,
2. the suggested meaning,
3. the meaning that can be deduced by investigation, and
4. the allegorical meaning.

In their thinking the allegorical was the high point of the various meanings. They would therefore take a simple Bible story and project various interpretations into it. While such meanings may not be convincing to us, they were to those trained in the rabbinic tradition (Barclay, pp. 44, 45).

Thus it is that Paul employs the story of Abraham and Sarah to make his point in a manner the Judaizers could understand. Sarah, as you will recall, was barren, and in line with the culture of her day she suggested to Abraham that he have children by Hagar her maidservant. The result of that union was Ishmael. Meanwhile, God promised Abraham and Sarah that they would have a child of their own. But that seemed ludicrous to them since Abraham was nearly 100 years old and Sarah 90. They both laughed because the promise involved a human impossibility. But in spite of their doubts, God fulfilled His promise through the "gift" of Isaac. Thus, so to speak, Ishmael had been born in the usual way of the flesh, but Isaac through a spiritual promise. After the birth of Isaac trouble erupted between the two women and their sons, with the older Ishmael persecuting Isaac.

That eventually led to Sarah's insistence that Abraham banish Hagar (Gen. 16:1-16; 17:15-25; 18:9-15; 21:1-21; Rom. 4:16-25; Heb. 11:11, 12).

Paul develops the story in the Galatians context on three levels. The first is the historical in Galatians 4:22, 23. In those verses he repeats the essence of the Old Testament story about the two women and their two sons. Both sons had Abraham as their father, but two major differences existed between them. For one thing, they had different mothers who had different statuses. Since both took after their mothers, Ishmael was born into slavery, while Isaac was born into freedom. A second difference that Paul highlights is the birth of one as happening in the usual manner of the flesh while the second's birth came about supernaturally through God's promise.

The second level of Paul's development of the Sarah-Hagar story is Paul's allegorization of it in verses 24-27. In those verses he compares the two women to two covenants and two cities.

The covenants here represent two ways of getting right with God. One Paul links to Mount Sinai, where Moses received the law from God. Those following that covenant are linked to Hagar and thus to the way of the flesh, the law, and slavery. The other he ties to Sarah and, by extension, to freedom and God's miraculous promise. The implicit question thus far in Paul's presentation, since both had the same father, is who is their mother? Are they children of freedom or of slavery? (For a fuller discussion of the covenants, see Knight, *Exploring Hebrews,* pp. 144-148).

With his treatment of the two cities Paul becomes a bit more specific. In a move that reverses the Judaizers' understanding he links the "present Jerusalem" to Hagar and Ishmael. Here Paul makes a major thrust at the Judaizers who held that the way things were done in Jerusalem (circumcision and so on) was how Christians should do them in Galatia. Paul contrasts the "present Jerusalem" with "the Jerusalem above," with the former being a place of slavery and the latter the abode of the free—the children of Sarah. Then in verse 27 he cites Isaiah 54:1 to the effect that the woman to receive the blessing was the barren one—that is, Sarah, the one who lived by the promise rather than by the flesh. In this context, of course, those who live by the flesh are those who rely on circumcision and the observance of law to get right with God, while those living by the promise are those who accept God's justification through faith in the promise to bless all the world through Abraham (Gal. 3:6-9).

That thought brings us to Paul's third level of treatment in the Sarah-Hagar story—the personal (verses 28-31). Here he identifies the Galatian Christians with Isaac, the child of the promise. Thus they were not to follow those "missionaries" from the earthly Jerusalem, but should stand with Paul on the promise of justification by faith made to the patriarch (Gal. 3:6-9; Gen. 15:6). But if they did so, they could expect persecution (verse 29), just as Paul himself was experiencing. On the other hand, they could also look forward to the blessing of Abraham. Meanwhile, the Judaizers and those who held that keeping the law was the way to get right with God would eventually get thrown out by Him (verse 30). Paul concludes with the resounding statement that the Galatians "are not children of a maidservant but of the free women" (verse 31).

Galatians 4:21-31, despite all of its obscurities to the modern mind, has extremely important lessons for those in the twenty-first century. For one thing, the church is still divided into the camps of those who live according to the flesh in spiritual matters and of those who rely on God through the promise—that is, those who would be justified by legal works and those who are justified by faith. Yet, as John R. W. Stott points out, the present troublers of the church are not "the Jews or Judaizers to whom Paul was writing, but people whose religion is legalistic, who imagine that the way to God is by the observance of certain rules" (Stott, pp. 121, 122).

The plain fact is that every church member is either an Ishmael or an Isaac—that is, they are either clinging to God's promise through faith or they are a slave still needing to be set free.

Stott sums up the matter nicely when he writes that "the religion of Ishmael is a religion of *nature,* of what *man* can do by himself without any special intervention of God. But the religion of Isaac is a religion of *grace,* of what *God* has done and does, a religion of divine initiative and divine intervention, for Isaac was born supernaturally through a divine promise. And this is what Christianity is, not 'natural' religion but 'supernatural.' The Ishmaels of this world trust in themselves that they are righteous, the Isaacs trust only in God through Jesus Christ. The Ishmaels are in bondage, because this is what self-reliance always leads to; the Isaacs enjoy freedom, because it is through faith in Christ that men are set free" (*ibid.,* pp. 128, 129). Or to put it another way, the Ishmaels spend all their lives seeking to master the law, while the Isaacs live their lives surrendering to the Master.

Part IV

Ethics:
The Responsibilities
of Liberty

Galatians 5:1–6:10

19. A Tale of Two Ways

Galatians 5:1-12

¹For this freedom Christ freed us; stand firm therefore and do not become enslaved again by a yoke of slavery.

²Behold I, Paul, tell you that if you receive circumcision, Christ will profit you nothing. ³Now I testify again to every man who receives circumcision that he is under obligation to keep the whole law. ⁴Whoever is seeking to be justified by law is separated from Christ; you have fallen away from grace. ⁵For we by the Spirit, by faith, earnestly await the hope of righteousness. ⁶For in Christ Jesus neither circumcision nor uncircumcision avails anything, but faith working through love.

⁷You were running well. Who hindered you from obeying the truth. ⁸This persuasion did not come from the One who calls you. ⁹A little leaven leavens the whole lump. ¹⁰I have confidence in you in the Lord that you will set your mind on no other view. And the one disturbing you will bear his judgment, whoever he may be. ¹¹But if I, brothers, still proclaim circumcision, why am I still being persecuted? Then the stumbling block of the cross has been abolished. ¹²I wish that those disturbing you would even emasculate themselves.

With chapter 5 we come to one of the great turning points of Galatians. The first two chapters focused on history as Paul defended both his apostleship and his gospel of liberty from the attacks of those who had come from Jerusalem and had challenged both. The next two chapters built upon the historical as Paul presented his theological understanding of the gospel of Christian liberty. Now in chapters 5 and 6 Paul turns to the ethical outworking of the gospel of freedom in the lives of believers.

According to James Dunn, "Paul reaches the climax of his exposition and appeal" in Galatians 5:1. "The whole reason for his writing to the Galatians is summed up in the passionate cry of v. 1" (Dunn, p. 260): "For this freedom Christ freed us; stand firm therefore and do not become enslaved again by a yoke of slavery."

Paul is at his passionate apex in Galatians 5:1-12. He, so to speak, pulls out all the stops as he pours out his heart and emotions. "He must have seen this as the critical moment," asserts Dunn. "If he could not convince his Galatian audiences now he might never have another chance; his work with them, and their freedom in Christ might be lost irretrievably" *(ibid.)*. Thus his passionate intensity.

Freedom is the obvious theme of verses 1-12, as it is of the entire epistle. The problem he was facing was that some of his Galatian converts had been led to see acceptance of circumcision and Jewish law as an advance on what Paul had taught them about getting right with God through faith. Thus his urgent call for them to stand fast in the freedom that Christ had died on the cross to provide for them (verse 1). That freedom, John Stott notes, "is freedom of conscience, freedom from the tyranny of the law, the dreadful struggle to keep the law, with a view to winning the favour of God. It is the freedom of acceptance with God and of access to God through Christ" (Stott, p. 132).

The focal point of the crisis was circumcision, a point made crystal clear in verses 2-4. The false teachers declared that "unless you are circumcised according to the custom of Moses, you cannot be saved" (Acts 15:2, RSV). Now Paul knew that circumcision in itself was a trivial matter and he didn't always oppose it (see, e.g., Acts 16:3). But in the way it was being urged in the Galatian context he saw it as the leading teaching of a way of religion that nullified the gospel of Christ. It was the entering wedge of a theology that taught salvation by good works in obedience to the law. That perspective regarded faith in Christ as insufficient for getting right with God. The Judaizers held that justification consisted of faith plus circumcision and obedience to the law, a position equivalent to saying that the sacrifice of Christ on Calvary was not enough, that believers must add something to that sacrifice behaviorally.

Paul refused to give an inch to such theology. Against it he makes four points in verses 2-4:

- "If you receive circumcision, Christ will profit you nothing" (verse 2).

- "Every man who receives circumcision . . . is under obligation to keep the whole law" (verse 3).
- "Whoever is seeking to be justified by law is separated from Christ" (verse 4).
- Such ones "have fallen away from grace" (verse 4).

It was no trivial matter for him. He argues that the two ways (faith versus faith + works) are not two varieties of Christianity but two entirely different religions. Dieter Lührmann helps us see that "once again Paul asserts an alternative where Judaism does not have one. For the Jews, submitting to the yoke of the law means the realization of freedom," but for Paul it is enslavement (Lührmann p. 95). He himself had spent his early life trying to please God by observance of the law (Phil. 3:4-6). But he failed. It was only after his salvation by grace that he saw that the function of the law was to point out sin rather than to save people from it (Gal. 3:21; Rom. 3:20-24). He had come to realize that if people were to please God by obedience to the law, they would have to keep every aspect of it flawlessly (Gal. 3:10; 5:3). The apostle recognized that trying to please God through keeping the law was the way of slavery (5:1) and failure (Rom. 3:9-24). No one had ever observed it perfectly except Christ. And Paul had come to understand that Christ's dying on the cross redeemed men and women from the curse of the broken law (Gal. 3:10, 13). For him the "gospel" of law keeping was a Satanic deception. It led only to enslavement and death. Thus his passion on the topic in Galatians 5:1-12.

> ## A Description of Christian Freedom
>
> "The person who is truly free is a person who
> (1) trusts, loves, and obeys God through Christ and in the Spirit,
> (2) loves and serves others, and
> (3) lives before God with a clear conscience as he or she grows before God in holiness and love"
> (McKnight, p. 259).

On the positive side, Paul asserts two things about those who accept the gospel. First, that it is by faith that they "await the hope of righteousness," evidently a reference to the Second Advent (verse 5). Second, a saved person's faith will work through love (verse 6). With that thought

125

Paul opens a line of argument that will dominate Galatians 5:13-6:10. Commenting on verse 6, Leon Morris writes that "we are not to think that the fact that we receive salvation by faith in Christ, not by any good deeds of our own, means that the Christian life is a life of blessed idleness. The way this faith is put into practice is by *working through love* ('expressing itself through love,' REB)" (Morris, p. 158).

In Galatians 5:7-12 Paul moves away from his discussion of the Galatian believers to focus on the false teachers who seek to lead them astray. Who are they? he asks in verse 7. Certainly not God he asserts in verse 8. But in verse 9 he notes that the false teaching of the Judaizers will spread throughout the whole church just as yeast leavens a lump of flour.

Paul shifts his appeal a bit in verse 10 through his assertion that he has confidence that the Galatians will stay by his gospel rather than side with the Judaizers. But the very thought of such apostles of doom raises his ire and his thoughts turn to their final judgment for the trouble they have caused. Not the least of their evils, as he sees it, is that they apparently, in his absence, had sought "to gain acceptance for their teaching" by pointing out "that Paul had himself been circumcised and suggested that in the matter of circumcision his teaching was much the same as theirs" (Morris, p. 161, cf. Bruce, p. 237). If that latter point was true, Paul queried, "why am I still being persecuted" by the Judaizers and others who rejected the full sufficiency of the cross (verse 11)?

The cross itself was a stumbling block (verse 11) to those who prided themselves in their law achievements. The cross reminds us that people can do nothing to save themselves from sin, no matter how hard they try. Calvary leaves no room for human pride (cf. Eph. 2:9). Nothing can be added to the cross. We must either accept it by faith or reject it. Those are the only two ways to relate to it.

Galatians 5:12 represents Paul's ultimate emotional outburst against the Judaizers, as he cries out that those who are teaching circumcision should follow their logic to its natural conclusion and emasculate themselves. Why just go part of the way, he argues. Instead, "they ought to make a full sweep of themselves and remove the the whole organ" (Keener, p. 533). William Barclay helps us see the force of Paul's outburst when he points out that "Galatia was near Phrygia and the great worship of that part of the world was the worship of Cybele; now it was the practice that priests and really devout worshippers of Cybele mutilated themselves by castration. The Cybele priests were eunuchs. So Paul says, 'If you go on in this way, of which circumcision is the beginning, you might as well end up by castrating yourselves like these heathen priests.' It is a grim illustration at which a polite society raises its eyebrows, but it would be intensely real to the Galatians who knew all about the priests of Cybele, who, in fact, lived among them" (Barclay, p. 48).

20. The Paradox of Freedom

Galatians 5:13-15

> *¹³For you, brothers, were called to freedom; only do not use your freedom for an opportunity for the flesh, but through love serve one another as slaves. ¹⁴For the entire law may be summed up in one word, "You shall love your neighbor as yourself." ¹⁵But if you bite and devour one another, beware lest you are consumed by one another.*

Verse 13 marks the beginning of the intensely ethical section of Galatians. "For about four and a half chapters," writes C. K. Barrett, "Paul insists in the strongest possible terms on the principle of faith alone. Justification is for the ungodly; no man, however virtuous, can merit salvation; human works, obedience to the law, are of no avail. But from 5:13 onwards he warns his readers against the abuse of freedom" (Barrett, p. 56). They must not suppose that they have the right to do anything they might choose.

Here we come to the practical Paul. His mind may fly to the heights of theological discussion, but it is always for a practical purpose. Theology for him was not an end in itself, but was always a means to an end. "To Paul," writes William Barclay, "a theology was not of the slightest use unless it could be lived out in the world" (Barclay, p. 49). That was so in the book of Romans, where in the first 11 chapters he presents a masterly and complex argument on sin and salvation for both Jew and Gentile. But in chapters 12 through 15 he brings his teachings down to earth as he presents how transformed church members can live the life of love.

Paul does the same thing in Galatians. In the first four and a half chapters he argues complex theory, but in the last chapter and a half he presents its implication for everyday living in the church. Here is where many modern church members part company with the apostle. They are good at talking theology, but poor at expressing God's love in their community. That, of course, is nothing new. According to Galatians 5:15 the church members in Galatia suffered from the same spiritual disease.

The apostle sounds the great resounding truth of Galatians in 5:13, in which he tells us that Christians "were called to freedom." Please note once again that it is not we humans who initiate our personal salvation. Rather, it is God who first begins it. All we can do is respond positively or negatively.

It is freedom to which we are summoned. But one might not guess that by looking at some church members. All too many appear despondent and depressed. I find such types to be the strongest argument against Christianity. The tragedy is that they apparently don't know what they have been called from and what they have been called to. Some have merely left the bondage of sin for that of legalism. They act as if God is watching them with an intense desire to nail them if they step out of line in the slightest. Such church members are anything but free.

But those who have been justified by God's grace accepted through their faith are free indeed. However, we need to ask, what has the Lord liberated them from? Several things, including a conscience burdened by guilt, the condemnation of the curse of the broken law (Gal. 3:10), and the need to get right with God through endless rounds of law-oriented behavior. Such freedoms are good reasons for Christians to rejoice. They have been justified in Christ and accepted as children of the promise.

But, suggests H. D. Betz, they can lose that freedom in at least two ways: legalism and license (Betz, p. 258). Paul covered the first of those possibilities in Galatians 5:2-12. He treats the second in verses 13-24. Barrett writes that "the man who sets out to express his freedom by following nothing but his own pleasure will find himself bound to himself, the slave of his own lusts and passions" (Barrett, p. 56). Jesus spoke of such people when He told the Jews, "every one who commits sin is a slave to sin" (John 8:34, RSV), and Paul in his letter to Titus described those who were "slaves to various passions and pleasures" (3:3, RSV). Modern social scientists refer to such people as addicts.

Thus the freedom of which Paul speaks is not absolute. While it is freedom from some things, it is not a license to do whatever we please. Someone has said that it is a freedom *from* sin, not a freedom *to* sin.

That is where some people get confused with Paul's theology. Here lurks the danger facing those who don't listen to him carefully. They hear the part about the freedom and conclude that they can follow their bodily or other inclinations wherever they may lead. After all, they assume, they don't have to keep the law to get right with God, and grace ensures forgiveness. Paul encountered that challenge in Romans 6:1. His answer was that Christians cannot live a life of sin because they have died to sin and been born to walk in God's ways (verses 2-11). In Romans 12 he refers to the same experience as a transformation and a renewal of the Christian's mind (verses 1, 2). The plain fact is that saved Christians don't want to sin and they repent when they do. They are free from the rule of their flesh but under the direction of the Holy Spirit. Thus they should not view their freedom as "an opportunity for the flesh" (Gal. 5:13).

Rather—and here is the paradox of Christian freedom—they are "through love" to "serve one another as slaves" (verse 13). As H. D. McDonald puts it, Christians are "free as to legalism" but "bound as to love" (McDonald, p. 131). Thus Christians are those whom God has rescued from slavery to the flesh but who have become slaves in love to their neighbors.

And they are not free from the law. Rather, they have a new relationship to it. They no longer see the law as a ladder to get to heaven but as an opportunity to love God and other people. Paul makes that clear in Galatians 5:13 and 14. They no longer obey the law in an effort to get saved. Instead, they keep God's law because they are saved.

But their observance of it is on the basis of love rather than legal obligation. Echoing Jesus (Matt. 22:37-40), who was following the Old Testament (Deut. 6:5; Lev. 19:18), Paul summed up the entire law as "You shall love your neighbor as yourself" (Gal. 5:14).

Earlier in the chapter he had spoken of "faith working through love" (verse 6). Paul's theology displays a definite conflict between legalistic law keeping and faith, but not between faith and love. Rather, faith expresses itself in love.

Barrett unpacks the dynamics involved when he writes that "the opposite of flesh is love; and love means serving one another. This becomes clearer . . . as Paul goes on (5:14) to quote the commandment of love for neighbour. Flesh, therefore, defined by its opposite, means self-centered existence, egocentric existence; not specifically a proclivity to carnal sins (as we call them), but a concern focused upon oneself. . . . Again, . . . we see from a different angle how faith and love cohere. Each has equally turned away from self; faith looks away from the self and its achievements to God as the centre of its trust; love looks away from the self and its wishes, even its real needs, to the neighbour, and spends its resources on his needs" (Barrett, pp. 72, 73).

Thus the paradox is not as confusing as it first appears. The slavery of faith is a painless one for converted Christians. Their faith, under the empowerment of the Holy Spirit, naturally flows out in love to others.

Paul's theology has as its foundation free grace accepted by faith, but it is not a lawless theology. For him every Christian always has two obligations. The first is their duty to love God, and the second is to love other people. Beyond that, the apostle directly ties those responsibilities to the Ten Commandments in Romans 13:8-10, in which he explicitly links love to one's neighbor with the commandments on the second table of the Decalogue. As noted above, the way of faith means that a Christian is free from keeping the law as an avenue to salvation, but the way of faith also means that a Christian for the first time has the liberty and the power to live God's law of love from the right motive.

One of the problems with the Galatians was that they were not living the law of love through faith. To the contrary, they were biting and devouring one another (Gal. 5:15), words used in classical Greek to "suggest wild animals engaged in deadly struggle" (Burton, p. 297). One of the great problems of legalists is that they are essentially self-centered—focused on themselves and their achievements and, on the other side, the faults of others. As a result, suggests Dieter Lührmann, they are "in conflict with one another and show absolutely nothing of the love that is demanded by the law to which they want to commit themselves" (Lührmann, p. 104).

The end result of a law/obedience orientation rather than a faith/grace orientation down through church history has been bickering and destructive church members. So it was in Galatia, and so it is today.

If so-called Christians would put Paul's admonition about the law in Galatians 5:13-15 into practice, the church would be a more delightful place. Every congregation has its "pious members" who act as if they can love God while being rude to other people. Beyond that, we continually encounter those who are extremely careful about how they keep the Ten Commandments and/or what they eat but who are meaner than the devil himself. All such need to study Galatians 5:13-15 carefully and come to grips with the unity of faith and love as they relate to law and salvation.

21. The Way of the Flesh

Galatians 5:16-21

¹⁶But I say, walk by the Spirit and you will by no means perform the desire of the flesh. ¹⁷For the desires of the flesh are against the Spirit and those of the Spirit against the flesh, for these things oppose each other, so that you may not do whatever things you would. ¹⁸But if you are led by the Spirit, you are not under law. ¹⁹Now the works of the flesh are plain, which are: fornication, impurity, sensuality, ²⁰idolatry, sorcery, enmities, strife, jealousy, anger, selfishness, dissension, cliques, ²¹envying, drunkenness, carousing, and things like these, of which I warn you beforehand, as I said before, that those who practice such things will not inherit the kingdom of God.

Paul in Galatians 5:13-15 taught that God called believers to freedom not so that they may indulge their sinful nature, but so that they may in love "serve one another as slaves." But how, we need to ask, is that possible? After all, it was a task that the Galatian believers were obviously failing at (verse 15).

The apostle's answer to both the Galatians and to us is that only the Holy Spirit can keep us free. The Holy Spirit comes onto center stage in verses 16-25, being mentioned seven times. Uniting with the Spirit is the only path to maintaining Christian liberty. Without the work of the Spirit in our life our liberty either veers off toward legalism or toward license. Both legalism and license Paul thinks of as works of the flesh, even though they are quite different in some ways. After all, legalism is "religious" while license is quite irreligious. But they both are works of the flesh because they both focus inward on ourselves and our accomplishments rather than upon God and what He has done for us.

It is of the utmost importance to realize that not all sin is irreligious. Sin is just as happy to dress up in religious garb as in secular. The central problem of the Galatians is their desire to sin religiously, to seek to do for themselves through the law what only God could do for them in Christ on the cross. The church 2,000 years later is still full of those suffering from religious sins of the flesh. Such believers need to stop running ahead of the Spirit, and to let Him enter their lives so that they might be free in Christ.

One of the central problems that Christians face is that each is a battlefield between the Spirit and the flesh, that there is a great conflict between good and evil raging in their very being (Gal. 5:17). This is a serious problem. It means that we are not eternally safe when we accept Christ and join the church. James Dunn suggests that the believer "is on both sides of the conflict" (Dunn, p. 299). That is, a believer has the potential to go either way in the struggle between flesh and Spirit.

Some church members don't like this teaching. They claim that they died to sin when they became a Christian and have crucified the flesh once and for all. But, Paul points out here, that is not the way it is. We will struggle with temptations of the flesh as long as we are on this earth. Martin Luther recognized that fact when he wrote that God's true saints are not "stocks and stones (as the monks and schoolmen dream) so that they are never moved with anything, never feel any lust or desires of the flesh: but, as Paul saith, their flesh lusteth against the Spirit, and therefore they have sin and can sin" (Luther, *Commentary*, p. 508).

> ## A Note on "Religious Flesh"
>
> C. S. Lewis writes that "the true Christian's nostril is to be continually attentive to the inner cesspool" (quoted in Barton, p. 184).

Those who stand over against Paul on this plain teaching are usually the better than others types who often have much to say about law keeping and sinless perfectionism. What they fail to realize is that they haven't gotten rid of the "flesh," that it has merely become "religious flesh."

Such "good" people often become critical of others in the church who do not live on their "high" standard. So it was with those who sought to follow the Pharisee-influenced Judaizers in Galatia. They may have pushed the devil with all his nasty sins, so to speak, out the front door of their lives, but he came right in the back door masquerading in Christian/law-loving piety.

And what is the solution to the human dilemma? Paul is clear on that point. The only way to deal with it is to let the Holy Spirit guide our lives. That is the meaning of Paul's words at the end of Galatians 5:18 when he writes, "you are not under law." Commenting on that passage, Ronald Fung writes that "if the Judaizers upheld the law as the only safeguard against becoming slaves to the flesh, Paul asserts as an adequate safeguard the guidance of the Spirit" (Fung, p. 252). He had said much the same thing in verse 16 when he charged Christians to "walk in the Spirit," which means to be under the moment-by-moment guidance of the Spirit (see Ladd, p. 475).

If Paul is right in what he writes in Galatians 5:16-18, then nothing can be more important in a Christian's life than working with the Holy Spirit. Kenneth Wuest states that "the Holy Spirit has been given to" Christians "as the Agent to counteract the evil nature," and He does so when we surrender to Him. *"There must be a cooperation of the saint with the Holy Spirit in His work of sanctifying the life. The Holy Spirit is not a perpetual motion machine which operates automatically in the life of the believer. He is a divine Person waiting to be depended upon for His ministry, and expecting the saint to cooperate with Him in it. Thus the choice lies with the believer as to whether he is going to yield to the Holy Spirit or obey the evil nature"* (Wuest, vol. 1, p. 154). And, according to Paul, there is no more important choice to be made. Accepting the Spirit into our lives is just as vital as receiving the substitutionary atonement of Christ, who absorbed the curse of the broken law for us on the cross (Gal. 3:13).

If Paul's focus in Galatians 5:16-18 is on the necessity of the Holy Spirit for victorious Christian living, in verses 19-21 his emphasis shifts to the works of the flesh. We saw in our discussion of verses 13-15 that in the context of Galatians we must define flesh as anything against love. That is, as C. K. Barrett notes, "the opposite of flesh is love; and love means serving one another [5:13, 14]. . . . Flesh, therefore, defined by its opposite, means self-centered existence, egocentric existence; not specifically a proclivity to carnal sins (as we call them), but a concern focused upon oneself" (Barrett, pp. 72, 73).

That is much the same as saying that SIN is love perverted and loving yourself more than God and other people (see Knight, *I Used to Be Perfect*, pp. 13-24). The impulse toward the flesh and SIN is the same thing. Anything that makes us self-centered rather than other-centered is a work of the flesh. From that perspective, SIN in the mind leads to sinful actions, and a focus on the flesh leads to the works of the flesh. Thus if I believe that I am the most important person in my universe I may eventually begin to dishonor God, use your body, or take your things. Those, of course, are the more obvious works of the flesh. On a less visible level my fleshly self love may just lead me to be critical of you because I am more dedicated to living all of God's laws than you are. The fruit of that "religious" attitude is dissension and strife in the church, the very problem that the law–emphasizing believers in Galatia were causing (see Gal. 5:20, 15).

Barrett speaks to that point when he writes that "as far as the works of the flesh (5:19-21) are concerned, the thing to note is that they are not all what we should describe as carnal sins. Some are: fornication, uncleanness, lasciviousness, drunkenness, revellings. And the sexual sins stand first because they are the clearest of all examples of a man, or woman, arrogating to himself rights he does not possess, exploiting for his own indulgence not only another's property but another's person, and at the most sensitive point. But idolatry, sorcery, enmities, strifes, jealousies, wrath, factions, divisions, party spirit, envyings, these too are works of the flesh; and church history has been and is littered with them. Not all are carnal sins, but all are self-centered sins. They underline the fact that sin is egocentricity; and the flesh is man's innate tendency to egocentricity" (Barrett, pp. 76, 77).

Paul's list of the works of the flesh falls into roughly four categories:
• sexual sins,
• religious deviations,
• disorders in personal relationships, and
• sins of intemperance (see Fung, p. 254).

His final words are that those who "practice [the verb tense here suggests continue to practice on a regular basis rather than an isolated lapse] such things will not inherit the kingdom of God" (Gal. 5:21).

God will have to exclude them for at least two reasons. First, their works provide evidence that they are not in Christ and thus they are not of Abraham's seed and heirs according to the promise (3:29). And, second, they wouldn't be happy in the kingdom because they are totally out of harmony with its basic principle of outgoing love to other people. As a result, not only would they feel uncomfortable there with their fleshly principles, but their presence would be eternally disruptive.

22. The Way of the Spirit

Galatians 5:22-26

²²But the fruit of the Spirit is love, joy, peace, patience, kindness, goodness, faithfulness, ²³meekness, self-control; against such things there is no law. ²⁴Now those who belong to Christ Jesus have crucified the flesh with its passions and desires.

²⁵If we live by the Spirit, let us also walk by the Spirit. ²⁶Let us not become boastful, challenging one another, envying one another.

One of the first things that we should note as we compare the fruit of the Spirit and the works of the flesh is that fruit is singular while works is plural. Donald Guthrie writes that "it is significant that Paul uses the singular 'fruit' rather than the plural, because the latter would suggest a number of variegated products, whereas his real aim is to show the various aspects of the one harvest. Not one of those qualities which Paul names can be isolated and treated as an end in itself" (Guthrie, p. 139).

Another way of saying it is that the various aspects of the fruit will all be seen in every true believer's life. One cannot, for example, have love for God and other people without having peace, joy, and gentleness. Likewise, one cannot have patience without self-control, meekness, and so on. The same cannot be said about the works of the flesh. After all, a person can be an adulterer without being an idolater or a drunkard. Thus we should think of the fruit as a unified cluster rather than as a series of discrete virtues.

Another thing that stands out as one of the differences between works and fruit is that the latter represents a shift away from the human accomplishment signified by "works." As Ronald Fung puts it, the phrase "fruit of the Spirit" "directly ascribes the power of fructification not to the believer himself but to the Spirit, and effectively hints that the qualities enumerated are not the result of strenuous observance of an external legal code, but the natural product ('harvest') of a life controlled and guided by the Spirit" (Fung, p. 262). Such a perspective was especially pertinent to those Galatians who found themselves tempted toward the Judaizers' "lets do for God" stance and away from Paul's "let God do for us" orientation.

One other thing we should note about the fruit of the Spirit before we move on is that we must distinguish the fruit from the gifts of the Spirit. Paul is quite clear in other places that such gifts as healing, prophecy, and so on go to certain individuals for ministry and that not every Christian has every gift (1 Cor. 12:4-11). That is, no one has all the gifts of the Spirit, but each of us has one or more spiritual gifts that we can use to help others. But with the fruit, as noted above, every true Spirit-led Christian has every aspect of it. All in all, G. G. Findlay suggests, the verses on the fruit "contain the ideal of character furnished by the gospel of Christ." The fruit described in Galatians 5:22, 23 "is the religion of Jesus put in practice" (Findlay, p. 375). That being so, it is unfortunate that the legalists of Galatia and the perfectionists of every age tend to focus on the external and often negative aspects of the law rather than upon the fruit set forth by Paul and Jesus (see, e.g., Matt. 5:43-48).

Verses 22 and 23 describe the fruit itself. The first aspect listed is "love." H. D. McDonald argues that "the term 'love,' which heads the list of the Spirit's fruit, should not be regarded merely as one of the cluster; it is rather the stem upon which all the rest hangs. Love stands at the head of the list, but it is the heart of the whole" (McDonald, p. 137). Paul's previous emphasis on love, which he claims is the natural outflow of faith (Gal. 5:6) and the sum total of the fulfilling of the law (verse 14), supports the validity of such a perspective. Beyond that, it is the need of love in their community that he is urging on the Galatian Christians (verse 15). Also supporting the centrality of love thesis is the contrast between the self-centeredness of the works of the flesh versus the utter other-centeredness of outgoing love that we discussed in sections 20 and 21.

William Barclay reminds us that Greek has four words for love, but that the one Paul uses in verse 22 is *agapē*. That is the word John used when he wrote that "God so loved the world, that he gave his only begotten Son, that whosoever believeth in him should not perish, but have everlasting life" (John 3:16, KJV). It is the word Paul employed when he described the greatest of all Christian virtues in 1 Corinthians 13. And it is the word Jesus turned to when He said that we should love our enemies and pray for those who are persecuting us (Matt. 5:44). Above all, it is the characteristic that we must have if we are to be perfect or complete like our Father in heaven (verse 48).

> ## Four Greek Words for Love
>
> 1. *Eros,* which "means the love of a man for a maid."
> 2. *Philia,* which "is the warm love which we feel for our nearest and dearest."
> 3. *Storge,* which stands for "affection and is specially used of the love of parents and children."
> 4. *Agapē,* which signifies "unconquerable benevolence. It means that no matter what a man may do to us by way of insult or injury or humiliation we will never seek anything else but his highest good" (Barclay, p. 54).

To Paul *agapē* is the fruitiest part of the fruit. It is the sum of the law (Gal. 5:14; Rom. 13:8-10), and it is the virtue that stands at the very center of living the Christian life. Without it the professions of even the most zealous Christian are nothing but a loud and meaningless noise (1 Cor. 13:1).

But with *agapē* individuals have peace with God and other people (the focal points of the two tables of the Ten Commandments, see Matt. 22:37-40), joy because nothing that anyone does to them can truly offend them, and patience, kindness, goodness, meekness, and self-control, all because they form a part of the intrinsic nature of *agapē.*

"Against such things," Paul writes, "there is no law" (Gal. 5:23). "This," claims Leon Morris, "is a masterly understatement. It draws our attention to the fact that the kind of conduct that Paul has outlined is that which lawmakers everywhere want to bring about" (Morris, p. 175). But what legislators through the centuries have failed at the Holy Spirit can accomplish in those who let Him work out God's will in their lives.

For that to happen, however, Paul tells us and the Galatians that people must do two things. First, they must crucify "the flesh with its passions and desires" (Gal. 5:24). Please note that the verb "to crucify" is in the active voice. In this context it is not something done to individuals but rather something done by them. Paul borrows the crucifixion image from Jesus, who told His disciples that if anyone would follow Him, "let him deny himself and take up his cross" (Matt. 16:24, RSV). Under the guidance and empowerment of the Spirit we must accept the crucifixion of our selfish (flesh) orientation to living. That crucifixion, the Greek aorist tense of the verb signifies in Galatians 5:24, is a particular action at a particular time, pointing to the time of conversion. In fact, that is what conversion means—death to one set of principles (works of the flesh) and birth to another (fruit of the Spirit). Unfortunately, crucifixion historically was a slow process. As noted above in our discussion of Galatians 5:17, the old principles of life may have been crucified, but they still struggle for supremacy in our daily life. That is one reason that Jesus told us that every Christian must "take up his cross daily" (Luke 9:23, RSV).

But crucifixion of the flesh is only the first step in what every Christian needs to do. After all, what could be worse or more discouraging than a dead convert? The second step is a necessity for those who desire the fruit of the Spirit. That is, they need not only to be crucified (Galatians 5:24), but they need to "walk by the Spirit" (verse 25). The Greek word used here for walk has a special significance. It is not the same one in verse 16, which is the ordinary word for walking, but it is *stoicheō,* which means to come into line with or, by extension, to walk in a straight line (see Rogers, p. 432). A Christian who has a faith relation with God through Jesus will walk in line with His will. In such a person the Spirit can produce the fruit described in verses 22 and 23.

But for that fruit to be true fruit of the Spirit the Christian must live it rather than merely talk about it. That is where Paul's appeal to the Galatians (and us) in verse 26 comes in, in which he says, "let us not become boastful, challenging one another, envying one another." Ben Witherington points out that "verse 26 stands as the mirror opposite of vs. 25. Having told them what they ought to do, Paul now concludes this argument by telling them what they must not do" (Witherington, p. 413). While he was speaking directly to the problems of the Galatian believers, it is just as meaningful to us living in the twenty-first century.

23. Living by the Spirit: Part 1

Galatians 6:1-5
 ¹*Brothers, even if a person is overtaken in some fault, you who are spiritual should restore such a one in a spirit of gentleness, watching out for yourself, lest you also be tempted. ²Bear one another's burdens, and thus you will fulfill the law of Christ. ³For if anyone thinks he is something when he is nothing, he deceives himself. ⁴But let each person examine his own work, and then his ground for boasting will be in himself alone and not in comparison with other individuals. ⁵For each person will have to bear his own load.*

The church in Galatia, unfortunately, seems to be typical of too many congregations. Paul has already warned them by telling them not to devour, provoke, and envy one another (Gal. 5:15, 26), and by including such things as strife, jealousy, envy, and dissension in his list of the works of the flesh (verse 20). On the positive side, he has begun presenting a solution by claiming that the essence of Christianity is "faith working through love" (verse 6), that "the whole law is fulfilled in one word, 'You shall love your neighbor as yourself'" (verse 14, RSV), and that the foremost aspect of the fruit of the Spirit is love (verse 22).

The Galatians obviously had some serious problems along these lines. Thus after having told them to walk by the Spirit (verse 25), Paul is now ready to give them some concrete advice on how to do so in the light of the problems developing in their midst as they move from their reliance upon grace to an orientation in which their personal achievements in law keeping are tilting not only their theology but also their attitudes toward their own selves and toward one another in an unhealthy direction. A reading of Galatians 6:1-5 implies that they were no longer acting graciously to one another (verses 1, 2); had developed inflated ideas of their own selves, probably because of their "superior spiritual achievements" (verse 3); and had begun comparing themselves with other individuals in the church who were presumably less dedicated to the "advanced" teachings that saw circumcision and observing the Jewish regulations as a way to truly get right with God (verse 4).

Paul has heard enough of such attitudes and actions flowing out of their new theological orientation. He will begin to address them head on in Galatians 6:1-5, ending up with the fact that ultimately each person comes to judgment before God (verses 5, 7, 8). To put it bluntly, Paul will demonstrate in verses 1-5 that "the first and great evidence of our walking by the Spirit or being filled with the Spirit is not some private mystical experience of our own, but our practical relationships of love with other people" (Stott, p. 155).

The apostle's first practical admonition has to do with those believers who have not done everything right, who have been "overtaken in some fault" (verse 1). The word he selected for "fault" is an interesting one. It means "to stumble on something" (Kittel, vol. 6, p. 170) or to make "a false step so as to lose footing" (Danker, p. 770). As F. F. Bruce notes, the word does not represent "a settled course of action but an isolated action" (Bruce, p. 260). In other words, we are dealing with a church member who has sinned but is not blatantly and unashamedly and continually practicing sin in the sense Paul spoke of in Galatians 5:21, in which he declared that those who do such things will "not inherit the kingdom of God" (RSV). That is, the ones Paul is speaking about in Galatians 6:1 are not hardened rebels but sincere Christians who have temporarily fallen.

Now we as fellow church members can relate to those who have made a mistake (even a serious one) in two ways. We can encourage them and lead them to the throne of grace where they can confess their moral failure and be forgiven (1 John 1:9), or we can add our condemnation to the weight of their already guilty conscience. That latter course "seems to have been what was happening in the churches in Galatia. The zealots for the law were merciless to sinners" (Hansen, p. 184). For Paul, that is part of the tragedy of their new emphasis on the law that had usurped the central place of faith and grace in the gospel he had preached to them. As Hans Betz notes, "Paul seems keenly aware that a self-righteous posture of prosecutors can cause greater damage to the community than the offence done by a wrongdoer" (Betz, p. 298).

Condemning those who have been careless or willful might seem to be quite normal and right—at least from a human perspective. But Paul is telling the Galatians and us today that it is not Christian. To the contrary, Spirit-led people—people walking by the Spirit (Gal. 5:25) —will express the love fruit of the Spirit (verse 22), which includes the virtue of gentleness (verse 23), as they deal with those "overtaken in some fault" (6:1). And they need to not only be gentle with such people, they must remember who they themselves are. After all, none of us are above falling (verse 1). And, if we reflect for a moment, we will recall that we ourselves have been saved by grace and repeatedly forgiven by the gentle mercies of God. Just as God has repeatedly restored us, so we, if we are Christians, will "restore" one another rather than condemn. The word "restore" is a healing word, "used especially as a surgical term, of setting a bone or joint" (Lightfoot, p. 215). Mark 1:19 employs it for the Zebedee brothers "mending" their nets. Christians are to be healers of those amongst them who have fallen into sin. Therefore, we should not condemn those trapped in sin but "bear one another's burdens" and thereby "fulfill the law of Christ" (verse 2).

The expression "law of Christ" is an interesting one in the Galatians' context. It undoubtedly alludes to Galatians 5:14, in which Paul said that "the whole law is fulfilled in one word, 'You shall love your neighbor as yourself'" (RSV). And verse 14 may be based upon such ideas as those set forth by Jesus in Matthew 22:37-40, in which He defines the law in terms of love, and John 13:34, in which He claims that His "new commandment" is that His followers should "love one another; even as I have loved you" (RSV; cf. 15:12).

The tragedy of the Judaizers and many modern Christians is that their preoccupation with the outward laws of the Bible has led them into a transgression of the heart of God's Old and New Testament LAW—to love one's neighbor as one's self (Gal. 5:14; Rom. 13:8-10; Matt. 22:37-40; Deut. 6:5; Lev. 19:18). It is out of the heart of the LAW of love that the more particular commandments related to our neighbor flow (see Rom. 13:8-10; Matt. 22:40). Central to Paul's overall teaching is that those who have been freed from Jewish legalisms and from using the law as a way to get right with God in the end live out the law as they walk by the Spirit. As Paul puts it in Romans, those who are "in Christ Jesus" are free from the "law of sin and death . . . in order that the just requirement of the law might be fulfilled in us, who walk not according to the flesh but according to the Spirit" (Rom. 8:1-4, RSV).

In Galatians 6:3 Paul turns to the topic of personal evaluation. The most serious delusion faced by Christians is thinking they are something when in fact they are nothing. We begin to assume we are something when we begin to contrast our "good" achievements with others who may not be as "righteous" in their daily lives as we are. "God," cried the Pharisee, "I thank thee that I am not like other men. . . . I fast twice a week, I give tithes of all that I get" (Luke 18:11, 12, RSV). Oh, how good we appear to ourselves when we compare ourselves to others. But, oh how poor we are when we evaluate ourselves against God, when we remember that He has forgiven us our past sins by His free grace, and when we realize that He even deals gently with us in our current pride.

Paul's admonition is that we need to examine our own work (Gal. 6:4). In the context of Galatians that examination needs to take place in the light of the fruit of the Spirit and the works of the flesh (5:19-23). Are we walking in the flesh with its spiritual pride and strife or are we walking in the Spirit with its love and gentleness? It is, according to Paul, one or the other. What, I need to honestly ask myself, is the guiding principle of my life as I relate to other church members? Am I condemning of those who have sinned or am I gently serving them in love?

Only when I walk in the Spirit do I have ground for "boasting" (6:4). The Galatians indulged in two kinds of boasting. One group lauded their accomplishments through circumcision and other aspects of the law viewed as a way of getting right with God. The other group consisted of those who realized that they had been rescued from the curse of the broken law by the death of Christ (3:10, 13), transformed from the realm of the flesh to that of the Spirit (5:19-23), and empowered by the Holy Spirit to walk in the way of the Spirit (verse 25). Such boasting consists of extolling what God has done for us in Christ (see 2:20). It actually represents humility in that we see that we are nothing without God's free grace. And it leads to the loving and gentle bearing of one another's burdens (6:1, 2).

But then in verse 5 we come to a surprise: "Each person will have to bear his own load." How is it that we need to share each other's burdens (verse 2) yet carry our own loads (verse 5)? The answer lies in the fact that we are looking at two different Greek words. The burden *(baros)* of verse 2 is a crushing one, whereas the load *(phortion)* of verse 5 is like an individual soldier's quite manageable pack, from which "each is supplied with his own provisions" (Lightfoot, p. 217). Thus if we are walking by the Spirit we will be gently working to help other Christians down the pathway of life, but each of us also remains responsible for daily living personally in the Spirit in our journey. Our load is to be in God's will as we walk. John Calvin is undoubtedly correct when he links each person bearing his or her own burden to God's final judgment, "in which each man for himself and without comparison will render an account of his life" (Calvin, p. 111). Galatians 6:7, 8, which deal with the results of sowing to the flesh or to the Spirit, reinforces that conclusion.

24. Living by the Spirit: Part 2

Galatians 6:6-10

> [6]*The one being taught the word is to share all good things with the one teaching.*
>
> [7]*Do not be deceived; God is not mocked; for whatever a man sows, that also he will reap.* [8]*For the one sowing to his flesh will from the flesh reap corruption, but the one sowing to the Spirit will from the Spirit reap eternal life.* [9]*Now let us not become weary in well doing, for in due season we will reap if we do not give up.* [10]*Therefore, as we have opportunity we should do good to all people, and especially toward those of the household of faith.*

The Christian freedom of which Paul has been writing in his letter to the Galatians is a deliverance from the curse of the broken law and from the burden of having to establish a right relationship with God through law keeping, but it is not a license to do nothing. To the contrary, saved Christians will have a desire to serve one another in acts of love.

Galatians 6:5 tells us that "each person will have to bear his own load." As we noted in section 23, the most likely meaning of that verse is that our load is to be in God's will in our daily journey in the Spirit (5:25). And central to walking in the Spirit is living out the fruit of the Spirit. Beginning in Galatians 6:1, Paul has been laying out specific ways in which Christians can walk in the Spirit:

- They can in gentleness restore those who have fallen (verse 1);
- They can share one another's burdens (verse 2);
- They can stop comparing their supposed accomplishments with

those of other believers and start focusing on God's will for their personal lives (verses 3-5).

Verses 3-5 imply not only the importance of self-examination and personal responsibility, but, by extension, judgment. Those themes surface again in verses 7 and 8. "Do not be deceived; God is not mocked; for whatever a man sows, that also he will reap," Paul asserts in verse 7.

The apostle is in actuality issuing a call for the individual believers in the Galatian churches to decide if they are going to live according to the flesh or the Spirit. There is no way that they can live by some mixture of the two (see Matt. 6:24). It is one or the other.

Part of his appeal is a warning based upon well-known agricultural principles. Farmers know that if they want a harvest they must sow seed in their fields. Beyond that, they understand that the type of seed that they plant will determine the kind of harvest they will have. If they sow thistles, they would not expect to reap wheat. Good seed produces a good crop and bad seed a bad one. Again, farmers realize that if they only plant one-third of their field they can not expect a good harvest in those parts left fallow.

"Precisely the same principle," John Stott writes, "operates in the moral and spiritual sphere. *Whatever a man sows, that he will also reap.* It is not the reapers who decide what the harvest is going to be like, but the sowers. If a man is faithful and conscientious in his sowing, then he can confidently expect a good harvest. If he 'sows wild oats,' as we sometimes say, then he must not expect to reap strawberries! On the contrary, 'those who plough iniquity and sow trouble reap the same' (Jb. 4:8). Or, as Hosea warned his contemporaries (8:7), 'they sow the wind, and they shall reap the whirlwind' (sc. of divine judgment)" (Stott, p. 166).

The law of sowing and reaping is built into the fabric of God's world in both the natural and spiritual realms. And, claims Paul in citing a proverbial warning, "God is not mocked." "There can be no double-dealing with God, for He knows all the thoughts and intents of the heart" just as He is aware of which seed a farmer has sown (Rendall, pp. 189, 190).

At the surface level all of us would agree that no one can fool the omniscient God. "Yet," G. Walter Hansen perceptively notes, "there is a common tendency to think that there is one exception to this universal principle: 'Though it proves true for everyone else, it is not true for me. I will not have to reap a harvest from the seeds I sow. I can sow whatever seed I want and still expect a good harvest.' This common line of thought only proves the words of the prophet Jeremiah, 'The heart is deceitful above all things and beyond cure' (Jer 17:9). Our capacity for self-deception is frightening. It is amazing how blind otherwise brilliant people can be to their own spiritual direction in life. In fact, the more brilliant people are, the more skilled they are at developing rationalizations to deceive themselves and to hide from God. The story of Adam and Eve's hiding from God behind their skimpy clothes and even skimpier excuses is our common human experience. Paul's warning ['do not be deceived'] needs to be heard, and to be heard often, to warn us against our most brilliant self-delusions" (Hansen, p. 194).

The apostle has already mentioned deception twice in his letter to the Galatians: "who has bewitched you" in 3:1 and self deception in 6:3. And just what is it that the Galatian believers (and us) are in danger of being deluded about? From the overall context of the book the two focal points of deception are the nature of true religion and how we need to express it in daily living. In Galatians 3 and 4 he dealt with the first aspect of their deception and in Galatians 5 and 6 he has focused on the second. He has repeatedly asserted that they need to live by the Spirit rather than by the flesh.

Now in Galatians 6:7, 8, Paul expands the flesh and Spirit motifs into a judgment scenario, claiming that "the one sowing to his flesh" will reap corruption, whereas the "one sowing to the Spirit" will harvest eternal life. It is not exactly certain what he means by "corruption" but it seems safe to say that at least part of what he has in mind would be the opposite of "eternal life."

But, what, we need to ask, is "sowing to his flesh"? In the Galatians' context it in the most general sense involves living a selfish, self-centered life. More specifically, it includes the works of the flesh listed in Galatians 5:19-21. And even more relevant to the context of 6:8, it speaks to those who were biting, devouring, provoking, and envying one another (5:15, 26) as they shifted away from Paul's grace/faith-based gospel to the legalistic solution promoted by the Judaizers. The crisis was literally destroying the Christian community in Galatia. Peter's and Barnabas' defection (2:12, 13) only illustrates the disharmony resulting from the false teachings.

And what does Paul mean here by "sowing to the Spirit"? He obviously has in mind living the God-centered/other-centered lifestyle expressed as the "fruit of the Spirit" (5:22, 23), which he also has referred to as walking by the Spirit (verse 25).

Paul, in the first five verses of Galatians 6, set forth several concrete examples of how the Galatians needed to walk in the Spirit or "sow to the Spirit." He continues with more specific examples in verses 6-10 in the context of a judgment illustration.

In verse 6, for example, he raises the issue of support of the ministry. The very fact that he mentions it suggests that it had become a problem in the Galatian congregations. Given the divisions in the church, it is easy to see how the situation might have developed. From Paul's allusion to the topic we can learn several things about the early Christian church. First, that he advocated formal teaching in correct doctrine and practice and that such instructors were active in Galatia. Second, verse 6 implies that these teachers were either full time or were at least giving a major portion of their time to their calling, since he admonishes that the members should support them. Paul said much the same thing in 1 Corinthians in which he wrote that "the Lord commanded that those who proclaim the gospel should get their living by the gospel" (9:14, RSV). Third, his counsel in its context suggests that if the church was to be united and strong it needed "gifted teachers . . . to devote themselves to an accurate interpretation and application of the 'truth of the gospel'" (Hansen, p. 193). That has been true throughout the history of the Christian church. But the devil is always active to both undermine wholesome teaching and to discourage good teachers through a lack of remuneration.

Paul's final admonition in verses 6 to 10 deals with doing good to others in the community, but especially to fellow believers (verse 10). He realized, however, that it is easy to get discouraged in well doing, especially in a divided congregation in which no one seems to appreciate what is being contributed. Such was the situation in Galatia, where even Paul himself had become discouraged, fearing he had labored in vain (4:11).

The only way that the Galatian believers could hope for spiritual health both collectively and individually was to move away from the divisive spirit of the Judaizers and to adopt fully the fruit of God's Spirit into their lives. That is just as true for us living 2,000 years later. The greatest need of the church is members who fully realize their humble part in the plan of salvation and who let God's Spirit live out His love, joy, and gentleness in their lives. Only when that happens will God's family on earth begin to look like His family in heaven.

Part V

Wrapping It Up

Galatians 6:11-18

25. Final Counsel and Benediction

Galatians 6:11-18

[11]See with what large letters I am writing to you with my own hand. [12]It is those who desire to make a good showing in the flesh who are trying to compel you to be circumcised, only so that they will not be persecuted for the cross of Christ. [13]For those who are circumcised do not themselves keep the law, but they desire you to be circumcised so that they may boast in your flesh. [14]But may I never boast except in the cross of our Lord Jesus Christ, through which the world has been crucified to me and I to the world. [15]For neither is circumcision anything nor uncircumcision, but a new creation. [16]And peace and mercy be upon as many as walk according to this rule, even upon the Israel of God.

[17]From now on let no one cause trouble for me, for I bear the marks of Jesus in my body.

[18]The grace of our Lord Jesus Christ be with your spirit, brothers, Amen.

With verse 11 Paul begins a final wrap-up written in his own hand. He had dictated the rest of his letter to one of his colleagues. Now the apostle goes out of his way to point out the "large letters" that he is using. The text doesn't tell us why he writes so large, but three suggestions have emerged to explain it. One possibility is that he had bad eyesight and, as a result, penned with an outsized script. Those who hold that position refer to his "bodily ailment" of Galatians 4:13 and to the fact that believers would have given him their own eyes (verse 15). A second suggestion is that Paul was not a professional scribe and thus formed rather sprawling and untidy letters.

Those suggestions may have some validity, but, given the content of his final few verses, it is most likely that he employed the large letters for emphasis. We still do the same thing today when we use capital letters, italics, or underlining. Such literary techniques signal the reader to pay attention because what follows is important. Along that line, Hans Betz writes that the final section "contains the interpretive clues to the understanding of Paul's major concerns in the letter as a whole and should be employed as the hermeneutical [i.e., interpretive] key to the intentions of the Apostle" (Betz, p. 313).

Certainly Paul highlights and pounds home in verses 12-16 themes evident throughout the epistle. One of them concerns his problem with the Judaizers which has been central from the first verse of chapter 1. Here in his most straightforward manner he outlines the techniques of those seeking to lead the Galatian believers away from the gospel truth that Paul had taught them. Circumcision was undoubtedly at the center of their message. They were apparently the same men that the book of Acts represents as claiming that "unless you are circumcised according to the custom of Moses, you cannot be saved" (15:1, RSV). Such a teaching was the ultimate heresy for Paul, whose message centered on salvation by grace accepted through faith (Gal. 2:16; Eph. 2:8).

But the good news is that they were as yet still "trying to compel" the Galatians to be circumcised (Gal. 6:12). Some of the believers may have already gone that direction, but from this verse it appears that many if not most had not yet taken that step. Thus Paul's urgent, vigorous, and aggressive style in writing to the Galatians. They were, as he saw it, in the midst of a life and death struggle. The word "compel" points to the pressure that the Judaizers were applying to the Galatian believers. "These teachers," Leon Morris writes, "were not saying that circumcision was a helpful rite for people who chose to accept it, but that it was necessary for true Christian initiation" (Morris, p. 187).

Paul has two things to say about such tactics. First, those pushing circumcision had a "desire to make a good showing in the flesh" (Gal. 6:12) so that "they may boast in your flesh" (verse 13). R. Alan Cole suggests that Paul's point was that the Judaizers "wanted 'ecclesiastical statistics'; so many circumcisions in a given year was certainly something to boast about. It is easy to smile at them. But 'baptismal statistics' in mission areas can at times be just as dangerous" (Cole, p. 181).

Second, Paul uplifted the cross of Christ. If the symbol of the Judaizers' theology was circumcision, that of Paul's was the cross. The first was a well recognized emblem in the Roman system. Circumcision saved Jews from persecution, because the authorities officially recognized the Jewish religion and officially allowed Jews (i.e., those who were circumcised) to practice it. Christians who were not circumcised did not have that protection. We need to remember that Rome viewed the earliest Christians as belonging to a Jewish sect. They did not yet classify them as a distinct religion.

On the other hand, the Romans regarded the cross as a despicable thing. In fact, it was "the most ignoble of all objects—a matter of unrelieved shame, not of boasting. It is difficult, after sixteen centuries and more during which the cross has been a sacred symbol, to realize the unspeakable horror and loathing which the very mention or thought of the cross provoked in Paul's day. The word *crux* [cross] was unmentionable in polite Roman society (Cicero, *Pro Rabirio* 16); even when one was being condemned to death by crucifixion the sentence used an archaic formula which served as a sort of euphemism: *arbori infelici suspendito,* 'hang him on the unlucky tree' (Cicero, *ibid.,* 13)" (Bruce, p. 271).

Yet the image of the cross was at the center of Paul's life and thought. Donald Guthrie notes that "in no more conclusive way could Paul express the centrality of the cross in his thinking than by exalting it as the sole object of his boasting. . . . For him it is the key to man's salvation, and he assumes that his readers will know what he means when he refers to it. It clearly stands for much more than the mere historical fact that Jesus was crucified. It stands for the whole significance of the event, not only for mankind in general but for Paul in particular. He could understand how the cross was a stumbling-block for Jews, but he could never understand how Christians could ever fail to see it as their greatest glory. It may well be that a major part of the weakness of much of the witness of the modern Church lies in a failure to boast in the cross" (Guthrie, p. 150).

One of the great paradoxes of Christian history is that so many calling themselves Christians have avoided the substitutionary death of Christ on the cross that is so central to Paul's letter to the Galatians (see especially 3:10-13). Perhaps one reason for that distortion is that the crucifixion reflects upon all of us humans in an unflattering light. It points to the fact that we are sinners who are unable to save ourselves, whoever we are or whatever we do. The cross shrinks us to our true size. In the process it provides the only possible foundation for a theology of salvation by grace. The only alternative to grace is some sort of salvation by human achievement. Whether that achievement be circumcision, dietary rigidity, or some other holy practice makes no difference. Paul's gospel is crystal clear—salvation by grace through faith on the basis of the cross and resurrection (Eph. 2:8-10; 1 Cor. 15:1-4). But, in spite of his clarity on the topic, people are still fascinated with the Judaistic perversion (or some form of it) some 2,000 years after the penning of his "large letters."

Paul's jest at the Judaizers that they wanted others to keep the law, but didn't truly observe it themselves is another recurring theme in Galatians. That is, the necessity of those who seek salvation through law to obey the whole law and the actual impossibility of doing so (3:10; 5:3; 3:21, 22). While to Paul the Judaizers were nothing short of hypocrites, they were at least consistent in their claim regarding the Gentiles that it was "necessary to circumcise them, and to charge them to keep the law of Moses" (Acts 15:5, RSV). Still, Paul regarded their claim as nothing but a human religion. Basing itself on what people could do for God rather than on what He could do for them, it was self-centered rather than cross-centered. But it must be one or the other, either by faith or by works, either the "worship" of the accomplishments of one's self that is so dear to the unrenewed human heart or a prostrating of self at the foot of the cross.

In Galatians 6:15 Paul hits upon the importance of a total renewal or rebirth or reorientation for every Christian. Christianity is not an outward change. It is not being circumcised or even baptized. Rather, it is letting God make us into "a new creation" (cf. 2 Cor. 5:17). Jesus calls that same experience being "born anew" by the Holy Spirit (John 3:3, 5). Paul in Romans 12:2 refers to it as a transformation. Other places speak of it as getting a new heart and a new mind (Phil. 2:5; Heb. 8:10; Rom. 12:2) or as being converted (Matt. 18:3; Acts 3:19). All those metaphors describe the same life changing event. For Paul Christianity is always an inner experience rather than an outward one. Yet the Judaizers down through history have always emphasized external symbols. Thus Paul's counsel to the Galatians is still as relevant as it was the day he wrote it.

The apostle notes in Galatians 6:16 that those who walked (lived) according to the rule (standard) of his gospel of grace would be blessed with the mercy they needed so badly and with that peace with God and with others that comes through justification by faith (Rom. 5:1, 10). He also reminds them of his teaching in Galatians 3:29 that it is those who have the faith of Abraham who are truly "the Israel of God." His final appeal is for them not to continue to cause him trouble by questioning his apostolic authority (see on 1:1), since he himself bears the marks of a slave to Jesus in his own body. Undoubtedly he had in mind the scars of his many persecutions (see 2 Cor. 11:23-28).

Paul ends his great epistle with a reference to grace. It is a fitting conclusion to a letter that began with the same word (1:3) and alluded to it throughout.

Exploring
Ephesians

Introduction
to the Letter to the Ephesians

The Epistle to the Ephesians holds a treasured place in Christianity. J. Armitage Robinson views it as "the crown of St Paul's writings" (Robinson, p. vii), while William Barclay asserts that it is "The Queen of the Epistles" (Barclay, p. 71).

We will see in the following pages that this short letter speaks to our needs today just as powerfully as it did to the church and its members two millennia ago. As a result, Ralph Martin asserts that "no part of the New Testament has a more contemporary relevance than the letter to the Ephesians" (Martin, p. 1). While that is true, it is also true that we will understand the letter better if we grasp some background issues related to it.

A Note on Authorship, Date, and Recipients

The letter to the Ephesians twice refers to the apostle Paul as its author (1:1; 3:1). For most of the history of Christianity believers took those claims at face value, but in the past 200 years they, like so many other aspects of the Bible, have been challenged, with some arguing that it is the work of one of Paul's disciples who used his name to gain acceptance. F. F. Bruce cautiously reflects that perspective when he writes that "if the Epistle to the Ephesians was not written directly by Paul, but by one of his disciples in the apostle's name, then its author was the greatest Paulinist of all time—a disciple who assimilated his master's thought more thoroughly than anyone else ever did. The man who could write Ephesians must have been the apostle's equal, if not his superior, in mental stature and spiritual insight. . . . The author, if he was not Paul himself, has carried the apostle's thinking to its logical conclusion." Bruce significantly adds that "of such a second Paul early Christian history has no knowledge" (Bruce, *Epistle to the Ephesians,* pp. 11, 12). To the contrary, early Christian writers, following the letter's own claims, regarded Paul as the author. That position received no significant challenge until 1792 (see Hoehner, pp. 2-6). And when all is said and done it is best to let the letter speak for itself in regard to its own authorship. In Ephesians we have the crowning summation of Paul's thought.

While the authorship of Ephesians is clear from the letter itself, the exact identity of its recipients is not. The problem is that the oldest and best Greek manuscripts omit the words "at Ephesus" in Ephesians 1:1. Thus the most accurate English translation is "to the saints who are also faithful in Christ Jesus" (RSV) rather than "to the saints which are at Ephesus, and to the faithful in Christ Jesus" (KJV).

Beyond the fact that the earliest manuscripts do not have the words "at Ephesus," the letter is also distinctive among Paul's correspondence in that it does not have any personal greetings to his friends and colleagues. That is especially strange when we recall that he worked in Ephesus longer than in any other place. According to Acts, he labored almost three years in the city (see 18:19-21; 19:1-20; 20:17-38).

In addition to the lack of personal greetings, Ephesians also makes no specific reference to any particular problems in the congregation and has no counsels on special aspects of faith and conduct—matters of content that we would expect if Paul wrote his letter to a single congregation. A comparison of Ephesians with his letters to Galatia or Corinth will highlight the differences between them. The issues raised in Ephesians are quite general and could apply to Christians in any Gentile community of the time.

Because of its generalities, it appears that Paul most likely wrote his masterful work as a circular letter meant to be read in all the churches in that part of Asia Minor for which Ephesus was the central city and the most prominent Christian community. If that is the case, it is probable that with the passage of time the name of Ephesus eventually found its way into later Greek manuscripts of the letter as a mark of identification that made its first verse parallel with the designations found in Paul's other letters.

The letter itself was apparently one of his later ones. Several times he notes that he was in prison (Eph. 3:1; 4:1; 6:20). As we look at his overall life it appears that our best estimate is that he wrote Ephesians sometime during A.D. 60–A.D. 62, just a few years before his death in Rome, which probably took place during the persecution of Nero in A.D. 64.

The Relationship Between Ephesians and Colossians

The letter of Ephesians did not travel alone from Paul's Roman prison to Asia Minor. H.G.C. Moule is undoubtedly correct when he suggests that "two other apostolic messages go by the same bearers; a letter to the outlying mission-church of Colossae, on some special dangers just now present there and at Laodicea [Col. 4:16], and a shorter missive, a note rather than a letter, for an individual Colossian, Philemon; it commends to him his slave Onesimus, once a runaway and perhaps a thief besides, now 'begotten' to the new life in the miracle of a true conversion, and returning at all costs to duty" (Moule, pp. 23, 24).

Not only did the Ephesian and Colossian letters journey to their destinations together, but we find more similarities between those two epistles than between any other letters in the New Testament. In fact, "with varying degrees of similarity, 75 of the 155 verses of Ephesians are found in Colossians" (Foulkes, p. 25). The most extensive example is the commendation of Tychicus, who delivered both letters, which evidences a verbatim correspondence between 29 consecutive words (see Col. 4:7, 8; Eph. 6:21, 22). Beyond those passages we observe many other striking parallels (see, *e.g.,* Eph. 5:22–6:9 and Col. 3:18–4:1 and the extensive graphic comparisons in Hoehner, p. 34 and Lincoln, p. xlix).

The echoes between the two epistles are not only striking but easily understood. Those of us who often write several letters in one day find ourselves molding similar material in varying ways for somewhat different purposes. Historians as they work with archival letter files are well aware of the phenomenon. Meanwhile, a comparative reading of Ephesians and Colossians in one sitting is both a blessing and an edifying and enlightening exercise. A contextual understanding of the phrasiology of one book at times helps us unpack Paul's intended meaning in the other.

Purpose of Ephesians

Paul had labored extensively in Ephesus and the surrounding territory from about A.D. 52 to A.D. 55. In the years since that time widespread evangelism had taken place among the Gentiles. As a result, many of the new believers did not know him personally, even though they apparently respected his reputation as an apostolic missionary.

C. E. Arnold notes that "being converts from a Hellenistic religious environment—mystery religions, magic, astrology—these people needed a positive grounding in the Pauline gospel from the apostle himself. Their fear of evil spirits and cosmic powers was also a great concern, especially the question of where Christ stands in relation to these forces" (in Hawthorne, p. 246).

In addition to that necessary theoretical grounding, they also required more background in how to live a Christian lifestyle free from the vices of their Greek culture, such as drunkenness, sexual immorality, and thievery. And beyond that, both the Gentile converts and what had become a Jewish Christian minority needed instruction that would help them overcome the tensions that had grown up between them as well as guidance as to how they might better unite as one in the church, or body, of Christ.

Thus Paul had definite issues to deal with in Ephesus and its surrounding region, even if they did not have the specificity of those addressed in most of his other letters.

Ephesians' Major Themes

Ephesians is rich in both theology and praise. The letter has at least six major theological themes. But running across them is an understanding of how God's grace not only provides salvation for individual Jews and Gentiles but brings them together in a united church that is an extension of the heavenly realm. "The author," Martin asserts, is gripped with the grace of God, "a single theme that runs like a thread through the treatise" (Martin, p. 6). With that thought in mind, *we can view grace as a presupposition that undergirds and contextualizes the epistle's other theological themes.* Those themes are:

1. *The Greatness of God and the Exaltation of Christ.* The first major section of Ephesians (1:3-14) is an unparalleled praise to the God who is working His great cosmic plan of salvation in human history. Fundamental to the epistle's concept of God is how His will (1:9, 4) and His love (1:5; 2:4) inspires Him to act for His people.

Introduction to the Letter to the Ephesians

God the Father is absolutely central to Ephesians. Of the 40 references to God as Father in Paul's writing, eight appear in Ephesians (1:2, 3, 17; 2:18; 3:14, 15; 4:6; 5:20; 6:23). The most that any other Pauline book mentions the Father is four.

Coupled with Ephesians' emphasis on God the Father is its exaltation of Christ. The epistle doesn't neglect the death of Christ (see, e.g., 1:7; 2:13, 16; 5:2, 25), but its focus is on His resurrection and glorification in heavenly places as He unites with the Father in working out Their great plan (see, e.g., 1:20-23).

2. *The Cosmic Struggle.* Ephesians is the New Testament document that more than any other enables us to see the cosmic forces behind earthly ones in the great spiritual struggle of the ages. On the one side is the "heavenly places" realm of the Father, which Christ entered at His resurrection (1:20). In that realm He is "far above all rule and authority and power and dominion, and above every name that is named, not only in this age but also in that which is to come" (verse 21, RSV).

Standing over against Christ are "the spiritual hosts of wickedness in the heavenly places" (6:12, RSV). Arnold notes that "the devil and various categories of 'powers' are mentioned sixteen times in the epistle" (Arnold, *Ephesians,* p. 1).

Not only does the epistle refer to the struggle between the opposing supernatural powers but chapter 6 has an extended section instructing earthly believers in regard to spiritual warfare against the powers of darkness (verses 10-20). It was absolutely essential for them to realize that Christ's power was superior to the various agencies of the other side that they feared.

3. *Salvation as an Accomplished Fact.* The letter does not totally neglect end-time salvation (see 1:10, 14; 4:30; 5:27), but the focus is on believers' salvation as an accomplished fact. That perspective is evident in Ephesians 2:5 and 8 with its use of the past tense: "You have been saved" (RSV). Believers, however, have not only been saved but also "raised up" with Christ and made to sit with Him in "heavenly places" (verse 6).

The central phrase expressing the saved state of believers is that they are "in Christ," a thought occurring some 34 times in Ephesians. James Stewart notes that Paul uses the phrase 164 times altogether, 11 times (counting pronouns and synonyms) in one of the great opening sentences of Ephesians (1:3-14). Stewart points out that "the heart of Paul's religion is union with Christ. This more than any other conception . . . is the key which unlocks the secrets of his soul" (Stewart, pp. 147, 152, 153).

The great "mystery" of the ages (see 3:3, 4, 9; 5:32; 6:19) is God's salvation of both Jews and Gentiles and the uniting of them in one body in the Church through Christ. The mystery of salvation was not an afterthought on God's part, but a part of His plan "from the foundation of the world" (3:9; 1:4, 5, RSV). Its fulfillment has begun with those who accept it, but it will not come to completion till the "fullness of time" (2:7; 1:10, RSV). Thus the "fruits of Christ's victory" are already possessed by believers but "have 'not yet' been fully realized" (O'Brien, p. 33).

4. *Walking the Christian Life.* The already but not yet approach to salvation in Ephesians leads to certain tensions in the lives of believers. They may be seated with Christ in "heavenly places" (2:6), but in their daily lives they are still living on earth, with all of its problems and temptations. As a result, Paul offers ethical guidelines along two paths. First, he appeals to believers to give up the vices that characterized their pre-Christian conduct, such as covetousness, fornication, impurity, idolatry, and so on (see, e.g., 5:3-13). Second, Paul desires that they "be continually renewed" in their minds (4:23), that they "put on the new nature, created after the likeness of God in true righteousness and holiness" (4:24, RSV), and that they be "imitators of God . . . and walk in love" (5:1, 2, RSV). Along that line, the apostle goes out of his way to give extended instruction on living in family and employment contexts (5:21-6:9). Thus, as in Galatians, the first half of Ephesians is theological while the second is ethical.

5. *The Unity of Jew and Gentile.* Also echoing the main theme of Galatians is the emphasis in Ephesians that salvation in Christ removes all racial and social barriers between Jews and Gentiles (Eph. 2:14; cf. Gal. 3:28, 29). In fact, God reconciled both to Himself "in one body through the cross, thereby bringing hostility to an end" (Eph. 2:16, RSV). Unity of the "one body" is a central theme in the epistle (see, e.g., 3:6; 4:3-6).

6. *The Nature of the Church.* Ephesians has a pervasive ecclesiological focus. The word *ekklēsia,* church, occurs nine times in the letter (1:22; 3:10, 21; 5:23, 24, 25, 27, 29, 32), in each case referring to the universal church rather than to a local congregation. In his other letters Paul addresses specific congregations, such as in 1 Corinthians 1:2, in which he

writes "to the church of God which is at Corinth" (RSV). But in Ephesians the church has what Ralph Martin calls "a sort of transcendental status" (Martin, p. 7). That is, the church on earth is a part of and participates in the life of the church in the heavenly places (Eph. 1:22, 23; 2:6; 5:27). Ephesians, to say the least, has an exalted view of the church. It is a body that spans not only earth but includes all God's people throughout the universe. Local congregations to Paul, Peter O'Brien suggests, "were concrete, visible expressions of that new relationship which believers have with the Lord Jesus. Local gatherings, whether in a congregation or a house-church, were earthly manifestations of that heavenly gathering around the risen Christ" (O'Brien, p. 26).

The epistle has varied metaphors for the church. Unlike much modern discussion, however, the letter does not describe the church institutionally. Rather, it views it architecturally as a building, with Christ as the cornerstone (Eph. 2:19-22); biologically as a unified body or organism, with Christ as its head (1:22, 23; 4:16; 5:23); and sociologically as a family unit, with Christ being the loving and caring husband of His bride (i.e., the church, 5:23-32). Each of those metaphors gives us a snapshot of the church from a different perspective.

Structure and Outline of Ephesians

Like several other Pauline letters, Ephesians falls into two main parts. Chapters 1-3 focus on theology, while the last three chapters demonstrate how doctrine translates into everyday conduct in the lives of believers.

I. Address and greeting (1:1, 2)

II. Doctrinal affirmations (1:3-3:21)

   A. Praise to God and Christ for Their many blessings (1:3-14)

   B. Prayer for the "Ephesians," that they might be able to grasp the greatness of what God has done in Christ (1:15-23)

   C. The saving grace of God, the foundation of the church (2:1-10)

   D. Reconciliation with God also means reconciliation with one another in the church, grace being the basis of Christian unity (2:11-22)

   E. Paul's ministry of grace in relation to the mystery of God (3:1-13)

   F. Paul concludes his prayer for the Ephesians and their need to understand the love of Christ and be filled with God's fullness (3:14-19)

   G. Praise to God (3:20, 21)

III. Practical exhortations (4:1-6:20)
    A. The importance of unity in the church (4:1-16)
        1. A plea for unity (4:1-3)
        2. A confession of unity (4:4-6)
        3. The role of the gifts of the Holy Spirit in producing unity (4:7-16)
    B. The importance of living a Christian life (4:17-5:20)
        1. Putting off the old nature and being renewed in the likeness of God (4:17-24)
        2. Specific instruction on living the Christian life (4:25-32)
        3. Imitating God (5:1, 2)
        4. Avoiding evil and living in the light (5:3-20)
    C. The importance of Christian relationships (5:21-6:9)
        1. Between husband and wife (5:21-33)
        2. Between parents and children (6:1-4)
        3. Between slaves and masters (6:5-9)
    D. The importance of fighting the powers of darkness in the strength of God (6:10-20)
IV. Personal report and final greetings (6:21-24)

Ephesians' Relevance for the Twenty-first Century

"This letter," writes Klyne Snodgrass, "is the most contemporary book in the Bible. Apart from a few terms and the treatment of slavery, Ephesians could have been written to a modern church. It is about us. It describes human beings, their predicament, sin, and delusion, but much more it describes God's reaching out to people to recreate and transform them into a new society" (Snodgrass, p. 17).

At the center of Ephesians' relevance is its portrayal of a victorious Christ who rules with God in heaven. As we pass through life we may feel powerless and even hopeless, but the letter to the Ephesians pounds home the truth that we have nothing to fear if we maintain our faith and put on the whole armor of God. The good news is that Christ has defeated the powers of darkness and that victory belongs both to the church and to each of us who is "in Christ."

A second aspect of significance to the contemporary scene is Ephesians' firm picture of salvation. We may have been lost in sin and addiction, "but God, who is rich in mercy, out of the great love with which he loved us, even when we were dead through our trespasses, made us alive together with Christ (by grace you have been saved), and raised us up with him, and made us sit with him in the heavenly places in Christ Jesus" (2:4-6, RSV). What a powerful truth. Here is comfort. But it's just the beginning of what God wants to do for each of us. "In the coming ages," he will "show the immeasurable riches of his grace in kindness toward us in Christ Jesus" (verse 7, RSV). Here Christians find both hope and an anchor for the soul.

A third highlight for us today is Ephesians' picture of the church as a community of the saved. John Stott writes that "one of our chief evangelical blind spots has been to overlook the central importance of the church. We tend to proclaim individual salvation without moving on to the saved community. We emphasize that Christ died for us 'to redeem us from all iniquity' rather than 'to purify for himself a people of his own' [Titus 2:14]. . . . Our message is more good news of a new life than of a new society. Nobody can emerge from a careful reading of Paul's letter to the Ephesians with a privatized gospel. For Ephesians is the gospel of the church" (Stott, p. 9). And the doctrine of the church may be one of the most neglected biblical concepts in the twenty-first century. As modern Christians we need the teaching of Ephesians on this point.

A related perspective desperately needed in the church today is Ephesians' instruction on unity. It not only sets forth the relationship of God's people both in heaven and on earth, but it moves beyond to teach the breaking down of "the dividing wall of hostility" (2:14, RSV) that has separated even members of God's church. The church of today needs to heed Paul's message and let it dissolve the racial and other impediments that block its oneness in Christ.

Other points of relevance in this "Queen of the Epistles" (Barclay, p. 71) are its instruction on family life and employer/employee relationships and its powerful illustrations of praise and prayer. A close study of those topics in Ephesians will benefit each one of us.

List of Works Cited

Abbott, T. K. *A Critical and Exegetical Commentary on the Epistles to the Ephesians and to the Colossians.* The International Critical Commentary. Edinburgh: T. & T. Clark, 1897.

Ante-Nicene Fathers, 10 vols. Alexander Roberts et al., eds. Peabody, Mass.: Hendrickson, 1994.

Apostolic Fathers, 2d ed. J. B. Lightfoot and J. R. Harmer, trans. Michael W. Holmes, ed. Grand Rapids: Baker, 1989.

Arnold, Clinton E. "Ephesians." In *Zondervan Illustrated Bible Backgrounds Commentary.* Clinton E. Arnold, ed. Grand Rapids: Zondervan, 2002, III:300-341.

_____. *Ephesians, Power and Magic: The Concept of Power in Ephesians in Light of Its Historical Setting.* Cambridge: Cambridge University Press, 1989.

_____. *Powers of Darkness: Principalities and Powers in Paul's Letters.* Downers Grove, Ill.: InterVarsity, 1992.

Barclay, William. *The Letters to the Galatians and Ephesians,* 2d ed. The Daily Study Bible. Edinburgh: The Saint Andrew Press, 1958.

Barth, Markus. *Ephesians: Introduction, Translation, and Commentary on Chapters 1-3.* Anchor Bible. Garden City, N.Y.: Doubleday, 1974.

_____. *Ephesians: Translation and Commentary on Chapters 4-6.* Anchor Bible. Garden City, N.Y.: Doubleday, 1974.

Barton, Bruce B. et al. *Ephesians.* Life Application Bible Commentary. Wheaton, Ill.: Tyndale House, 1996.

Best, Ernest. *A Critical and Exegetical Commentary on Ephesians.* The International Critical Commentary. Edinburgh: T. & T. Clark, 1998.

Bratcher, Robert G., and Eugene A. Nida. *A Handbook on Paul's Letter to the Ephesians.* UBS Handbook Series. New York: United Bible Societies, 1982.

Bromiley, Geoffrey W., ed. *The International Standard Bible Encyclopedia,* rev. ed. 4 vols. Grand Rapids: Eerdmans, 1979-1988.

Bruce, F. F. *The Epistle to the Ephesians: A Verse-by-Verse Exposition.* n.p.: Fleming H. Revell, 1961.

_____. *The Epistles to the Colossians, to Philemon, and to the Ephesians.* New International Commentary on the New Testament. Grand Rapids: Eerdmans, 1984.

Calvin, John. *The Epistles of Paul the Apostle to the Galatians, Ephesians, Philippians and Colossians.* T. H. L. Parker, trans. Calvin's Commentaries. Grand Rapids: Eerdmans, 1965.

Dale, R. W. *The Epistle to the Ephesians: Its Doctrine and Ethics,* 7th ed. London: Hodder and Stoughton, 1893.

Danker, Frederick William, ed. *A Greek-English Lexicon of the New Testament and Other Early Christian Literature,* 3d ed. Chicago: University of Chicago Press, 2000.

Edwards, Mark J., ed. *Galatians, Ephesians, Philippians.* Ancient Christian Commentary on Scripture. Downers Grove, Ill.: InterVarsity, 1999.

Findlay, G. G. *The Epistle to the Ephesians.* The Expositor's Bible. New York: A. C. Armstrong and Son, 1905.

Foulkes, Francis. *The Letter of Paul to the Ephesians,* rev. ed. Tyndale New Testament Commentaries. Grand Rapids: Eerdmans, 1989.

Hawthorne, Gerald F., and Ralph P. Martin, eds. *Dictionary of Paul and His Letters.* Downers

Grove, Ill.: InterVarsity, 1993.

Hodge, Charles. *Commentary on the Epistle to the Ephesians*. Grand Rapids: Eerdmans, 1994.

Hoehner, Harold W. *Ephesians: An Exegetical Commentary*. Grand Rapids: Baker, 2002.

Horn, Siegfried H. *Seventh-day Adventist Bible Dictionary*. Washington, D.C.: Review and Herald, 1960.

Johnston, Robert M. *Peter and Jude: Living in Dangerous Times*. Bible Amplifier. Boise, Ida.: Pacific Press, 1995.

Josephus. *Complete Works*. William Whiston, trans. Grand Rapids: Kregal, 1960.

Knight, George R. *My Gripe With God: A Study in Divine Justice and the Problem of the Cross*. Washington, D.C.: Review and Herald, 1990.

Kreitzer, Larry J. *The Epistle to the Ephesians*. Epworth Commentaries. Peterborough, U.K.: Epworth Press, 1997.

Liefeld, Walter L. *Ephesians*. The IVP New Testament Commentary. Downers Grove, Ill.: InterVarsity, 1997.

Lincoln, Andrew T. *Ephesians*. Word Biblical Commentary. Dallas: Word, 1990.

Lloyd-Jones, D. Martyn. *Christian Unity: An Exposition of Ephesians 4:1-16*. Grand Rapids: Baker, 1998.

_____. *Darkness and Light: An Exposition of Ephesians 4:17-5:17*. Grand Rapids: Baker, 1998.

_____. *God's Ultimate Purpose: An Exposition of Ephesians 1*. Grand Rapids: Baker, 1998.

_____. *God's Way of Reconciliation: An Exposition of Ephesians 2*. Grand Rapids: Baker, 1998.

_____. *Life in the Spirit in Marriage, Home, and Work: An Exposition of Ephesians 5:18-6:9*. Grand Rapids: Baker, 1998.

_____. *The Unsearchable Riches of Christ: An Exposition of Ephesians 3*. Grand Rapids: Baker, 1998.

Mackay, John A. *God's Order: The Ephesian Letter and This Present Time*. New York: Macmillan, 1953.

Maclaren, Alexander. *Ephesians*. Expositions of Holy Scripture. Grand Rapids: Eerdmans, 1938.

Martin, Ralph P. *Ephesians, Colossians, and Philemon*. Interpretation: A Bible Commentary for Teaching and Preaching. Louisville: John Knox, 1991.

Meyer, F. B. *Power for Living: Studies in Ephesians*. Greenville, S.C.: Ambassador, 1997.

Mishnah: A New Translation. Jacob Neusner, trans. New Haven, Conn.: Yale University Press, 1988.

Mitton, C. Leslie. *Ephesians*. New Century Bible Commentary. Grand Rapids: Eerdmans, 1973.

Morris, Leon. *Expository Reflections on the Letter to the Ephesians*. Grand Rapids: Baker, 1994.

Moule, Handley C. G. *Ephesian Studies*. London: Hodder and Stoughton, n.d.

Neufeld, Thomas R. Yoder. *Ephesians*. Believers Church Bible Commentary. Scottdale, Penn.: Herald Press, 2002.

Nichol, Francis D., ed. *The Seventh-day Adventist Bible Commentary*. Washington, D.C.:

Review and Herald, 1953-1957, VI:991-1047.

O'Brien, Peter T. *The Letter to the Ephesians.* Pillar New Testament Commentary. Grand Rapids: Eerdmans, 1999.

Patzia, Arthur G. *Ephesians, Colossians, Philemon.* New International Biblical Commentary. Peabody, Mass.: Hendrickson, 1990.

Perkins, Pheme. *Ephesians.* Abingdon New Testament Commentaries. Nashville: Abingdon, 1997.

Ridderbos, Herman. *Paul: An Outline of His Theology.* John Richard De Witt, trans. Grand Rapids: Eerdmans, 1975.

Robinson, J. Armitage. *St Paul's Epistle to the Ephesians: A Revised Text and Translation With Exposition and Notes,* 2d ed. London: James Clarke, n.d.

Rogers, Cleon L., Jr., and Cleon L. Rogers III. *The New Linguistic and Exegetical Key to the Greek New Testament.* Grand Rapids: Zondervan, 1998,

Schnackenburg, Rudolf. *Ephesians: A Commentary.* Helen Heron, trans. Edinburgh: T. & T. Clark, 1991.

Scott, E. F. *The Epistles of Paul to the Colossians, to Philemon and to the Ephesians.* Moffatt New Testament Commentary. New York: Richard R. Smith, 1930.

Snodgrass, Klyne. *Ephesians.* The NIV Application Commentary. Grand Rapids: Zondervan, 1996.

Stedman, Ray C. *Expository Studies in Ephesians 1-3: Riches in Christ.* Waco, Tex.: Word, 1976.

Stewart, James S. *A Man in Christ: The Vital Elements of St. Paul's Religion.* New York: Harper & Row, n.d.

Stoeckhardt, George. *Ephesians.* Concordia Classic Commentary Series. St. Louis: Concordia, 1987.

Stott, John R. W. *The Message of Ephesians: God's New Society.* The Bible Speaks Today. Downers Grove, Ill.: InterVarsity, 1979.

Thompson, G.H.P. *The Letters of Paul to the Ephesians to the Colossians and to Philemon.* The Cambridge Bible Commentary. Cambridge: Cambridge University, 1967.

Trench, Richard Chenevix. *Synonyms of the New Testament.* Robert G. Hoerber, ed. Grand Rapids: Baker, 1989.

Westcott, Brooke Foss. *Saint Paul's Epistle to the Ephesians.* London: Macmillan, 1906.

White, Ellen G. *Christ's Object Lessons.* Washington, D.C.: Review and Herald, 1941.

_____. *The Desire of Ages.* Mountain View, Calif.: Pacific Press, 1940.

_____. *Education.* Mountain View, Calif.: Pacific Press, 1952.

Wood, A. Skevington. "Ephesians." In *The Expositor's Bible Commentary.* Frank E. Gaebelein, ed. Grand Rapids: Zondervan, 1978. XI:1-92.

Yoder, John Howard. *The Politics of Jesus.* Grand Rapids: Eerdmans, 1972.

Part I

Saying Hello

Ephesians 1:1, 2

1. A Meaningful Greeting

Ephesians 1:1, 2
>¹*Paul, an apostle of Christ Jesus by the will of God.*
>*To the saints [at Ephesus*] who have faith in Christ Jesus:* ²*Grace to you and peace from God our Father and the Lord Jesus Christ.*

---

*The words "at Ephesus" are not in the best and oldest Greek manuscripts.

Paul was a remarkable letter writer. Even his greeting could be pregnant with Christian meaning. While largely following the letter writing conventions of his day, he adapted them to his own needs. The prologue to Ephesians has three sections:

- the identity of the sender,
- the recipients, and
- a greeting.

One of the first things to note about those three sections is that Christ is mentioned in relation to each of them. For Paul, Christ and what He did for him (and us) is always central. Ephesians is full of Christ Jesus from beginning to end.

Paul immediately wants his readers to know that he is "an apostle of Christ Jesus" (1:1). The word *apostle* is a transliteration of the Greek *apostolos,* which means one sent as a messenger or an agent. "An apostle," writes Robert Johnston, "is one who is sent out on a mission. The word *missionary* comes from a Latin word that means the same thing (mitto, 'to send')" (Johnston, p. 39).

The word itself had a strong heritage in Judaism. The Jewish leaders in Jerusalem sent out representatives to those Jews scattered throughout the world. "When such an *apostolos* went out," William Barclay notes, "he did not go out simply in his own authority and in his own strength. Behind him, and in him, there lay the authority of the Sanhedrin, whose representative he was" (Barclay, p. 86). Paul had before his conversion been an apostle of the Sanhedrin. In fact, he had been on an apostolic mission from the Sanhedrin when the Lord Jesus met him on the road to Damascus and converted him to Christianity (Acts 9:1-9). After that blinding experience he was no longer an *apostolos* of the Sanhedrin but an *apostolos* of Christ Jesus. From that point onward to his death he would be a servant of Christ.

Paul went out of his way to emphasize that his apostleship was "by the will of God" (Eph. 1:1). That is, he was under God's appointment and not his own. E. F. Scott points out that his "claim must be interpreted in the light of the opening chapter of Galatians. Paul's opponents had sought to weaken his authority by insisting that while he called himself an apostle he was not on the same footing as the immediate disciples. Any right he had to teach the gospel was derived from them, and wherever he differed from them he must be wrong. His answer was that his commission, just as much as theirs, was from God" (Scott, p. 13).

Thus right up front Paul asserts the authority that lay behind his message, meaning that it is therefore one that others must listen to. It is not from some private person expressing an opinion, but from God Himself, given through Paul, the one whom He has sent. He comes as the authoritative representative of Christ, and, as Charles Hodge notes in a burst of enthusiasm, "in no portion of the Sacred Scriptures are the self-evidencing light and power of divine truth more concentrated than they are here" in Ephesians (Hodge, p. xv).

After giving his own identity, Paul refers to the recipients of his letter. He describes them as:

1. "the saints [at Ephesus],"
2. "who have faith in Christ Jesus" (1:1).

A "saint" in the Bible is not some Mother Teresa, some individual martyred for the faith, or a hero of the faith, such as Saint Peter. To the contrary, a biblical saint is an ordinary Christian. The basic meaning of the word is to be "set apart." The idea is that God has set Christians apart for

Himself. The word in the Greek also implies to be holy. Thus a saint is one whom God has set apart for holiness.

The New Testament regards those individuals who believe in Jesus as Savior and Lord as saints. Thus Paul could note that even the individuals in the rather disorderly Corinthian church were "called to be saints" (1 Cor. 1:2, RSV). It was the same in Ephesus. And so it is with you and I. We are saints in the biblical sense because God has summoned us to Himself and away from the world.

The saints that Paul writes to in Ephesians he describes as having faith (1:1). The word he uses *(pistos)* can have either a passive or an active meaning. That is, it can mean either "being faithful" or "having faith." Of course, we might argue that a person who has faith will be faithful in daily life. Likewise, it is true that one who is faithful also possesses faith. Thus J. Armitage Robinson is undoubtedly correct when he asserts that " 'faithful in Christ Jesus,' [is] an epithet in which the two senses of *pistis,* 'belief' and 'fidelity,' appear to be blended" (Robinson, p. 141).

> ## Paul's Intent Is Clear
>
> "We must listen to the message of Ephesians with appropriate attention and humility. For we must regard its author neither as a private individual who is ventilating his personal opinions, nor as a gifted but fallible human teacher, nor even as the church's greatest missionary hero, but as 'an apostle of Christ Jesus by the will of God,' and therefore as a teacher whose authority is precisely the authority of Jesus Christ himself, in whose name and by whose inspiration he writes" (Stott, pp. 21, 22).

Many translations refer to the faithful saints Paul addresses as being "in Ephesus." But since, as I noted in my introductory remarks under authorship and recipients, those words do not appear in the oldest and best Greek manuscripts, I have put them in brackets in my translation. Having said that, however, there is no doubt that the letter originally went to the region of Asia Minor and Ephesus was most likely one location at which Paul wanted it read. Ephesus, as you will recall from Acts 19, was the center of the cult of the goddess Diana or Artemis. In fact, the city's inhabitants attacked Paul because his evangelistic success threatened the livelihood of those silversmiths who made their living by creating images to Artemis (verses 23-41). The widespread reverence and fear of such gods in Ephesus and its vicinity finds significance in the letter to the Ephesians in its oft-repeated references to principalities and powers that wage warfare with Christians and Christianity (see Eph. 6:12, for example).

But perhaps the most important point about the saints Paul is writing to is that they lived somewhere. As a result, they had two homes. That is, they were both "in Christ" and "in Ephesus" (or some other location). The same is true of you and I. We are already citizens of heaven but at the same time we also exist on earth. John Stott points out that "many of our spiritual troubles arise from our failure to remember that we are citizens of two kingdoms. We tend either to pursue Christ and withdraw from the world, or to become preoccupied with the world and forget that we are also in Christ" (Stott, p. 23). We need to balance our citizenships by learning to live in the world according to the principles of Christ.

Being "in Christ Jesus," as we noted in the introduction, is Paul's favorite description of a person who has salvation in Christ. The apostle will have much to say on that phrase throughout his letter.

Three words have special significance in the greeting of Ephesians 1:2. The first is "grace," a word that forms a theme throughout the letter. Grace in Paul is always God's free gift of salvation through Christ. "By grace you have been saved through faith; and this is not your own doing, it is the gift of God" (2:8, 5, RSV). That verse is a high point in both Ephesians and in Paul's theology. It is the core of his gospel.

A second great word in verse 2 is "peace." We have peace with God because of the healing gift of God's grace. And in Pauline thought such peace is not only with God but also with one another and within our own lives. "Peace" in the New Testament stems from the Hebrew concept of *shalom*. More than the absence of conflict and trouble, it is rather "the presence of something wonderful: the blessing of God in all its fullness" (Morris, p. 13). It represents "a state of well-being" (Danker, p. 287) and comes from being right with God. There is only one way to get that peace. And that is by accepting God's forgiving grace through an act of personal faith (see Rom. 5:1, 9, 10).

The final word we want to examine in Paul's greeting is "Father" (Gal. 1:2). Once again we are dealing with a general Pauline theme that receives special treatment in Ephesians. All Christians in the epistle are children of God. Thus they belong to the one universal family of God (2:19; 3:15) and have each other as brothers and sisters. Being a part of that family is a result of grace and a part of the peace of the gospel.

In two short but forceful verses Paul has raised several of his letter's themes. He will have more to say on these topics throughout his insightful letter.

Part II

Doctrinal Affirmations

Ephesians 1:3–3:21

2. The Purpose of God, Part 1

Ephesians 1:3-10

> [3]*Blessed be the God and Father of our Lord Jesus Christ, who has blessed us in Christ with every spiritual blessing in the heavenly realms,* [4]*even as He chose us in Him before the foundation of the world, that we might be holy and blameless in His sight. In love* [5]*He predestined us to adoption as sons through Jesus Christ to Himself, according to the good pleasure of His will,* [6]*to the praise of the glory of His grace, which He freely gave to us in the Beloved.* [7]*In Him we have redemption through His blood, the forgiveness of trespasses, according to the wealth of His grace,* [8]*which He gave to us overflowingly. In all wisdom and understanding* [9]*He made known to us the mystery of His will, according to His kind intention which He purposed in Him [Christ].* [10]*This mystery, which God as a steward will complete in the fullness of time, is to bring all things together in Christ, the things in the heavens and the things on the earth.*

Ephesians 1:3-14 in the Greek original composes a single sentence. Markus Barth describes it as "one infinitely long, heavy, and clumsy sentence, replete with dependent clauses, excurses, specifications, repetitions, and the like" (Barth, *Ephesians 1-3*, p. 77). And E. Norden calls it "the most monstrous sentence conglomeration . . . I have ever met in the Greek language" (in *ibid.*). In a more positive light, R. W. Dale refers to verses 3-14 as a "golden chain" of many links (Dale, p. 40) and J. Armitage Robinson speaks of them as a "kaleidoscope of dazzling lights and shifting colours" (Robinson, p. 19).

All in all, verses 3-14 are one of the most complex yet one of the most spiritually loaded sentences in the Bible. It is as if Paul in his praise and excitement runs from one thought to the next without taking time to breathe. The problem facing the reader will always be to grasp the majesty and the intricacies of its content. As an aid in that endeavor, all translations that I know of break Paul's one majestic sentence into several shorter ones. Beyond that, commentators cluster his ideas into categories. But after all is said and done the full meaning of the passage itself still eludes our earthly minds. Both its praise and its full meaning soars beyond us. It is truly one of those passages that we could read aloud every day and continue to gain new insights.

Verse 3 begins the apostle's great burst of praise to all three members of the Trinity. First he praises the Father, "who has blessed us in Christ with every spiritual blessing" (verse 3). The Father is the source of every blessing that we receive as Christians. As John Stott points out, "his initiative is set forth plainly, for he is himself the subject of almost every main verb in these verses" (Stott, p. 33). Thus it is God the Father who has

- "blessed us" (verse 3),
- "chose[n] us" (verse 4),
- "predestined us" (verse 5),
- freely given His grace to us (verse 6; gave "overflowingly," verse 8),
- "made known to us the mystery of His will" (verse 9), and
- will bring His plan to completion in the fullness of time (verse 10).

If we could sum up in one sentence the role of God the Father in Ephesians 1:3-10 it would be that He had a plan and a purpose that is rooted in His will to save sinners.

Paul next praises Christ, the Son, whom he mentions some 15 times in verses 3-14. Beyond that, the phrase "in Christ," "in whom," or "in Him," occurs 11 times. The apostle presents Christ as "the sphere within which the divine blessing is given and received" (O'Brien, p. 91). It is in Him and through His blood that we have redemption (verse 7). And it is through Christ that God will complete His plan and unite all things in the heavens and on the earth (verse 10).

The Holy Spirit is also prominent in verses 3-14, although only verses 13 and 14 mention Him by name. But the Spirit's presence appears also in verse 3, since He is the agent of "spiritual blessings."

One way to come to grips with the meaning of verses 4-10 is to view God's blessings as past, present, and future. First, verses 4 and 5 take us "before the foundation of the world" when God "chose" us for holiness (verse 4). He not only selected us but He "predestined" or elected us to become His sons and daughters (verse 5).

Now some people don't like the doctrine of predestination, but the plain fact is that it is a biblical teaching in both the Old and New Testaments. In the Old we find God summoning the nation of Israel to be His special people, and the New finds Him calling a worldwide group "to his eternal glory in Christ" (1 Peter 5:9, 10, RSV). The plan of salvation was not an afterthought. Rather, God saw the issues from "the foundation of the world" and had a plan in place (Eph. 1:4).

While the doctrine of predestination is a biblical teaching, it is one that has been misunderstood. Some, unfortunately, have taught that Christ predetermined some people for heaven and others for hell, each individual having nothing to do with their fate. But in reality God desires each and every person to be saved eternally. He predestined all to be saved. Christ died "once for all" (Heb. 9:26), but there is a condition to receiving that grace His death made possible—faith. That is, individuals must accept God's gift in order to become a part of the family of God. As Paul puts it in Ephesians 2:8, "by grace you have been saved *through faith*" (RSV). And

> ## A Past Blessing of Believers
>
> God predestines sinners to salvation (verses 4, 5), but that predestination:
> - must be accepted by faith
> - must be viewed primarily in terms of service rather than privilege

that faith is one rooted in the sacrifice of Christ on the cross (Rom. 3:21-25) and the "blood" of the "Lamb of God" whose sacrifice of Himself took away the sin of the world (Eph. 1:7; John 1:29).

It is important to realize that God predestined every person to salvation, but that it is only those who accept His gift who become a part of the family of God that finds its home in the "heavenly realms" (Eph. 2:19; 3:14; 1:3).

A second misunderstanding regarding the biblical teaching of predestination is that God is not summoning a people to privilege but rather to service. Of course, it is a privilege to be a Christian. But if people only sit around and boast of their status they haven't quite figured out what God's call is all about. In short, the blessings of salvation lay upon those elected a life of responsibility to both their Lord and their fellow humans. And just as Jesus gave Himself as a servant to others, so each of His followers will do the same if they have truly accepted Him into their hearts (Matt. 20:26-28). In other words, God not only appointed us to be saved from sin but also to be His agents here on earth. The biblical doctrine of predestination is a beautiful and meaningful teaching. And, like Paul, we should not reject the concept but rejoice in it. It filled the great apostle with nothing but praise.

Ephesians 1:3-10 not only deals with past blessings, but also present. That theme dominates verses 5-8. In particular, we find three great Pauline words that highlight the present condition of Christians. First, God had adopted them into His family (verse 5). Whereas once they were alienated from Him and His other children, now they are united to Him as a part of His heavenly family. The church doesn't speak enough of adoption, but Paul realizes its significance. So does the apostle John, who tells us that we become children of God the very moment we believe on and receive Christ (John 1:12, 13). For too long have some taught that we are born as God's children. Not so according to the Bible. Individuals become sons and daughters when they make a faith decision for Jesus and are born again from above (John 3:3, 5; Rom. 8:14-17).

> **The Present Blessings of Believers**
>
> 1. Adoption (verse 5)
> 2. Redemption (verse 7)
> 3. Forgiveness (verse 7)

A second present possession of Christians is redemption (Eph. 1:7). The ancient world often applied the term to the buying of slaves or hostages so that they could be freed. In Paul's writings redemption has to do with being freed from bondage to sin and the penalty of the broken law (Rom. 6:16, 18, 20; Gal. 4:8-10). And, as with all his other metaphors of salvation, he always ties redemption to the blood of Christ and/or the cross of Calvary (see Knight, p. 77). Paul knows of no theory of salvation that is not linked to Christ's substitutionary sacrifice as the Lamb of God.

The third present blessing for every Christian is forgiveness of sin (Eph. 1:7). All of these present blessings—adoption, redemption, forgiveness, and others—are the result of God's grace, which He dispenses "overflowingly" (verse 8). God is not stingy with His grace. Paul's wording is as if He cannot give us enough of His grace. Because of that grace Christians are saved people. Their salvation is a present reality.

But present salvation is not all there is. According to Ephesians 1:3-10, God also has a future blessing for His people, the topic of verses 9 and 10. In the fullness of time He will, as a faithful steward, bring to completion His great plan. When time merges with eternity at the second advent of Jesus, the Lord will unite more fully all of His people into one great family. That uniting has already

> **The Future Blessing of Believers**
>
> In the "fullness of time" God will complete His plan and unite "the things in the heavens and the things on earth (verse 10).

begun through the work of Christ in the establishment of His church, but there will come a time when all discord in the universe will cease. Then God will fully bring together "the things in the heavens and the things on the earth."

Thus even though Christians are already saved, they still await the fullness of their salvation. Paul sees our salvation as both present and future, as both a now and a not-yet experience. In short, whatever blessings we have here and now will multiply when the fullness of time finally arrives and God brings the plan (mystery, verses 9, 10) that He developed "before the foundation of the world" (verse 4) to its climax. The problems that we face as Christians here on earth will not always be. No wonder Paul refers to the Second Advent as the "blessed hope" (Titus 2:13).

3. The Purpose of God, Part 2

Ephesians 1:11–14
In Him in whom also we were appointed, having been predestined according to the purpose of the one who works all things according to the determination of His will, that we who were the first to hope in Christ might be for the praise of His glory. In Him you also, having heard the message of the truth, the good news of your salvation, and also having believed in Him, you were sealed with the Holy Spirit of promise, which is the pledge of our inheritance until the redemption of God's possession for the praise of His glory.

In verses 9 and 10 the apostle spoke of the "mystery" of His will. Mystery in the writings of Paul "is something which has long been kept secret, and which has now been revealed; and it is something which is still incomprehensible to the person who has not been initiated into its meaning" (Barclay, p. 96). More specifically, in Ephesians the mystery centers on the fact that the gospel is available to Gentiles as well as to Jews. God is beginning to unite His people in His church on earth but the mystery will not be completed until "in the fullness of time" God brings "all things together in Christ, the things in the heavens and the things on the earth" (verse 10). His ultimate goal is the universal unity of those who accept His Lordship. Its full completion, as we noted in section 2, is still in the future.

But already God has made great progress toward bringing the Gentiles into His salvation on an equal basis with the Jews. That step in the fulfillment of the mystery we see reflected by the pronouns in Ephesians 1:11-14. The flow is from *we* to *you* to *our*.

First, the *we* refers to the Jewish people, including Paul himself. "We were appointed, having been predestined" according to God's will (verse 11). "We . . . were the first to hope in Christ" (verse 12). Those verses reflect the truth of the Old Testament, in which the Jews were God's chosen people. It is also echoed in the New, in the sense that the Gospel message went first to the Jews and only later to the Gentiles (Acts 1:8; Rom. 1:16).

But in Old Testament times the Jews were God's people to the exclusion of the other nations. The only way a Gentile could become a part of God's people was to convert to Judaism. But, Paul tells his readers, that has changed.

That is where the *you* of Ephesians 1:13 comes in. Now "you also, having heard the message of the truth, . . . and also having believed in Him, you [also] were sealed with the Holy Spirit of promise." Wonder of wonders to a Jew, mystery of mysteries, those Gentiles who have accepted Christ are also a part of God's people.

And now the *our* of verse 14 finds its significance. The inheritance of the promises made to Abraham and the Jewish people are *ours*. They belong to *both* Jews and Gentiles. To highlight that idea Paul employs the word "possession." In the Old Testament, F. F. Bruce points out, that term is "used of God's people Israel—notably in Exod. 19:5, where Yahweh calls Israel 'my own possession among all peoples.' . . . That such language should now be applied to Gentile believers is a token of the security of their new standing within the community of God's own people, fully sharing present blessing and future hope with their fellow-believers of Jewish stock" (Bruce, *Epistles to Colossians* . . . , p. 267).

Paul's use of "we," "you," and "our" in Ephesians 1:11-14, Peter O'Brien notes, "anticipates the motif of the reconciliation of Jews and Gentiles in Ephesians 2:14-18, a reconciliation with God and with one another which has been effected through Christ's death on the cross" (O'Brien, p. 115).

Looking a bit more closely at the Gentile's new position, we note that their inclusion results from God's initiative. He predetermined their inclusion, sent the Savior, and dispatched such messengers as Paul so that they might hear the message of the Gospel and come to belief. All through the Bible it is not humans who find God but God who goes after them. It was so with Adam and Eve in the Garden of Eden after they sinned (Gen. 3:8-10); it was so with the lost coin and the lost sheep (Luke 15:4, 8); it was so in Jesus' ministry (John 3:16; Luke 19:10); it was so with the election of the Jews (Rom. 9:9-13); and it is so with the inclusion of the Gentiles (Eph. 1:4, 11-14). Salvation is always rooted in unmerited grace, and is always at God's initiative.

That does not mean that people are inactive in the plan of salvation. Ephesians 1:13 sheds insight on certain aspects of the human part in it. First, we hear "the message of the truth, the good news of [our] salvation." There is, we should note, different ways of "hearing" God's message. Some merely listen to the words, but nothing happens in their hearts and lives. They gain no understanding. Others hear and understand, but don't do anything about it. And then there are those who hear, understand, and respond in faith.

That brings us to the second aspect of the human role in salvation. People choose to say yes to God rather than no. That is, they accept the gospel message that they have heard rather than reject it. Even though faith—the ability to believe, the capacity to say yes to God—is a gift from Him, it is still up to us to utilize our will to use His gift of faith in accepting His gospel.

Hearing and believing are important aspects of the plan of salvation. They make preaching and witnessing vital also. As Paul put it in Romans, " 'every one who calls upon the name of the Lord will be saved.' But how are men to call upon him in whom they have not believed? And how are they to believe in him of whom they have never heard? And how are they to hear without a preacher? And how can men preach unless they are sent? . . . So faith comes from what is heard, and what is heard comes by the preaching of Christ" (Rom. 10:13-15, 17, RSV). No wonder God wants us to be His witnesses to the ends of the earth until the close of time (Matt. 28:18-20). His plan of uniting His people throughout the universe is not yet completed (Eph. 1:10, 14). And, wonder of wonders, He desires each of us to have a part in it—not only in hearing and believing, but in witnessing so that others might also hear and believe.

Before we move on from the concept of hearing and believing, we need to note one more thing. Some interpreters of Ephesians 1:10 (that God in the end will bring "all things together in Christ" in the "fullness of time") have concluded that He will eventually save everybody (universalism). But that is not Paul's message. For him the gospel or good news of salvation is for those who both hear and respond in faith. All such, he tells us, are "sealed with the Holy Spirit of promise." And that sealing is God's pledge or guarantee of future redemption when He completes the redemption of His possession—His special people who have accepted His Lordship (Eph. 1:13, 14).

We learn three things about the Holy Spirit in these verses. First, He is the "Spirit of promise." O'Brien suggests that Paul probably used the phrase to refer to the fact that the Old Testament promised the Holy Spirit (see Joel 2:28; Ezek. 36:27) and that He was "poured out by the exalted Jesus at Pentecost" (O'Brien, pp. 119, 120). Jesus, of course, also promised that the Holy Spirit would come to guide His people (see John 14-16; Acts 1:4, 5). Paul is telling the Ephesians that they themselves have the Spirit of the promise. And the good news is that we as twenty-first century Christians still have the Spirit's power and gifts amongst us and will continue to do so until the end of time.

Second, the Holy Spirit is God's seal. The Holy Spirit has sealed all Christians. A seal is a mark of ownership. The Roman world branded cattle and slaves with a seal to signify ownership. In the book of Ezekiel God put a mark or a seal on His people to distinguish them as His personal possession and save them from destruction (Eze. 9:4-9). And by sealing Gentile believers God stamps them as His own. Later in Ephesians Paul tells them that they "were sealed for the day of redemption" (Eph. 4:30, RSV). That is, God will be with His people throughout the trials of this life until "the fullness of time" (1:10) arrives, when He redeems His possession (i.e., His people, verse 14).

The third thing God says about the Holy Spirit is that He is a "pledge" or guarantee. In the biblical world the word used for pledge meant a *"first installment, deposit, down payment, pledge . . . ,* which secures a legal claim to the article in question" (Danker, p. 134). The gift of the Spirit indicates that God is not merely promising final victory to those who accept His gift through belief but guaranteeing it. In fact, the Spirit is the first part of God's ultimate gift.

The last thing we should note about Ephesians 1:11-14 is its focus on praise, an emphasis initiated in verses 3 and 6. Praise to God is in many ways both a central theme of Ephesians 1 and the only proper response to what God has done for us in Christ. Here the human-centeredness of natural humanity comes into direct collision with the God-centeredness of His children. John Stott writes that "fallen man, imprisoned in his own little ego, has an almost boundless confidence in the power of his own will, and an almost insatiable appetite for the praise of his own glory. But the people of God have at least begun to be turned inside out. The new society has new values and new ideals. For God's people are God's possessions who live by God's will and for God's glory" (Stott, p. 50). They reserve all of their praise for God.

4. A Powerful Prayer for Understanding

Ephesians 1:15-23

[15]*Therefore I also, having heard of the faith in the Lord Jesus that is among you and of your love toward all the saints,* [16]*do not cease giving thanks for you, mentioning you in my prayers,* [17]*that the God of our Lord Jesus Christ, the Father of glory, may give you a Spirit of wisdom and of revelation in a full knowledge of Him,* [18]*having the eyes of your heart enlightened, that you may know what is the hope of His calling, what are the riches of the glory of His inheritance in the saints,* [19]*and what is the exceeding greatness of His power to us who believe according to the working of the might of His strength,* [20]*which He accomplished in Christ when He raised Him from the dead and seated Him on His right hand in the heavenly places,* [21]*far above all rule and authority and power and dominion and every name that is named, not only in the present age but also in the one to come.* [22]*And He has put all things under His feet and gave Him as head over all things to the church,* [23]*which is His body, the fullness of Him who fills all in all.*

In Ephesians 1:15-23 Paul moves from the breathless praise of verses 3-14 to equally breathless prayer. In both passages the apostle rapidly heaps phrase upon phrase as he exudes his understanding of God and what the Lord has done for His people in Christ. The first chapter of Ephesians contains what may be the most tightly packed prose of the New Testament.

Paul in verses 3-14 praises God who has blessed His people in Christ. Now in verses 15-23 he prays that His people might more completely understand from their hearts the fullness of divine blessing. The following outline will help us grasp the main points of his prayer.

The Structure of Ephesians 1:15-23

1. The occasion for Paul's prayer (verse 15)
2. The core of the prayer (verses 16-18a)
   a. Thankfulness for the Ephesians (verse 16)
   b. A petition for their enlightenment (verses 17, 18a)
3. The focal point of the prayed-for enlightenment (verses 18b, 19). That they might more fully comprehend
   a. "the hope of His calling" (verse 18b)
   b. "the riches of the glory of His inheritance in the saints" (verse 18c)
   c. "the exceeding greatness of His power" (verse 19)
4. The shape of the greatness of God's power (verses 20-23)
   a. He raised Christ from the dead (verse 20a)
   b. He enthroned Christ with Himself. As a result, Christ possesses incomparable power (verses 20-22a)
   c. He made Christ to be the head of the church (verse 22b, 23)

The first thing to note about verses 15-23 is the occasion for Paul's majestic prayer. He had heard of their faith in Christ and of their love for one another (verse 15). Now that is good news—much better news than what he had heard about the "bewitched" Galatians (Gal. 3:1). Here is a group of people on the right track who demonstrate "the two things which must characterize any true church": *"loyalty to Christ and love to men"* (Barclay, p. 102). Some have one but not the other. After all, some people claim to be loyal to Christ but are careless of others. On the other hand, some individuals care very much about other people but despise Christ and the message of the cross. Both groups are misguided. The Ephesians, however, possess the two essential aspects of Christianity.

The most remarkable thing about Paul's prayer, D. Martyn Lloyd-Jones observes, is that he chose to offer such a fervent prayer for such balanced Christians. "We might have thought," he pens, "that there was no need to pray for people who had experienced such great blessings." But we find a lesson here. "Conversion is not the end, it is merely the beginning; it is only the first step" in the Christian life (Lloyd-Jones, *Ultimate Purpose,* pp. 338, 339). God wants His children to grow in a heart knowledge throughout their existence. Throughout the ceaseless ages of eternity the glory of what God did for us in Christ will be our study.

Another important aspect of Paul's prayer that we must emphasize is that he is not praying that the Ephesians will receive the blessing, but rather that they might more fully understand what they already possess. According to the apostle, Christians are saved people (in Eph. 2:5, 8 "saved" is in the past tense). It is our joy as Christians to understand ever more fully what it means to be a saved person, to belong to God's redeemed people, and to grasp more clearly the Father's, Christ's, and the Holy Spirit's roles in that salvation. Such themes are not only those of the praise and the prayer of Ephesians 1 but of the whole letter. But such knowledge, of course, is impossible without the ministry of the Holy Spirit, who provides Christ's followers with both wisdom and revelation (1:17).

Paul especially wants the Ephesians to comprehend three things more fully. The first is "the hope of His calling" (verse 18). We noted in our study of verses 4 and 5 that our salvation is God's initiative. We didn't just wake up one day and feel a need for Him and salvation on our own. Not so! The biblical teaching from first to last is that it is He who first calls us. We merely respond to His wooing. And the hope to which God has summoned us is not merely a better life on this earth but eternal life in Christ (cf. Rom. 6:23). That eternal life a Christian already possesses (John 3:36; 5:24), but with the second advent of Christ it will take on a fullness impossible for us to fully grasp in our earth-bound state.

The second thing Paul desired the Ephesians to more fully realize was "the riches of the glory of His inheritance in the saints" (Eph. 1:18). A great deal of discussion has centered on whether the inheritance is God's or the saints'. It can be translated either way from the original Greek. And while the saints' "hope" is certainly tied to their heavenly inheritance, the overall context of Ephesians suggests that the phrase should be translated as the saints being God's inheritance (see section 2 on verse 14), in much the same way that the Old Testament writers taught that God's people were His "inheritance" or "possession" (see, e.g., Deut. 4:20; Ps. 33:12; Jer. 10:16). In Ephesians all of God's people—both Jews and Gentiles—are His inheritance "in whom he will display to the universe the untold riches of his glory" (O'Brien, p. 136). As F. F. Bruce notes, "we can scarcely realize what it must mean to God to see His purpose complete, to see creatures of His hand, sinners redeemed by His grace, reflecting His own glory" (Bruce, *Epistle to the Ephesians,* p. 40).

The third thing Paul prays for the Ephesians is that they might more fully comprehend "the exceeding greatness" of God's power and "the might of His strength" (Eph. 1:19). Paul warms to that topic even more than the other two. As a result, in verses 20-23 the apostle waxes exuberant on three of the most important things a Christian can know about God's power.

The first is that He raised Christ from the dead (verse 20). The resurrection of Christ was absolutely central in Paul's understanding of the Gospel. In 1 Corinthians 15:1-4 he gives the resurrection equal billing with the death of Christ in his definition of the Gospel. And for a good reason. After all, a dead Savior offers no hope. As John Mackay points out, "Had it not been for the Resurrection all that Jesus Christ was and said and did in His life and in His death would have been futile and in vain. His memory would most likely have been forgotten" (Mackay, p. 93). But the grave couldn't hold Christ. God raised Him up. As a result, He has "the keys of hell and of death" (Rev. 1:18, KJV). His victory over death He will share with all who believe in Him. That is part of the "hope of His calling" (Eph. 1:18; 1 Thess. 4:13, 18). Having power over death is no small thing.

A second item Paul wants his readers to understand more fully about God's power is that He not only raised Christ from the dead, but He also seated Him on His right hand in Heaven. Here Paul refers to the Messianic promise of Psalm 110:1, one of the most frequently cited Old Testament texts in the New (see, e.g., Matt. 26:64; Mark 14:62; 16:19; Luke 22:69; Acts 2:33-35; 7:56; Rom. 8:34; 1 Cor. 15:25; Col. 3:1; Heb. 1:3; 8:1; 10:12). "The Lord says to my lord," we read in the psalm, " 'Sit at my right hand, till I make your enemies your footstool' " (Psalm 110:1, RSV). Not only would the resurrected Christ share God's throne, but He was also certain of final victory. And rightly so if He was "far above all rule and authority and power and dominion" in both the present age and the age to come (Eph. 1:21). Here Paul has in mind those "world rulers of this present darkness" or "spiritual hosts of wickedness in the heavenly places" that he will later call on Christians to fight (6:12, RSV). And Christ was also above "every name that is named" (1:21). That phrase, Clinton Arnold points out, "would have communicated in an especially powerful way to people who had formerly been involved in magical practices—like many of the Christians at Ephesus. Knowing the right names and invoking the most powerful names was crucial to the practice of magic." Thus "Paul argued for the superiority of Christ in no uncertain terms. There is no conceivable god, goddess, power, spirit or demon who does not fall under the dominion of Christ" (Arnold, *Powers,* p. 107). That was good news then and it is good news now. Christians—those who serve and worship Christ—have nothing to fear from any quarter.

The third thing Paul desires his readers to realize about Christ is that God not only "put all things under His feet" (verse 22), but that He also made Him head of the church, "which is His body" (verse 23). In some of his earlier epistles Paul had set forth the idea of the church as the body of Christ, which should work together harmoniously as do the parts of a healthy organism. But in such passages as 1 Corinthians 12 the head is merely one part of the body. Here in Ephesians 1:22, 23 the apostle sets Christ forth as the unique and all powerful head that fills the rest of the body. John McVay points out that "Christ is designated as 'head'" not merely in a metaphorical sense, "but as an important means to communicate the uniqueness and importance of Christ" (in Hawthorne, p. 378). The church has only one head and He is both all powerful and active. Through His power He is "filling up *all* things in every conceivable way (1:23). The church is inextricably related to this *fullness* as both recipient and dispenser" (Neufeld, p. 88). It is the members of the body, working under the direction of its head, who carry out Christ's mission in the world. Thus the gospel song suggests that we are His mouth to preach His truth and His feet to take the Gospel message to the far corners of the earth.

5. What We Were

Ephesians 2:1-3

¹And you were dead in your trespasses and sins, ²in which you formerly walked according to the way of this world, according to the ruler of the power of the air, the spirit now working in the sons of disobedience. ³Among them we too all formerly lived in the passions of our flesh, indulging the desires of the flesh and of the mind. And we were by nature children of wrath, even as the rest.

Ephesians 1 began with praise for all that God has done for us in Christ (verses 3-14) followed by a majestic prayer regarding the power of both God and Christ that guarantees the Christian hope (verses 15-23). Chapter 2 starts with an equally forceful portrayal of exactly what God has done for us in Christ. We who were dead in sin have been saved in Christ (verses 1-10). Paul tells the story of salvation in those verses in two stages. His Ephesian readers (and us) are "reminded [of] what they have been delivered from, as well as what they have been lifted to" (Moule, p. 66). Verses 1-3 set forth the first stage and verses 4-10 present the second.

Before looking at the flow of verses 1-3 we should note Paul's use of pronouns. Verse 1 employs "you" and "your," a reference to the Gentiles. No one doubted their past condition. It was obvious to all that they had been lost in sin. But in verse 3 he switches to "we," thus bringing in himself and other individuals with a Jewish background. The end result is that all (both Gentiles and Jews) are sinners, all are children of wrath, all are equally dead in trespasses and sins, and all, therefore, are in need of salvation by grace through faith (verses 4-10).

The sequence of the argument is the same as that found in Romans 1-3. In Romans 1:18-32 Paul describes the "nasty sins" of the Gentiles as well as their hopeless condition. One can only imagine the saints nodding their heads in agreement. But then comes Romans 2:1, which tells the Jews that they were also sinners and had no room to gloat. It is all too easy for us "righteous" church people with our "more harmless vegetarian sins" to look down our noses at the coarser types. But Paul speaks to the religious segment of the population in Romans 2:1-3:23, concluding that all, both Jews and Gentiles, "have sinned and fall short of the glory of God" (3:23, RSV). Then he immediately in Romans 3:22-26 presents the only solution for both groups: salvation by grace accepted by faith.

The two great themes of both Romans and Ephesians are humanity's universal lostness and God's solution through His grace, which all must accept by faith. Paul is quite certain that he has a message needed by both Jews and Gentiles. Both require the cross and grace. Before the cross all is level ground. No one group stands higher than the other. Jews and Gentiles are both lost and both can only find salvation in Christ.

And in both Romans and Ephesians Paul goes to great pains to note that the absolute dependence of both Jews and Gentiles on the grace of God should unite them as a people. That unity is the climaxing theme of Romans 9-11, and it is central also in Ephesians 2:11-22, in which the apostle speaks of the breaking down of the dividing wall (verse 14) and of a unified church family built upon the foundation of Christ (verses 19-22). Thus lostness and grace are central both to Paul's soteriology (doctrine of salvation) and his ecclesiology (doctrine of the church).

Moving beyond the pronouns of Ephesians 2:1-3, we need to focus on the concept of power. Just as God had power to raise Christ from the dead (1:20), so He also has power to rescue Christians from death (2:1) through "the exceeding riches of His grace in His kindness toward us in Christ Jesus" (2:6-8). The theme of God's power ties Ephesians 1 and 2 together.

The key word in Ephesians 2:1-3 is "dead." According to Paul, it is the condition of all of those outside of Christ. The apostle gives the cause of that death as sins and trespasses. The great reformer John Calvin writes that Paul "does not mean only that they were in danger of death; but he declares that it was a real and present death by which they were overwhelmed. As spiritual death is nothing else than the alienation of the soul from God, we are all born dead, and we live dead until we are made partakers of the life of Christ" (Calvin, p. 139). Jesus referred to that partaking of the life of Christ as a new birth (John 3:5, 7), a topic that will move to center stage in Ephesians 2:4-10 in which the key concept is life.

According to verses 2 and 3, the Ephesians had previously been under the control of three powerful influences. The first Paul describes as walking "according to the way of this world" (verse 2). Walking is an important word throughout the Bible. "Our walk," F. B. Meyer points out, "is a synonym for our life. Life is a walk from the cradle to the grave" (Meyer, p. 109). From Paul's perspective a person is either walking without God and living according to the self-centered values of contemporary culture or walking with God and reflecting the God-centered/other-centered standards of Christ.

The temptation of walking "according to the way of this world" threatens each and every person. A constant part of our environment, it lures us to adapt to the ways of the surrounding culture rather than to those of God, thus becoming secular, materialistic, immoral, unjust, and so on. For many it is the temptation to live the kind of life portrayed on the TV screen which daily saturates the bulk of modern humanity. The fallen world around us seeks to mold us in its image.

Leading to a form of cultural bondage from which it is next to impossible to escape, walking the path of the world makes us dead to the things of God and exuberantly alive to the thrills of "this world."

The second influence working to drag people down is "the ruler of the power of the air, the spirit now working in the sons of disobedience" (verse 2). Here we find the personal force behind the world's spirit and values. The letter to the Ephesians has more to say about the personal source of evil than any other New Testament letter, climaxing with a call to meet the "spiritual hosts of wickedness" in spiritual warfare (6:12-17). At least twice in Ephesians Paul refers to the ultimate origin of evil as the devil (4:27; 6:11). Here in chapter 2 he calls him "the ruler of the power of the air" (verse 2).

It is absolutely central to realize that the devil was no fiction to Paul. To the contrary, he was the cause of the spiritual problem. Satan would like nothing more than to convince people (including Christians) that he does not really exist, something he has been quite successful at. As a result, he has blinded multitudes to the reality of his personal influence in the world both at large and in individual lives. Thereby the "ruler of the power of the air" has left many defenseless in the warfare between good and evil. We need to come to grips with Paul's vivid portrayal of the spiritual forces that seek to keep people in a state of spiritual death and lostness.

Not only do individuals face environmental and personal spiritual forces, but they host a problem within themselves. The third influence that holds people in bondage to sin and death is "the passions of our flesh" (Eph. 2:3). The flesh, Clinton Arnold notes, "is Paul's favorite expression to convey the inner drive of people to act in ways deviant to the standard of God's righteousness. It points not only to the inner motivating force behind actions that are associated with the body, such as sexual sin, but also to aspects of the thought life as well, such as envy and anger. This inner impulse to do evil is set in contrast to the new impulse to live with moral integrity provided by God's gift of the Holy Spirit (see Gal. 5:19-23)" (Arnold, *Powers,* p. 125).

Paul's teaching relates the idea of the flesh to the concept of walking in the sense that a person can either walk according to the flesh or according to the spirit. The "passions of our flesh" do not refer to the quite natural fulfillment of our God-given appetites, but rather to their perverted gratification. Thus, for example, the devil is always around to have people move from marital sex to adultery, from a natural enjoyment of food to gluttony, and from life's natural excitement to dangerous and/or perverted thrill seeking. And, as we might expect, the influence of the "ruler of the power of the air" (Eph. 2:2) and the environmental cultural forces unite with the wayward pull of "the flesh" to make the perverted form of any drive more attractive and exciting than the God-intended one.

In summary, Paul portrays human beings in their natural state as being deeply affected by evil from at least three sources:

1. the environment,
2. a supernaturally powerful opponent, and
3. an inherent inclination toward evil.

Their combined force leads to failure and spiritual death. Such was the condition of the Ephesians in their former life. They had been powerless to win against the unholy trinity daily influencing their lives. That's the bad news of the human condition according to Paul.

But it is the bad news that leads to the good news in Ephesians 2:4-10. Christ's power, as we saw in Ephesians 1:21, far exceeds "all rule and authority and power and dominion" (RSV). And He makes that power available to each of us. That is where the "BUT GOD" of Ephesians 2:4 comes in. "BUT GOD" are the most important two words in our lives.

6. What We Are in Christ

Ephesians 2:4-10

⁴But God, being rich in mercy, because of His great love with which He loved us, ⁵even when we were dead in our transgressions, made us alive together with Christ (by grace you have been saved), ⁶and He raised us with Him and seated us with Him in the heavenly places in Christ Jesus, ⁷that in the coming ages He might display the exceeding riches of His grace in His kindness toward us in Christ Jesus. ⁸For by grace you have been saved through faith; and that is not of yourselves, it is God's gift—⁹not because of works, lest anyone should boast. ¹⁰For we are His work of art, having been created in Christ Jesus for good works, which God previously prepared, that we should walk in them.

"BUT GOD!" We find no more important words in all the Bible. Ernest Best notes that Ephesians has just finished describing unbelievers as "dead in sin, under the power of evil supernatural beings, controlled by their own wicked desires and subject to God's wrath." They are in a position in which "they could expect no mercy from God" (Best, p. 213). Paul hadn't described unbelievers as partially lost, but as totally lost and hopeless. That was the message of Ephesians 2:1-3.

It is at that very juncture that the apostle drops in his "BUT GOD." A fundamental aspect of the mystery of the gospel is that the Lord rescues sinners in spite of themselves. The "BUT GOD" stands at the very foundation of the good news or gospel. God didn't stand idly aside as sinners walked (2:2) the path to eternal destruction (Rom. 6:23). No! He stepped in and did for them what they could not do for themselves. Instead of giving them what they deserved, He offered what they did not deserve. He provides them with grace rather than wrath. And Paul introduces that gift with the attention catching phrase "BUT GOD."

Andrew Lincoln helps us fit Ephesians 2:1-10 into the overall context of the letter. In the thanksgiving section (1:15-23), he notes, "the writer had told his readers that his prayer for them was that they might know the surpassing greatness of God's power toward them as believers. Now [in 2:1-10] he plays his own part in helping them to gain such knowledge by reminding them how God's power has affected their lives and what an immense change it has wrought" (Lincoln, p. 116).

Ephesians 2:4-10 tells us several things. First, it forces us to face what we are outside of Christ. It can be summed up in one word—"dead" (verse 5). Human sins and transgressions separate us from God, the source of life (Isa. 59:2). Sin in Paul's thought leads to bondage, condemnation, and death.

The Four Characteristics of God

1. Merciful (verse 4)
2. Loving (verse 4)
3. Kind (verse 7)
4. Full of grace (verses 5, 8)

It is those characteristics that undergird the "BUT GOD" of Ephesians 2:1-10.

Second, the passage reveals a great deal about God. Paul uses four helpful descriptive words as he informs us of those divine characteristics that undergird the "BUT GOD" of verse 4. One is that He is "rich in mercy" (verse 4). The Old Testament often characterized Him as being merciful. When He met Moses upon the Mount, for example, God referred to Himself as "the Lord, a God merciful and gracious, slow to anger, and abounding in steadfast love and faithfulness, keeping steadfast love for thousands, forgiving iniquity and transgression and sin" (Ex. 34:6, 7, RSV; cf. Ps. 103:8; Jonah 4:2; Micah 7:8). As a God of mercy He does not give rebellious people what they deserve if they are willing to respond to His call and humbly come to Him.

A second great description of God is love. The good news that He "loved us" with a "great love" follows the "BUT GOD" of Ephesians 2:4. That love, in fact, stands at the basis of who He is (1 John 4:8) and the reason that He sent the Savior (John 3:16).

A third divine trait is "kindness" (Eph. 2:7). Such kindness is not a meaningless abstraction for Paul, but rather a "kindness toward us in Christ

Jesus." The fourth is the magisterial concept of "grace," a characteristic so central to his theology that he mentions it in both verses 5 and 8.

Grace is a central theme in Ephesians. In Paul's praise in chapter 1 he claims that it was "freely bestowed on us" in Christ (verse 6, RSV), that it was lavished on us (verse 8), and that we have redemption through the blood of Christ "according to the riches of his grace" (verse 7, RSV). Because of His grace, God gives us what we don't deserve. He offers us salvation rather than wrath. Without grace Paul never would have written "BUT GOD."

Ephesians not only reveals a great deal about people outside of Christ and about the character of God, it also graphically portrays what the Lord has done for His people in Christ. The key word expressing what He has done is "saved." Twice Paul tells us that we "have been saved" (2:5, 8). It is absolutely essential to recognize that the word is in the past tense. Salvation, according to Ephesians, is not something that people hope for. No! It is an accomplished fact in the life of a Christian. Of course, as we noted previously, even though believers have already been saved, they will not receive salvation's fullness until Christ comes in the clouds of heaven and rescues them from the ongoing problems of a sinful world.

But according to Paul in Ephesians God has already accomplished three things for His people. He has:

1. "made us alive together with Christ" (verse 5),
2. "raised us with Him" (verse 6), and
3. "seated us with Him in the heavenly places in Christ Jesus" (verse 6).

Interestingly enough, those three blessings parallel "the three successive historical events in the . . . career of Jesus, which are normally called the resurrection, the ascension, and the session" in heaven at the right hand of God (Stott, p. 81). Paul explicitly referred to the first and third of those events in his discussion of Christ's power in Ephesians 1:21, 22.

But the amazing thing about the apostle's treatment of salvation in Ephesians 2:4-10 is that he is writing about believers and not Christ. John Stott states that "He is affirming not that God quickened, raised and seated Christ, but that he quickened, raised and seated us with Christ. Fundamental to New Testament Christianity is this concept of the union of God's people with Christ. What constitutes the distinctness of the members of God's new society? Not just that they admire and even worship

Jesus, not just that they assent to the dogmas of the church, not even that they live by certain moral standards. No, what makes them distinctive is their new solidarity as a people who are 'in Christ.' By virtue of their union with Christ they have actually shared in his resurrection, ascension and session" *(ibid.)*. In short, a part of Paul's Gospel is that we as Christians already belong to God's universal church in the heavenly places. That is a spiritual reality in spite of the fact that we as church members still exist on planet Earth for a time.

The apostle's understanding of salvation goes way beyond what most of us have grasped. It is little wonder that he can scarcely restrain his praise for what God has done for His people in Christ (Eph. 1:3-14) or cease to pray that we might understand the magnitude of our present salvation (verses 15-23).

Ephesians 2:4-10 not only tells us of the greatness of our salvation, it also describes how God accomplished it. The passage does so by the use of both negatives and positives. On the negative side the apostle makes two assertions. Salvation is

- "not of yourselves" (verse 8) and
- "not because of works, lest anyone should boast" (verse 9).

Paul never ceases to drum home the truth that humans can do nothing to merit or add to God's salvation in Christ. According to him that is not only true but also, given the human temptation toward pride, essential. The great nineteenth-century evangelist Dwight L. Moody caught the apostle's thought when he claimed that if anybody ever got to heaven because of anything they had done the rest of us would never hear the end of it.

On the positive side, we can sum up Paul's description of salvation in one word—grace. Grace means that God gives us what we don't deserve, that He blesses and forgives us when we should actually receive condemnation and death.

But, the apostle notes, God's grace has a condition to it. That is, we

> ## The Human Part in Salvation
>
> "The only thing that a man can contribute to his redemption is the sin from which he needs to be redeemed" (William Temple, in Barton, p. 46).

must accept it. We do so through faith. Faith, it is important to recognize, is not some human work of a different flavor. No, it also is a gift of God (Acts 18:27). The Lord Himself makes it possible for us to have faith. Our part is to choose to accept that possibility. Faith is our "hand" reaching out to receive God's grace. He is more than willing to present us with His gifts, but He forces them upon no one. Thus faith is our saying "yes" to God.

The final thing that Ephesians 2:4-10 teaches us is that God's saved people are to be a witness to the wonders of His grace. Verse 7 tells us that throughout eternity God will "display the exceeding riches of His grace in His kindness toward us in Christ Jesus." Reflecting on that passage, F. F. Bruce suggests that God's saved people will "serve as a demonstration of his grace to all succeeding ages" (Bruce, *Epistles to Colossians . . .* , p. 288; cf. Best, p. 223).

Ephesians 2:10 adds to the dynamics of that display. There the apostle tells us that saved by grace people are "His work of art." They are not only individual examples of what He can do for human beings, but as God's church they were "created in Christ Jesus for good works, which God previously prepared, that we should walk in them."

We need to make an important distinction in verse 10. Christians do not earn their salvation through their works (verse 9), but once saved and recreated (verse 10) in Christ they will live a life in harmony with their new heart and mind that is no longer in rebellion against God. As one sage put it, Christian works are not the *root* of salvation but the *fruit* of it. Again Paul expresses the new direction of the born of the Spirit Christian by the word "walk" (verse 10). A Christian walks in the good works of God's love as a result of a new relationship to Him through Jesus. That contrasts to their previous condition, mentioned in verse 2, when they walked in the ways of the secular world. The ability to empower His saved by grace people to live a new life is a part of the demonstration of the power of God's grace.

Paul is excited about what he is writing concerning the heighth and depth and width and breadth of salvation. And if we begin to grasp what he is telling us in Ephesians we will progressively share in his breathless excitement.

7. Before Christ: The Great Division

Ephesians 2:11, 12

[11]Therefore remember that formerly you, the Gentiles in the flesh, those called the uncircumcision by those called the circumcision, which is performed in the flesh by hands—[12]remember that you were at that time without Christ, having been alienated from the commonwealth of Israel, and strangers to the covenants of the promise, having no hope and without God in the world.

The two great themes of Ephesians 2 are alienation and reconciliation. The first three verses dealt with human alienation from God, whereas verses 11 and 12 explore that existing between people. Similarly, verses 4-10 treated the reconciliation of sinners with God, while verses 13 to 22 present the bringing together of people. And in the structure of the chapter the second reconciliation is dependent upon the first. That is, when people get right with God (verses 4-10) they are in a position to get right with one another as they join the great family of God (verses 13-22).

The tragedy of some believers both then and now is that they think they can be right with God without having true respect for one another. That was true in the Jewish/Gentile split in the Ephesian congregations. Most of us don't have that exact problem in the twenty-first century, even though antisemitism is still a difficulty for some. The greater source of estrangement for us today comes from questions of race, economics, and even marginal theological issues. But the problem of alienation is just as serious and just as disastrous for the unity of God's church as it was 20 centuries ago. Reconciliation is an ongoing need as the church and its members seek to approximate God's ideal.

The point that we can never forget as we study Ephesians 2 is that we can never be truly right with God until we have love and demonstrate that love to all of His other children—even those *different* in some significant way from us. Paul is clear that God's church is the "family of God" (verse 19) rather than a cluster of social or racial clubs. Ephesians 2 is just as relevant today as the day Paul penned it.

I once pastored a church in which one of the members drove 100 miles round trip each week to attend another congregation because a person of another race attended our local one. There is only one thing that can be said about such a person—he was sick, lost, and confused about the very meaning of church attendance. He was still suffering from the alienation that should be a part of our "Before Christ" past. Listen carefully, because in chapter 2 Paul is not merely addressing some ancient people about their problem. To the contrary, he is speaking to you and me about our problems.

The key word in Ephesians 2:11 is "formerly," contrasted with the "but now" of verse 13. Paul in verses 11 and 12 is writing about the condition of the Gentiles before their encounter with Christ. For the purpose of his argument in chapter 2 the apostle presents them in their pre-Christian life as being "alienated from the commonwealth of Israel, and strangers to the covenants of the promise, having no hope and without God in the world" (verse 12).

And the Jews and Gentiles of the first century certainly found themselves separated from each other by a number of barriers. One was circumcision, which the Jews rightly saw as the sign of Abraham's covenant with God (Gen. 17:9-14). But in their arrogance in being God's chosen people they failed to remember that to really belong to His people means also a circumcision of the heart (Rom. 2:28, 29). As in Christian baptism, in God's eyes the outward act in the flesh is only significant as a sign of an inward change. One of the problems of religious people down through history is that they have sought to substitute external symbols for the reality of a life transformed by God. In the first century that led to racial/religious slurs, with the Jews referring to the Gentiles as the uncircumcised or uncircumcised dogs, and the Gentiles retaliating by alluding to Jewish circumcision in an unflattering way.

The barrier between Jews and Gentiles even entered into the prayer life of Jewish men, who daily thanked God that they had not been born a slave, a woman, or a Gentile. But the most visible institutionalized barrier between the two groups appears in the very architecture of the Jewish Temple in Jerusalem. The first century Temple compound had several courts, each progressively more distant from the Temple proper. The closest was the court of the priests. Next was the court for Israelite men. Then came the court of the women. Those three courts were all on a level with the Temple itself. On a lower level and behind a wall was the court of the Gentiles. That was as close to the Temple that a Gentile could get. Separating the court of the Gentiles from the Jewish courts stretched a wall displaying warning signs in both Greek and Latin. Josephus, the first-century Jewish historian, describes those signs. "There was," he writes, "a partition made of stone . . . , whose height was three cubits [about five feet] . . . ; upon it stood pillars, at equal distances from one another, declaring the law of purity, some in Greek, and some in Roman letters, that 'no foreigner should go within that sanctuary'" (Josephus, *Wars* V.5.2). In another place Josephus writes that the inscription "forbade any foreigner to go in under pain of death" (Josephus, *Antiquities* XV.11.5).

In the past 150 years archaeologists have recovered at least two of those inscriptions. And Paul himself had experienced the strength of the alienation related to the Temple a few years before writing to the Ephesians when a Jewish mob almost lynched him because it thought he had brought a Greek into the Temple area. Interestingly enough, the Gentile in question had been an Ephesian (Acts 21:27-30).

Speaking of the alienation between Jew and Gentile, William Barclay writes that "the Jew had an immense contempt for the Gentile. The Gentiles, said the Jews, were created by God to be fuel for the fires of Hell. God, they said, loves only Israel of all the nations that He had made. . . . It was not even lawful to render help to a Gentile mother in her hour of her sorest need, for that would simply be to bring another Gentile into the world. . . . If a Jewish boy married a Gentile girl, or if a Jewish girl married a Gentile boy, the funeral of that Jewish boy or girl was carried out. Such contact with a Gentile was the equivalent of death. . . . Before Christ the barriers were up" (Barclay, p. 125).

Paul labored hard to bring Jew and Gentile into the same church. From our historical distance we generally fail to see the magnitude of the task he sought to accomplish. It led to battles again and again in such places as Rome and the churches in Galatia. In his letter to the Romans, for example, after writing for three chapters on the topic, he said that God through His grace would "have mercy upon all"—both Jew and Gentile (Rom. 11:32, RSV). And in the hard-fought battle reflected upon in his letter to the Galatians he told them that "in Christ Jesus you are all sons of God, through faith. For as many of you as were baptized into Christ have put on Christ. There is neither Jew nor Greek, there is neither slave nor free, there is neither male nor female; for you are all one in Christ Jesus. And if you are Christ's, then you are Abraham's offspring, heirs according to promise" (Gal. 3:26-29, RSV).

As in his letters to the Romans and to the Galatians, so it is in the epistle to the Ephesians: Paul proclaims the fact that those who had once been "alienated from the commonwealth of Israel, and strangers to the covenants of promise" (Eph. 2:12) were now one with God's Jewish people. In short, before Christ the barriers were up. After Christ they are down. Their removal is the topic of Ephesians 2:13-22.

But before turning to that passage we should reflect upon the issue of hope. In verse 12 Paul asserts that before the Gentiles found Christ they had "no hope and [were] without God in the world." For the apostle hope is a historical reality. The basic idea is that history is not aimless or cyclical but is going somewhere. The Bible is a book of hope. Things perhaps aren't going as we would like them, but God's people do not need to worry, because He has a plan for them. J. M. Everts points out that "in the OT hope is closely related to the character of God. Those who hope in God, trust God and His promises. . . . Paul understands Christian hope as a fulfillment of God's promises to Israel," which included the assurance that the seed of Abraham would bless all the nations of the earth. In fact, the Old Testament sets forth Abraham "as an example of someone who never doubted that God would fulfill his promises," in spite of his outward circumstances (in Hawthorne, pp. 415-417).

The hope of the Jews, of course, was the coming of the Christ. That hope was fulfilled in the birth of Jesus of Nazareth, who is "God with us" (Matt. 1:23, RSV), a child who would "save his people from their sins" (verse 21, RSV). And that fulfillment provides the foundation for a post-Christ philosophy of history. History for Christians is the same as for the Jewish nation—it is going somewhere! For the ancient Jewish nation hope's climax was the first coming of Christ. For Christians it is the Second Coming, an event Paul refers to as "the blessed hope" (Titus 2:13).

With that first climax of hope Jesus "saved" (Eph. 2:5, 8) those people (both Jews and Gentiles) who accept His grace, while the second one will physically unite all of God's people with the rest of His followers in the heavenly places. Perhaps the most important thing that we can say about Christians is that we are a people who have hope. Hope keeps us going when life becomes thin or even vicious. When things really get bad we need to heed Paul's admonition to "remember" (verse 11) how much worse they appear without Christ—without hope.

8. After Christ: The Great Unity

Ephesians 2:13-18

¹³But now in Christ Jesus you who were formerly far off have been brought near by the blood of Christ. ¹⁴For He is our peace, who has made both groups into one and in His body of flesh has broken down the partition of the dividing wall, ¹⁵nullifying the law of the commandments contained in ordinances, that in Himself He might create the two into one new man, thus making peace, ¹⁶and that He might reconcile the two in one body through the cross, by it having put to death the hostility. ¹⁷And He came and preached peace to you who were far off and peace to those near, ¹⁸for through Him we both have access in one Spirit to the Father.

"BUT NOW!" Those two words in Ephesians 2:13 hold a place analagous to the "BUT GOD!" of verse 4. Both signal a radical contrast between what went before and what follows them. Yet there is a difference. The "BUT GOD" of verse 4 transitions from the total lostness of all humanity (described in verses 1-3) to the salvation of those who accept God's grace through faith (verses 4-10), whereas the "BUT NOW" of verse 13 moves from the alienation and hopelessness of the Gentiles (verses 11 and 12) to their inclusion in the one great family of God (verses 13-22). Each "BUT," however, serves a crucial role in Paul's presentation in Ephesians 2. Both emphasize the sharpness of the contrast in the journey from before Christ to after Christ in the experience of both individuals and communities.

The "BUT NOW" of verse 13 reflects on the Gentiles, "who were formerly far off" but who have now "been brought near" through the "blood of Christ." In the presentation running from verses 13 to 18 it is significant that three times Paul refers to the efficacy and importance of the blood and or sacrifice of Christ.

- Those "who were formerly far off have been brought near by the *blood of Christ*" (verse 13).
- Christ "made both groups into one and in *His body of flesh* has broken down the partition of the dividing wall" (verse 14).
- He reconciled "the two in one body *through the cross*" (verse 16).

The cross of Calvary on which Jesus died for the sins of each and every person is absolutely central to the apostle's theology. Why? Because on Calvary Christ took the penalty of the broken law and became a "curse for us" (Gal. 3:10, 13, RSV). The cross stands at the foundation of grace. On it Christ not only made forgiveness possible through the shedding of His blood (Heb. 9:22), but His sacrifice created the moral foundation for the extension of grace to those willing to accept it through faith (see Rom. 3:24-26). For Paul, without the substitutionary sacrifice there is no gospel.

Another key word in Ephesians 2:13-18 is "peace," mentioned four times.

- "He is our peace" (verse 14).
- Christ is the one "making peace" (verse 15).
- He "preached peace to you who were far off" (verse 17).
- And He also preached "peace to those near" (verse 17).

Central to Paul's thought is that Christ "is our peace" (verse 14). He not only reconciles, unites, and brings peace, but He is peace. His very being is peace, a concept undoubtedly tied in the apostle's mind to the Messianic title of Isaiah 9:6, a passage that refers to the coming one as the "Prince of Peace" (KJV).

One of the functions of valid Christianity is to bring peace to each and every Christian:

- peace between the individual and God,
- peace between various identifiable groups, such as the Jews and Gentiles of Ephesians 2:11, 12,
- and peace within each individual Christian because of the removal of personal guilt and condemnation (cf. Rom. 5:1, 8-10).

Given Paul's emphasis on peace, one of the great tragedies among Christians is that some of them individually and as groups have so little peace. Perhaps we really haven't grasped what God has done for us in terms of our salvation and in tearing down ethnic, social, and national walls. Our modern tribalisms and discriminations may not be between Jew and Gentile, but they are just as disruptive. And the words of Paul are just as much needed today as they were in the Ephesian congregations. Has Jesus really brought peace to you? Do you have a calm assurance that you are saved in Christ? Are you as a church member a peacemaker or a troublemaker? Think about those questions. Don't just pass them off. They stand at the very center of what it means to be a Christian.

Barrier Breakers

"Christianity is the only religion in the world that can truly be described as an equal-opportunity faith. All Christians stand on level ground before the cross of Christ: young and old, male and female, Jew and Gentile, rich and poor, black, white, and every other color. We all are sinners in need of salvation. Other religions set up barriers between people. Hindus believe in a caste system; Muslim men will not worship with Muslim women; until very recently, black people could not join [certain so-called Christian congregations]. Christ alone abolishes all these barriers. Are there barriers in your church (or in your heart) based on race, economics, or sex? Check your attitudes and actions against Scripture. If you find yourself out of accord with it, repent and ask God to help you. Don't put up walls where Christ has torn them down" (Barton, p. 54).

One way that Christ brought peace was through breaking down "the partition of the dividing wall" (Eph. 2:14). Some have seen that barrier as the wall in the Temple that separated the court of the Gentiles from the courts of the Jews, and beyond which a Gentile passed at the risk of life itself. We discussed that wall earlier in section 7. While that is an attractive explanation, still, as Peter O'Brien observes, "whether the Gentile readers of this letter, living in Asia Minor, would have recognized such an allusion is questionable" (O'Brien, p. 195). We find the best contextual candidate for the wall in the next phrase in Paul's sentence. He closely ties the breaking down of the dividing wall to "nullifying the law of the commandments contained in ordinances" (verse 15).

The wording of that phrase has caused endless discussion in terms of its exact meaning. Perhaps the best way to get at Paul's meaning is to examine other New Testament passages that infer that the law acted as a barrier between Jew and Gentile. In Acts 15:1 we read that "some men came down from Judea and were teaching" the Gentiles, "'Unless you are circumcised according to the custom of Moses, you cannot be saved'" (RSV). Those missionaries of the law created endless havoc in the churches of Galatia with their emphasis on circumcision (Gal. 6:12) and the Jewish ceremonial calendar (4:10). The same problem seems to have arisen in Colossae, where some of the believers were judging others about the observance of those Jewish holy days that were "a shadow of what is to come" (i.e., pointed to the coming of Christ, such as the Passover, which found its fulfillment in Christ as the Passover Lamb, Col. 2:16, 17, RSV; 1 Cor. 5:7; cf. Rom. 14:5, 6). In the immediate context of Ephesians 2:15, with its nullification of "the law of the commandments contained in ordinances" passage, we find evidence that such issues as circumcision also created problems in the Ephesian community (see verse 11).

Thus it appears that circumcision, the Jewish calendar, and other aspects of the Jewish ceremonial law did indeed isolate Jews from Gentiles. As a result, by "nullifying" those ordinances through His death, Christ did indeed break down "the partition of the dividing wall" (Eph. 2:15, 14).

Francis Foulkes highlights the logic of that conclusion when he writes that "much of the law (e.g., the sacrificial ritual) was preparation for, and foreshadowing of, the Christ, and so was fulfilled by what he did when he came." On the other hand, Foulkes points out that "the moral demands and principles of the law were not lightened by Jesus, but made fuller and more far-reaching" (Mt. 5:21-48)" (Foulkes, p. 91).

John Stott takes the same position, noting that Paul could not be speaking of a nullification of the moral law "when Christ himself in the Sermon on the Mount specifically declared the opposite, that he had not come to abolish" the law but "to fulfill it." As a result, "Paul's primary reference here . . . seems to be to the *ceremonial* law. . . . He did it *in his flesh* (surely a reference to his physical death) because in the cross he fulfilled all the types and shadows of the Old Testament ceremonial system" (Stott, pp. 99, 100).

By breaking down "the partition of the dividing wall" (Eph. 2:14) Paul asserts that Christ accomplished at least two other objectives. First, He opened the way to create a new humanity from both Jews and Gentiles, or as Paul puts it, to "create the two into one new man" (verse 15). That one new collective "man" he will discuss as God's church in verses 19-22, a topic we will focus on in section 9.

The second accomplishment Paul refers to as reconciliation (verse 16), another peace-oriented word. Reconciliation is a family word. The rebellion of sin had shattered the unity between God and humans and between people and their neighbors. Healing both human and human/divine relationships, reconciliation brings peace to the family of God, a theme Paul will pick up again in verse 19.

The apostle is excited about what God has done in Christ. The Lord not only saves all on the same basis (grace), but that identical approach to salvation leads to a profound equality among Christians (see Gal. 3:26-29) that breaks down barriers and airs of superiority (see Eph. 2:9) and provides the basis for the unity of all of God's people in His universal church. Such is the profound mystery (see 3:3-6) that Paul has grasped and so enthusiastically shares with both his Ephesian audience and those of us who read his epistle in the twenty-first century.

9. The Church of God

Ephesians 2:19-22

[19]So then, you are no longer strangers and aliens, but you are fellow citizens with the saints and members of the family of God, [20]having been built upon the foundation of the apostles and prophets, Christ Jesus Himself being the cornerstone, [21]in whom all the building is joined together and is growing into a holy temple in the Lord, [22]in whom you also are being built together into a dwelling place of God in the Spirit.

So then" are the key words that link verses 19-22 with the discussion in verses 13-18 of the one new humanity and of peace through the cross of Christ. Now that the work of Christ has united Jews and Gentiles, so what?

That is where Paul's "so then" comes in. Up through verse 18 he has been discussing the process of unity, but "now he contemplates the thing itself" (Lloyd-Jones, *God's Way*, p. 302). And the "thing itself" is three snapshots of a racially-united Christian church.

The first is from a political angle: "You are no longer strangers and aliens, but you are fellow citizens with the saints" (Eph. 2:19a). The saints in this case are the Jewish Christians. In the Old Testament period God had set the Jewish people apart as a holy nation. Thus the Jews had been God's saints, those appointed for holy living. As Paul noted earlier, the Gentiles were not a part of that restricted group. Outsiders, they were "alienated from the commonwealth of Israel, and strangers to the covenants of the promise" (verse 12).

But that has all changed through the work of Christ. Now they are *politeia* or citizens along with the Jews. They belong to the kingdom of

God, and the Lord Himself is their ruler. That reality signaled a radical shift in their status. As part of God's international community of saints, they have equal status to the Jews. From their new perspectives the Gentile believers can exclaim, "We no longer live on a passport, . . . we really have our birth certificates, . . . we really do belong" (Lloyd-Jones, *God's Way,* p. 302).

In this teaching Paul makes it clear that Christians are a people (or a nation) distinct from all others. Some of the earliest Christian writers picked up on that idea. The Epistle to Diognetus (cir. A.D. 200) calls Christians a "new race of men" (chapter 1), while Clement of Alexandria (cir. 155-cir. 220) distinguished Christian believers from Jews and Greeks by stating that they are "the one race of the saved people" (Clement, *Miscellanies* VI.5). The unity of that race centers on the fact that a common allegiance to a new Ruler, including His authority and the laws and mores of His kingdom, binds Christians together. Their new citizenship, of course, brings with it certain privileges, including:

- the right of admittance to the King (Eph. 2:18; 3:12; Heb. 4:16).
- access to the resources of the kingdom (John 16:23).
- protection from the King's enemies (Eph. 1:20-22), and
- ultimate hope in the victory of the King in His struggle against "the world rulers of this present darkness" and "the spiritual hosts of wickedness in the heavenly places" (Eph. 6:12, RSV; 1:10; 4:30).

As one can see, it is no small privilege to be a citizen of God's kingdom. And those rights and privileges also bring the responsibilities of citizenship. Paul will turn to that topic beginning in chapter 4.

Ephesians 2:19's second snapshot of the church pictures it as being the "family of God." This is not the only family-type imagery in Ephesians. In the first chapter he wrote that God "destined us in love to be his sons through Jesus Christ" (verse 5, RSV). And in Ephesians 4:6 he speaks of "one God and Father of us all" (RSV).

The good news for the Gentiles was that they were now part of God's universal family. That was a theme to rejoice about. "See," wrote John the apostle, "what love the Father has given us, that we should be called children of God" (1 John 3:1, RSV).

While it is true that the Gentiles could feel joy because God was now their Father in a new and special way, the context of Ephesians 2:19 suggests that it is the fact of brotherhood and sisterhood that Paul sought to emphasize. The early Christians styled themselves as brothers and sisters. And it was by those titles that they tended to greet each other. Unfortunately, it is all too easy to use such greetings without fully realizing their significance. They not only relate each and every Christian vertically to the same father, but they unite each Christian horizontally to every other Christian in a bond of affection. At least that is the ideal. Some individuals and congregations, however, have a difficult time putting it into practice. All such need to seriously meditate upon how they became a part of the family of God and what it means for their daily lives. When we realize God's love and sacrifice for us and His grace to us, it will inspire us to reach out in His spirit to our spiritual siblings. Perhaps Paul's snapshot of the family of God is an ideal. But it is one that he wants us to live out in our individual and corporate lives.

It is to the third snapshot that Paul devotes the most attention. In Ephesians 2:20-22 he refers to the church as a temple. The various temples in Jerusalem had been at the center of Israelite identity and worship since the time of Solomon. The Jews believed themselves to be God's people because they had God's Temple. But the death of Jesus supernaturally tore the curtain into the Temple in two (Matt. 27:51), signifying that the Temple in Jerusalem was no longer God's dwelling place.

Following the logic of Ephesians 2, if God had created a new people (verse 15), it naturally followed that He would have a new temple where He could dwell among them. That new holy temple was His church, made up of both Jews and Gentiles. Paul raises that same topic in 1 Corinthians 3:16, in which he describes the church as God's temple with God's Spirit dwelling in it.

The apostle has several quite specific things to say about the church as God's temple. He first discusses its foundation, declaring it to be built upon "the apostles and prophets" (Eph. 2:20a). Foundations, as any contractor knows, are absolutely central to a good structure. Jesus made that absolutely clear in his saying about building upon the sand versus upon the rock (Matt. 7:24-27).

Paul asserts that the foundation of God's church is "the apostles and prophets." The most natural interpretation of that phrase is to see the prophets as the authors of the Old Testament and the apostles as the authors of the New. Thus, as D. Martyn Lloyd-Jones points out, "the foundation . . . is the teaching of the apostles and prophets" (Lloyd-Jones, *God's Way,* p. 352). A church with a solid foundation is one whose teachings are based solidly in the Bible.

The second aspect of the church as God's temple that Ephesians highlights is that Jesus Christ is the cornerstone (Eph. 2:20b). C. Leslie Mitton argues that the most important part of a structure's foundation was its cornerstone, "because every line of the building was to be calculated from this keystone of the foundation. Only when this was well and truly laid could other bricks be added to it and set in their own place by aligning them to the brick at the corner. The first stone at the corner, the one to which all others will be aligned, this is the cornerstone of the foundation, as important to the foundation as the foundation is to the whole building" (Mitton, p. 114).

Paul in 1 Corinthians 3 refers to Christ as the foundation (verse 11), but here the apostle wants to highlight the fact that it is Christ who holds the church together. As John Stott reminds us, "unless it is constantly and securely related to Christ, the church's unity will disintegrate and its growth either stop or run wild" (Stott, p. 108).

The third constituent of the church as God's temple is the individual Christians who "are being built together into a dwelling place of God" (Eph. 2:22). It goes without saying, following Paul's logic, that Christians can only be correctly incorporated into the building when the foundation and the cornerstone each have their proper place. Any other approach to construction would be a total disaster. And so it is in the history of the church. The wreckage of religious groups who have either moved away from the Bible's central teachings or from a balanced understanding of the work of Christ and the meaning of His life and death litter church history.

It is important to note that God's church is a dynamic edifice. It *"is growing* into a holy temple in the Lord" (verse 21), and its members "are being built together into a dwelling place of God" (verse 22). The present tense of the verbs indicates "continual development. . . . Though the building is structurally complete, it continues to grow w[ith] the addition of individual stones" (Rogers, p. 438).

The word that Paul uses for temple in verse 21 also harbors an important insight. It is not *hieron,* which refers to the entire Temple compound with its courts, porches, and porticoes, but *naos,* a term applying to the Temple proper and limited to the holy and most holy places (see Trench, pp. 27, 28). It was in the *naos* that God met with the priests and dwelt among the shekinah glory. The church is where God now encounters His people. Or as Francis Foulkes points out, "now God seeks as his *dwelling place* the lives of men and women who will allow him to enter by his Spirit" (Foulkes, p. 96). But in the context of Ephesians that dwelling is not so much individual as it is corporate as the different stones and family members from a broad range of backgrounds unite in harmony to celebrate the fact of their mutual salvation by grace in Christ.

10. A Minister of the Mystery of God

Ephesians 3:1-13

¹For this reason I, Paul, the prisoner of Christ Jesus for the sake of you Gentiles—²if indeed you have heard of the stewardship of God's grace that was given to me for you; ³how the mystery was made known to me by revelation, as I wrote before in brief. ⁴In reading this then you will be able to understand my insight into the mystery of Christ, ⁵which in other generations was not made known to the sons of men, as it has now been revealed to His holy apostles and prophets by the Spirit; ⁶that is, how the Gentiles are fellow heirs and belong to the same body and are co-sharers of the promise in Christ Jesus through the gospel, ⁷of which I became a serving minister through the gift of God's grace that was given to me through the working of His power. ⁸To me, the very least of all saints, this grace was given, to preach to the Gentiles the unsearchable riches of Christ, ⁹and to enlighten all people regarding the administration of the mystery hidden for ages past in God, who created all things, ¹⁰that the many colored wisdom of God might now be made known through the church to the rulers and the authorities in the heavenly places, ¹¹according to the eternal purpose which He has accomplished in Christ Jesus our Lord, ¹²in whom we have boldness and confident access through faith in Him. ¹³Therefore, I ask you not to despair concerning my afflictions for you, which is for your glory.

Even a glance at Ephesians 3 reveals that the first three words of its two major paragraphs are the same. Both verses 1 and 14 begin with "for this reason." Paul was apparently beginning a prayer for the Ephesians when he got sidetracked by some additional insights that he desired to share with his readers. As G. G. Findlay notes, "verses 2-13 are in form a parenthesis. They interrupt the prayer which appears to be commencing in the first verse and is not resumed until verse 14. This intervening period is parenthetical, however, in appearance more than in reality. The matter it contains is so weighty and so essential to the argument and structure of the epistle, that it is impossible to treat it as a mere *aside*" (Findlay, p. 155).

What put the apostle off the track was his introduction of himself as "the prisoner of Christ Jesus for the sake of you Gentiles" (verse 1). It raised two items in his major theme of the inclusion of Jews and Gentiles into one body that he hadn't addressed in his first two chapters, namely:

1. the exact nature of God's "mystery" and the place of both Jews and Gentiles in it,
2. and his personal role in the preaching of God's mystery.

It was the biographical allusion in verse 1 that stimulated him to address both issues. There he introduced himself as "the prisoner of Christ Jesus." Now it should be obvious to any student of the New Testament that he was a prisoner of Nero rather than of Christ. After all "he *was* Caesar's prisoner." Yet "nowhere does Paul ever refer to himself as a prisoner of Caesar" (Steadman, p. 177).

What does Paul mean? The facts of the matter are that he had appealed his case to the Emperor and therefore was being sent under guard to Rome for trial (Acts 25:11, 12). But the initial cause of his arrest had been the alarm of certain Jews from Asia who had seen him in the Temple. "Men of Israel," they cried out, "help! This is the man who is teaching men everywhere against the people and the law and this place" (Acts 21:27, 28, RSV). That episode and the tempest that followed it in which Paul was "dragged . . . out of the temple" (verse 30) led to his arrest and eventual appeal to Caesar. Thus it was quite true that although Paul was a prisoner of Caesar, it was because of his preaching Christ to the Gentiles, including the position that Gentiles did not have to be circumcised and keep the Jewish ordinances since the only way into God's family was through grace alone (see Eph. 2:4-9).

Thus Paul was both a prisoner of Caesar and of Christ. But he always called himself a prisoner of Christ because it was his preaching of the Gospel that repeatedly brought him into conflict with human authorities.

Before moving away from Paul as a prisoner of Christ we should note a lesson we can learn from his words. William Barclay points that out when he writes that "if a man is in prison for some great cause he may either grumblingly regard himself as a poor and wretched and ill-used creature, or he may radiantly regard himself as the standard-bearer and protagonist of some great cause. The one man will regard his prison as a penance; the other man will regard it as a privilege. When we are undergoing hardship, unpopularity, material loss for the sake of Christian principles we can either regard ourselves as the victims of men, or as the champions of Christ. Our point of view will make all the difference. Paul is our example; he regarded himself, not as the prisoner of Nero, but as the prisoner of Christ" (Barclay, p. 142).

The two thematic concepts that dominate Ephesians 3:1-13 are mystery and minister. The word "mystery" surfaces in verses 3, 4, and 9. It also appears in Ephesians 1:9, in which Paul writes that God had "made known to us in all wisdom and insight the mystery of his will" (RSV) and in 6:19, in which he reiterates his commission to "proclaim the mystery of the gospel" (RSV).

With so much emphasis on mystery it is only natural to ask what it involves. Before answering that question it is important to remind ourselves that we should not equate the Greek *mystērion* with the English "mystery." In Paul's writings a *mystērion* is not something mysterious in the sense that it is difficult to understand. Rather, it represents a thing that has long remained secret, but now "something God wishes to make known to those who are willing to receive His revelations" (Horn, p. 747). It is a secret that God has opened for all to understand.

With that background, let us examine what Ephesians 3:1-13 has to say about the all-important mystery that is at its focal point. In verse 3 the apostle tells us that revelation had made it known to him. That is, the mystery was not something that he understood through human study. Rather, the Holy Spirit enlightened his mind as He revealed to him the exact nature of the mystery. Closely aligned with the idea that Paul received understanding of the mystery through revelation is the fact that God had *not* revealed it to previous generations (verse 5). Verse 9 reinforces that thought when it tells us that "the mystery [was] hidden for ages past in God." But in Paul's day it had at last "been revealed to His holy apostles [including Paul] and prophets by the Spirit" (verse 5). Ephesians 6:19 adds that Paul's commission from God was "to proclaim the mystery of the gospel" (RSV).

Well, so far we have danced all around the idea of *mystērion* without defining it. That is the contribution of Ephesians 3:6: that "the Gentiles are fellow heirs and belong to the same body and are co-sharers of the promise in Christ Jesus through the gospel." As Harold Hoehner puts it, "Ephesians views God's sacred secret as believing Jews and Gentiles united into one body. In the OT Gentiles could be a part of the company of God, but they had to become Jews in order to belong to it. In the NT Gentiles do not become Jews nor do Jews become Gentiles. Rather, both believing Jews and Gentiles become one new entity, Christians (Eph. 2:15-16). That is the mystery" (Hoehner, pp. 433, 434).

With that definition in mind it is easy to see that the *mystērion* of God is one of the centerpieces of Ephesians, being mentioned in the book's opening and closing sections, praised and prayed about in chapter 1, hammered home forcefully in terms of its meaning in chapters 2 and 3, and applied in the last half of the book.

And that brings us to the second key concept of Ephesians 3:1-13: minister. Paul tells us that the mystery had been supernaturally revealed to him (verse 3). That is, a revelation from the Holy Spirit had opened it to him. "By revelation," Markus Barth explains, "God opens and gives himself to man but does not make himself subject to man's intellectual or technical control. Revelation creates rather than annihilates wonder, awe, and respect" (Barth, *Ephesians 1-3,* p. 341). And Paul never got over the awe and wonder of what God had done through Christ for both Jews and Gentiles. That revelation turned him from a Jewish persecutor of Gentile Christians (Acts 8:1-3) to become the apostle of Christ to them (13:47). It led him to express his thoughts about God's gospel mystery in superlatives. And of all Paul's writings, Ephesians is the showplace of descriptive superlatives, not only in the praise and prayer of chapter 1, but right here in chapter 3. Phrases such as "the unsearchable riches of Christ" (Eph. 3:8) pepper the letter.

What revelation showed Paul regarding the mystery quickly transformed his life. He became a servant/minister of Christ to spread its good news. And given the nature of the world in which he lived, he spent much if not most of his time seeking to bring Jews and Gentiles together in the same community of faith. We see that not only in Ephesians, but also in Galatians, Romans, and his other letters. Thus *mystērion* takes its place beside gospel as being two words at the very center of Paul's theology and mission.

It overjoyed and overawed him that all of us who believe in Christ can "have boldness and confident access" to God "through faith" (Eph. 3:12). That is good news indeed. And like Paul, we need to let it energize us to enlighten others on what God has done for all humanity in Christ.

11. A Prayer for Mystery Comprehension

Ephesians 3:14-21

> [14]*For this reason I bend my knees to the Father,* [15]*from whom every family in the heavens and on earth is named,* [16]*that He may grant you, according to the riches of His glory, to be mightily empowered through His Spirit in the inner man,* [17]*and that Christ may dwell in your hearts through faith, and that you, having been rooted and grounded in love,* [18]*might be strong enough to comprehend with all the saints what is the breadth and length and height and depth,* [19]*and to know the love of Christ that surpasses knowledge, that you may be filled with all the fullness of God.*
>
> [20]*Now to the One who is able to do far more abundantly beyond all that we ask or think, according to the power working in us,* [21]*to Him be the glory in the church and in Christ Jesus to all the generations forever and ever. Amen.*

Do you ever think about your prayers? What we pray for and about paints a picture about us. It indicates our concerns, desires, and ambitions.

Paul's concerns in Ephesians are obvious. He has an overwhelming desire for the members of the Ephesian congregations to come to an ever-more complete understanding of what God has done for them in Christ and for what He yet wants to do for them both individually and corporately.

In Ephesians 3:14 Paul turns from teaching the Ephesians to praying for them. It seems that he has been trying to pray for them ever since the second half of chapter 1. In fact, he made a pretty good start of it in the prayer of Ephesians 1:15-23, but he got sidetracked in his desire to teach them more about God's gift of salvation in Ephesians 2:1-10 and what salvation by grace meant for their corporate life as a united body of Jews and Gentiles in verses 11-22.

A Prayer for Mystery Comprehension

The apostle starts off his prayer in Ephesians 1:15 with "for this reason." The next time we find those words are in Ephesians 3:1, in which the apostle tries to resume his prayer with "for this reason," only to break off in mid-sentence as he realizes he has more to teach them about God's mystery and his part in presenting it. That took him up through verse 13. His mind and heart appear to be overflowing all through the first half of his letter as he praises, teaches, and prays in onrushing sentences full of superlatives.

Finally in verse 14 he gets back to his prayer, for the third time starting off with "for this reason." But now he will complete it.

Interestingly enough, Paul goes out of his way to tell us that he bends on his knees before the Father, which undoubtedly means that he was kneeling. Markus Barth calls that an "extraordinary attitude of prayer" (Barth, *Ephesians 1-3,* p. 367). Kneel-

> **An Interrupted Prayer With Three Beginnings**
> 1. "For this reason" (1:15)—interrupted by teaching.
> 2. "For this reason" (3:1)—interrupted by teaching.
> 3. "For this reason" (3:14)—the prayer completed.

ing was not the usual position for prayer in the biblical world. People generally stood. Thus Jesus admonished, "whenever you stand praying" (Mark 11:25, RSV), indicating the usual posture. Again in Luke 18:11, 13 we find both the Pharisee and the tax collector standing while they prayed. But the New Testament does have instances when people did kneel. One is Jesus in Gethsemane (Luke 22:41) and a second is Stephen as the mob stoned him (Acts 7:60). Leon Morris concludes from the evidence that "every time Scripture speaks of prayer offered kneeling the occasion is serious" (Morris, p. 101). And so it was for Paul as he diligently prayed for the Ephesian believers.

The reason behind the repeated "for this reason" undoubtedly has to do with his desire for them to have a better understanding of God's great mystery—of what He has done through grace to form one united body of believers that will demonstrate their ability through Christ and the Spirit to live a new life in resurrection power. Words related to knowledge, wisdom, and comprehension tie the two parts of Paul's prayer (Eph. 1:15-23; 3:14-21) together. He knows that they are already in Christ, that they have begun to comprehend God's mystery of what He has done and is doing for them. But he also realizes that they can still expand both their comprehension and the depth of their Christian living as they are being built spiritually together as a united community and as they continue to be built in unity into the family of God. Thus Paul prays for their continued growth in empowerment (3:16) and comprehension that they might know "the breadth and length and height and depth" of God's love and be "filled with all the fullness of God" (verses 18, 19). Paul was using his "access" to the Father (2:18; 3:12) to pray for the Ephesian believers. Perhaps the very thought of that access may have led him back to his prayer in Ephesians 3:1 and again in 3:14 after the teaching segment running from 3:2-13 had interrupted his first attempt at completing the prayer.

The prayer itself contains five petitions for the Ephesian believers. First, he asks that they might be "mightily empowered through His Spirit in the inner man" (verse 16). Paul desires his readers to have the gift of all gifts, the power of the Holy Spirit. It alone gives individuals the desire and ability to renounce and overcome sin. In speaking of the gift, Paul once again slides into superlatives. The word he uses for empowered is amplified by the Greek word for power, *dunamis,* from which we get the English word dynamite. And as you know, dynamite can change the shape of things when you set it off in your back yard. It is through the power of the Spirit that God transforms human lives. But the apostle just doesn't pray for the Ephesians to be empowered but rather that they be "mightily empowered." And he would pray the same for us. He wants us to have the blessing of all blessings in full abundance.

> ### The Blessing of All Blessings
>
> The promised blessing of the Holy Spirit, "claimed by faith, brings all other blessings in its train. It is given according to the riches of the grace of Christ, and He is ready to supply every soul according to the capacity to receive" (White, *The Desire of Ages,* p. 672).

The second petition parallels the first: "that Christ may dwell in your hearts through faith" (Eph. 3:17). The Holy Spirit is the representative of Christ (John 14:26; 15:26; 16:12, 13), and Paul tends to use the indwelling of Christ and that of the Holy Spirit interchangeably, since in actuality a person can't have one without the other. Likewise the "inner man" of

Ephesians 3:16 and the "heart" in verse 17 represent that part of us with which we make decisions for or against God and His principles. If Christ dwells in our heart so that we are "rooted and grounded in love" the Spirit will be there to empower us to live the life of love.

The third petition is that believers "be strong enough to comprehend . . . the breadth and length and height and depth" of the love of God and its outworking in the mystery of salvation (verse 18). As noted previously, one of Paul's burdens all through Ephesians is that his readers might understand the magnitude of what God had done and was currently doing for them in Christ.

Closely paralleling the petition that they might comprehend God's gift is the fourth, which requests that God will grant them the privilege "to know the love of Christ that surpasses knowledge" (verse 19). "This petition," Peter O'Brien writes, "is remarkable, for although the apostle has said much in chapters 1-3 about his readers being in Christ, he assumes that they do not adequately appreciate Christ's love." And "God's almighty power is needed to grasp its dimensions; hence he prays for power to enable them to understand how immense it is" (O'Brien, p. 264). And yet that knowledge is to be not merely an intellectual exercise, but a personal, experiential one. But when all is said and done, the knowledge of the "love of Christ . . . surpasses knowledge" (verse 19). In other words, the subject is so vast that we can never fully grasp it. It will be the study of the saints throughout the ceaseless ages of eternity, but even then they will never plumb the depths of the mystery of the ages.

The final petition is that God's people might "be filled with all the fullness of God" (verse 19). With that request Paul set the stage for the last half of his letter to the Ephesians, which deals with the Christian life. The only way any person can live such a life is to be filled with God's power and love.

Following the petition Paul utters another doxology of praise (see also 1:3) in Ephesians 3:20, 21. Into that doxology he works a statement on God's ability to answer prayer. John Stott outlines that superlative ability in seven stages:

1. "He is able to *do* or to work *(poiēsai),* for he is neither idle, nor inactive, nor dead."
2. "He is able to do what *we ask,* for he hears and answers prayer."
3. "He is able to do what we ask or *think,* for he reads our thoughts,

and sometimes we imagine things for which we dare not and therefore do not ask."

4. "He is able to do *all* that we ask or think, for he knows it all and can perform it all."

5. "He is able to do *more . . . than* (*hyper,* 'beyond') all that we ask or think, for his expectations are higher than ours."

6. "He is able to do much more, or *more abundantly (perissōs),* than all that we ask or think, for he does not give his grace by calculated measure."

7. "He is able to do very much more, *far more abundantly,* than all that we ask or think, for he is a God of super-abundance. . . . There are no limits to what God can do" (Stott, pp. 139, 140).

What a God! Paul is excited about Him. "His soul and heart seem to be bursting with a desire to praise, and to thank, and to glorify, the God who has made such things possible for men" (Lloyd-Jones, *Unsearchable Riches,* p. 303). And our hearts will be also when we begin to grasp the magnitude of what God has accomplished for *each of us* in Christ.

Part III

Practical Exhortations

Ephesians 4:1–6:20

12. Living the Mystery in Unity

Ephesians 4:1-6

[1]Therefore I, the prisoner of the Lord, beg you to walk worthily of the calling by which you were called, [2]with all humility of mind and gentleness, with patience, showing tolerance to one another in love, [3]making every effort to guard the unity of the Spirit in the uniting bond of peace. [4]There is one body and one Spirit, just as you were called in one hope of your calling, [5]one Lord, one faith, one baptism, [6]one God and Father of all who is over all and through all and in all.

The "therefore" of verse 1 signals the major transition in the book of Ephesians. For three chapters Paul has praised God for what He has done in Christ, taught exactly what Christ had done, and prayed that they might understand it better. That half of the book was heavy on theological content and breathlessly written as the apostle strung together long lists of words and phrases in his exuberance. The entire discussion centered on the mystery of God in which He gave of Himself so that all, both Jew and Gentile, could be saved by grace (Eph. 2:5, 8) and be united in one body (3:6).

The last three chapters are different in both style and content. Paul's sentences are now shorter and more manageable, and the focus is no longer on instruction, but on living the saved life. As Pheme Perkins puts it, "Ephesians presumes that conversion leads to moral renewal" (Perkins, p. 94). Other students of Paul have viewed his sequence in terms of the indicative and the imperative. First, the apostle in the indicative mode tells his readers what God had done for them in Christ. Then comes the ethical imperatives, indicating what they should do in response. "Now as regards the relationship to each other of these two different ways of speaking," Herman Ridderbos writes, "it is immediately clear that the imperative rests on the indicative and that this order is not reversible. For in each case [in Paul's writings] the imperative follows the indicative by way of conclusion" (Ridderbos, pp. 254, 255). Repeatedly we find him using a thus or a therefore as he moves from the indicative of instruction to the imperative of apostolic command (see, e.g., Rom. 6:12; 12:1; Col. 3:5). So it is in Ephesians. First came the three chapters telling what God has done. Then follows chapter 4, verse 1: *"Therefore* I . . . beg you to walk worthily." That "therefore" is the lead word in the verse that shapes the bulk of the rest of the epistle. Putting the ethical section of Ephesians in its context, Ernest Best writes that "behaviour is thus seen in Ephesians as both response to what God has done in Christ, and as the proper accompaniment to the praise of God, the two themes present in chaps. 1-3" (Best, p. 353).

"Therefore . . . walk worthily" of your calling. "Walk," we noted in our discussion of chapter 2, indicates the direction of people's lives. Before they were saved in Christ they "walked" according to the principles of this world (2:1, 2), but after their conversion they were to "walk" in good works (verse 10).

And what does Paul mean by his imperative to "walk worthily"? Chapters 4 and 5 answer that question. Ephesians 4:1-16 indicates that they must walk in unity, while 4:17-5:20 proclaims that they must walk in purity.

You may have noticed that in the twenty-first century the church and its many congregations don't always walk in unity. In fact, the universal church at all levels maintains a fractured existence. So it was with the congregations in and around Ephesus. They not only had the usual personality difficulties, but they also struggled with the racial issue of their Jewishness and their Gentileness. God had made provision for their unity, but they were still struggling.

As a result, Paul suggests several characteristics that will help them to dwell in full harmony. His suggestions, if followed, would even make your local congregation a more pleasant place to be. (They might even help your marriage and other personal relationships.)

The first is that of humility. Before Christianity, society did not regard humility as a virtue. To the contrary, people saw it as a servile, cringing, shameful sort of thing, a characteristic that befitted the attitude and status of a slave. Jesus reversed all that and in the process gave the world (or at least His followers) a new model of life. Paul urges his readers in Philippians to "have this mind among yourselves, which is yours in Christ Jesus, who, though he was in the form of God, did not count equality with God a thing to be grasped, but emptied himself, taking the form of a servant [i.e., slave, *doulos*], being born in the likeness of men. And being found in human form he humbled himself and became obedient unto death, even death on a cross," the most shameful of all deaths (2:5-8, RSV). Again, Jesus described Himself as "gentle and lowly in heart" (Matt. 11:29, RSV).

It doesn't take a great deal of wisdom to realize that a church full of humble people can more easily achieve unity than one full of the proud and arrogant. Being humble is part of what it means to be like Jesus.

A second characteristic that leads toward unity is gentleness. Peter O'Brien points out that "this gentleness is not to be confused with weakness (as contemporary Graeco-Roman thought regarded it), but has to do with consideration for others and a willingness to waive one's rights" (O'Brien, p. 278).

> **Characteristics That Will Lead to Peace and Unity in Your Life**
>
> 1. "humility of mind,"
> 2. "gentleness,"
> 3. "patience,"
> 4. "tolerance,"
> 5. "love" (Eph. 4:2).

The third and fourth characteristics are closely related. Patience is being "longsuffering towards aggravating people" (Stott, p. 149), while "showing tolerance" (Eph. 4:2) indicates "giving patience to someone till the provocation is past" (Rogers, p. 440). Both are characteristics of God, who has shown unending patience and tolerance to sinners ever since the Edenic Fall (see Ex. 34:6; Rom. 5:6-8; 2 Peter 3:9). God has provided the model. As a result, Jesus taught in the parable of the forgiven servant, we need to act in a similar way to one another (Matt. 18:23-35; cf. 1 Thess. 5:14, 15).

The final characteristic that Paul advocated for unity in the church was love *(agapē)*. In Ephesians 3:17 he had prayed that the Ephesians might be rooted and grounded in love. Now he wants them to live it. *Agapē* is that attitude of heart and mind that always wants the best for other people, no matter how poorly they have treated us.

To live out those four characteristics will lead to peace (Eph. 2:3) and unity in the body of Christ. William Barclay helps us see the basic principle behind the five characteristics Paul has set forth when he writes that "every one of the . . . great Christian virtues depends on one thing—on the obliteration of self. So long as self is at the centre of things, so long as our feelings, our prestige, are the only things that matter, . . . oneness can never fully exist. It can only exist when we cease to make self the centre of things and when we think more of others than we do of ourselves. Self kills peace. In a society where self predominates, men cannot be other than a disintegrated collection of individualistic and warring units. But when self dies and Christ springs to life within our hearts, then there comes the peace, the oneness, the togetherness, which is the great hall-mark of the true Church" (Barclay, p. 165).

In Ephesians 4:1-3 Paul presented the personal characteristics that develop peace and unity in the body of Christ. Then in verses 4-6 he provides us with the theological basis for peace and unity. He bases it on seven ones.

First, there is one body. In the heart and mind of God the church is not a multitude of denominations and factions. It does not have a Jewish and a Gentile faction, or even Catholic, Methodist, or Adventist factions. He well knows the divisions that separate believers, but that was never His ideal. His will is that all believers might humbly submit to His word and experience the oneness of the Trinity (i.e., the Spirit, Lord, and Father of verses 5 and 6). "The body of Christ is, by definition, *one*" (O'Brien, p. 281), and God wants His people to experience as much unity as possible on this earth in both their local congregations and in the larger realm. In spite of the fact that the gap between His ideal and reality is great in this life, God will rectify it at the Second Advent.

Second, there is "one Spirit," who works to bring unity and cohesion to the body. Beyond that there is "one hope" because all Christians are moving toward the same goal, "one Lord" who is the focal point of all of their hope, and "one faith" in that one Lord that brings them a sense of unity. Jews don't have one faith and Gentiles another. And in an ultimate sense there do not exist various faiths for the differing groups of Christians in our day. That "one faith" is directly related to the "one Lord" who saves by grace.

And the church has "one baptism" through which people signify their desire to become a part of the "one body." Paul is not here speaking of the mode of baptism, but of the fact that every person enters the church through the rite of baptism. Again, Jews don't have one mode of entry and Gentiles another, "for as many of you as were baptized into Christ have put on Christ" (Gal. 3:27, RSV). It is no accident that Paul repeatedly connects baptism with Christian oneness here in Ephesians and in Galatians 3 and 1 Corinthians 12:13.

Lastly, there is "one God and Father of all who is over all and through all and in all" (Eph. 4:6). It is that "one God" who has made us a part of the one "family of God" (2:19) through the sacrifice of the "one Lord," through the work of the "one Spirit," and through the means of "one hope," "one faith," and "one baptism." As a result, "one body" unites all of God's people on both earth and in the heavenly places. Wonderful indeed is the mystery of God. It is worth living for.

13. Diversity in Unity: Spiritual Gifts

Ephesians 4:7-11

> [7]*But to each one of us grace was given according to the measure of Christ's gift.* [8]*Therefore it says, "When He ascended on high he led captive many captives, and He gave gifts to men." * [9]*(Now as to the meaning of "He ascended," what is it except that He had also descended into the lower parts of the earth?* [10]*He who descended is He who also ascended far above all the heavens, so that He might fill all things.)* [11]*And He gave some to be apostles, and some to be prophets, and some to be evangelists, and some to be pastors and teachers.*

Paul spoke of the gift that God had given him personally in Ephesians 3:2. It involved preaching to the Gentiles the mystery of the "unsearchable riches of Christ" (verse 8, RSV). Now in chapter 4 he raises the topic of the gifts that God has provided the various members of the Ephesian congregations.

Ephesians 3:7 implies three lessons. First, "each one of us" has a gift of some sort. According to the New Testament the entire church is a charismatic (from the Greek *charisma*, "gift") community. Each Christian has been born of both water and the Spirit (John 3:5, 7) and thus each person has a spiritual gift. Of course, as we will see below, Ephesians 4 does not list all the gifts, but each and every Christian receives something from the Lord.

A second implication is that there is a difference between *saving grace* and *serving grace*. We receive saving grace when God rescues us from the pit of sin (Eph. 2:1-10). He then follows it with a special gift of serving grace that we might reach out as Christ's agents to help others. There is something amiss with a people who believe they have saving grace without serving grace. Such is a biblical impossibility.

The third thing hinted at in verse 7 but made more explicit in verse 11 and in other parts of Paul's writings is that not every person receives the same gift. The body of Christ, as Paul so aptly puts it in 1 Corinthians 12, has different needs and God gives various gifts to fulfill each of them so that the body can be both balanced and healthy (see verses 4-31). Thus God's church possesses diversity. The diversity of Ephesians 4:7-11 may seem surprising, coming as it does on the heels of the strong emphasis on unity in verses 1-6. But, as we will see in verses 12-16, the very purpose of the variety of gifts is to bring about unity in the church.

It is a beautiful truth that the God who lives in heaven sees the individual talents of each of us here on earth and gives gifts to enhance our natural endowments. One side benefit of the diversity of gifts is variety in the church. Christians, so to speak, don't all come from the same cookie cutter. To the contrary, the body of Christ is a living organism of many parts. That's good. The church would be a dull place if everyone had exactly my strengths, weaknesses, and gifts. It might be very good at some things and very bad in others. But one thing for sure is that it would be boring. Thank God for diversity in unity. It makes the church more beautiful and more functional.

Many people get a bit more than confused when they read Ephesians 4:8-10. They don't seem to have any problem with the fact that Christ gave gifts to people soon after His ascension. After all, Acts 2:33 makes it clear that upon being "exalted at the right hand of God, and having received from the Father the promise of the Holy Spirit, he . . . poured out this which you see and hear" on the day of Pentecost (RSV).

That is clear enough. But what does it mean that He "led captive many captives" and that "He ascended" only after He had "descended into the lower parts of the earth"? We can grasp the captive part once we realize that Paul in verse 8 is quoting Psalm 68:18. "Initially," suggests Arthur Patzia, "the psalm celebrated an earthly triumph of the Israelites over their enemies and the return of the defeated foes with the spoils of war [including captives] to the capital city." It also served "as a picture of God's victory over all his enemies during the exodus and his enthronement in the holy city" (Patzia, p. 236).

Robert Bratcher and Eugene Nida suggest that "there is no way of determining who the New Testament writer considered these captives to be, whether human or angelic opponents. . . . The text is quoted for the purpose of using *he gave gifts to mankind* as the scriptural proof of Christ's bestowing gifts on his people" (Bratcher, p. 99).

While the latter part of Bratcher's statement is certainly true, especially since the Jews associated Psalm 68 with the feast of Pentecost, the New Testament does give a hint as to who the captives might be. Matthew 27:52, 53 tells us that at the crucifixion God raised many of His people from the prison house of death as a witness to Christ's resurrection. Ellen White for one believes that those resurrected ones "ascended with Him as trophies of His victory over death and the grave." They were no longer "the captives of Satan," but His redeemed ones (White, *The Desire of Ages,* p. 786).

Well, you may be thinking, *the captive part is as clear as need be and the idea of Christ's giving gifts during Pentecost after His ascension is quite evident from the book of Acts, but I am still confused about "into the lower parts of the earth"* (Eph. 4:9). You are not the only one. Ambrosiaster (4th century), utilizing the oft-misunderstood passage in 1 Peter 3:19 regarding Christ after His death preaching "to the spirits in prison" (RSV), writes that after Christ's "triumph over the devil, he descended to the heart of the world, so that he might preach to the dead, that all who desired him might be set free" (in Edwards, p. 164).

That interpretation was common among certain commentators and early fathers of the church, but a more likely explanation is that the descent and ascent of Ephesians 4 parallels the flow of Philippians 2:7, 8, in which Christ descended to this earth at the incarnation and even went down so far as to take the form of a servant and die the death of the cross. In Philippians an ascent follows that incarnational descent when after the crucifixion God "highly exalted him and bestowed on him the name which is above every name" (verse 9, RSV). That understanding fits both Ephesians 4 and the general flow of the epistle. In chapter 1, for example, we find Christ being raised "from the dead and seated" at the right hand of God in the heavenly places that He might fill all things (see 1:20 and cf. 1:23 with 4:10). Thus Ephesians 4:8-10 is not as difficult to understand as it first appeared.

The quotation from Psalm 68:18 does, however, have one serious problem. The psalm has *"received* gifts," whereas Paul cites it as *"gave* gifts."

A Diversity of Gifts

Rom. 12:6-8	1 Cor. 12:8-10	1 Cor. 12:28-31	Eph. 4:11	1 Peter 4:10
1. prophecy	prophecy	prophecy	prophecy	
2. service		helpers		service
3. teaching		teaching	teaching	
4. exhorting				
5. giving				
6. helping				
7. mercy				
	8. wisdom			
	9. knowledge			
	10. faith			
	11. healing	healing		
	12. miracles	miracles		
	13. discrimination			
	14. tongues	tongues		
	15. interpretation of tongues			
		16. apostles	apostles	
		17. administration		
			18. evangelists	
			19. teaching pastors	speakers

The discrepancy has two possible solutions. The first is that Paul may have been citing from an Old Testament understanding not reflected in the Hebrew and Greek versions familiar to us today. In support for that hypothesis is the fact that two ancient versions of the Hebrew Bible (one Aramaic and the other Syriac) do have "gave" in Psalm 68:18. A second explanation is that a certain logic does lead from a victor accepting gifts from the vanquished only to turn around and bestow gifts on his faithful followers. It finds a parallel on the day of Pentecost as Christ, after being exalted to the right hand of God, received the promise of the Holy Spirit from the Father, and then "poured out" the gift on His followers (Acts 2:33).

The important thing from Paul's perspective is that Christ endowed the church with gifts (Eph. 4:7, 8). Please note that in both verse 7 and again in verse 11 they come from Christ. That is of interest since 1 Corinthians 12 declares the Holy Spirit as the source of the gifts (see verses 4, 11), and Romans 12 has God the Father assigning or giving them (see verse 3). While it is quite appropriate to refer to serving grace as spiritual gifts, we need to realize that hidden away in this teaching is a Trinitarian lesson. All three members of the Godhead are coequal in giving them, even though the Holy Spirit is the Person of the Trinity who oversees the actual operation of spiritual gifts.

Ephesians 4:11 has one of the shorter lists of spiritual gifts in the New Testament. It focuses mainly on those leadership attributes that can bring unity to the church, but it is not a complete summary of all spiritual gifts. As the chart on page 245 demonstrates, the New Testament has five lists of spiritual gifts. A parallel listing shows that there is a wide diversity amongst them in order that all the work of the church might be accomplished by its various members. As 1 Corinthians 12:14-26 indicates, if church members each let God use their gift through their lives there will be unity in the body of Christ and the church will function well. Problems come in when some disown their gift, and, worse yet, others lust after the gifts of others. But God's ideal is for His children to utilize their diverse gifts so that the church might have both unity and efficiency.

You should note as you examine the five clusters of spiritual gifts in the New Testament that they are remarkable for their lack of overlap. Peter O'Brien writes that "each list diverges significantly from the others. None is complete, but each is selective and illustrative, with no effort to force the various gifts into a neat scheme. Even together all five do not present a full catalogue of gifts" (O'Brien, p. 298). Just as the needs of the church are extremely diverse and the abilities of individuals greatly varied, so are the gifts that God gives to believers that He might be glorified in both the earth and in the heavenly places.

14. The Purpose of Spiritual Gifts

Ephesians 4:12-16

12for the equipping of the saints for the work of ministry, for the building up of the body of Christ, 13until we all arrive at the unity of the faith and the fuller knowledge of the Son of God, to mature personhood, to the measure of the stature of the fullness of Christ, 14so that we should no longer be immature children, driven by waves and carried around by every wind of doctrine, by the trickery of men, by craftiness in deceptive scheming. 15Rather, speaking the truth in love, let us grow up in all things into Him who is the head, Christ. 16From Him the whole body is being joined together and united by every ligament provided. It grows and builds itself up in love when each part is working properly.

And He gave gifts to men" (verse 8). Verses 7-11 indicate two different categories of gifts. The first is that "each one of us" (every Christian) receives some gift from God for service (verse 7). Then in verse 11 Paul specifies certain leadership gifts (apostles, prophets, evangelists, and pastors and teachers).

Verse 12 begins an important discussion on the reason for spiritual gifts. Paul specifies two main purposes:

1. "for the equipping of the saints for the work of ministry" and
2. "for the building up of the body of Christ."

We need to note several things about the first purpose, beginning with the fact that the work of ministry is for all the saints. Now a saint is one who has been set apart for holy use. The New Testament does not regard them as some person who is especially "holy." To the contrary, every Christian is a saint. That includes you (and me). Thus Paul is definitely teaching in verse 12 that the work of ministry belongs to each and every converted individual.

We need to move away from the unbiblical concept that it is the paid (or unpaid) clergy who are responsible for ministry in the church and its surrounding community. No! No! No! The biblical teaching is that each of us has a role (verse 12) and each of us has received some gift to enable us to carry out God's ministry. Our serving grace is to be a ministering grace.

If that is so, some may be thinking, *then we have no need of a distinctive ministry for the clergy.* But that is not what the apostle is teaching. Ephesians 4:12 flows directly out of verse 11. And in verse 11, as we observed earlier, Paul lists the leadership gifts, including pastors and teachers. It is the function of pastors and teachers and other clergy types to *equip "the saints* for the work of ministry." Please note that it does not say that pastors and other leaders are to do all of the work themselves, but rather to prepare the entire church to do ministry. Thus the function of clerical leadership is to *enable* every church member to enter God's work. That entails both helping each saint to find his or her gift or gifts and also how to put that gift to use in the church and community. Thus pastors and other leaders need to move away from the *sin* of monopolizing ministry and to take up their roles as enablers.

John Stott helpfully reflects upon this important issue when he asks "what model of the church, then, should we keep in our minds? The traditional model," he responds, "is that of the pyramid, with the pastor perched precariously on its pinnacle, like a little pope in his own church, while the laity are arrayed beneath him in serried ranks of inferiority. It is a totally unbiblical image, because the New Testament envisages not a single pastor with a docile flock but both a plural oversight and an every-member ministry. Not much better is the model of the bus, in which the pastor does all the driving while the congregation are the passengers slumbering in peaceful security behind him. Quite different from either the pyramid or the bus is the biblical model of the body. The church is the body of Christ, every member of which has a distinctive function. Although the body metaphor can certainly accommodate the concept of a distinct pastorate (in terms of one ministry—and a very important one—among many), there is simply no room in it either for a hierarchy or for that kind of bossy clericalism which concentrates all ministry in the hands of one man and denies the people of God their own rightful ministries" (Stott, p. 167).

Thus the ministry of every church is its entire congregation. The role of pastors and other leaders, according to Paul, is to train and qualify them.

The second purpose of spiritual gifts set forth in Ephesians 4:12 is that they are "for the building up of the body of Christ." In that connection the apostle sets up three sub-goals that we must achieve in the process.

But before we look at those crucial sub-goals we need to focus on the word "until" in verse 13. That word provides us with the length of time during which the church will have need of the enabling, equipping gifts of verse 11. The church will require them "until" it has reached the sub-goals of verse 13. That is, spiritual gifts will be necessary until the Second Advent.

The first sub-goal consists of a "unity of the faith" among believers (verse 13). As we have repeatedly noted thus far in our study of Ephesians, unity is one of the key concepts of the letter, especially as it extends across racial/ethnic and Jewish/Gentile barriers.

But Christian unity according to Paul's ideal is not to be a mindless or blind conformity. It is to be a "unity of the faith." That thought brings us to the second sub-goal in the building up process: believers must come to a "fuller knowledge of the Son of God" (verse 13). They already have a salvational level of knowledge of Christ and His grace, but in his already but not yet format Paul states that they still have much more to learn as they grow up in Christ. The New Testament never sees salvation merely as a punctiliar event. To the contrary, it views it as a process. And the teaching ministry of pastors and other church leaders (verse 11) is absolutely essential in the growth of God's church. Christianity is not a religion of ignorance but rather one in which individuals and the church constantly come to know God better and better. Having a correct understanding of Him and His work for the church was important for Paul.

The third sub-goal is related to the other two. Certainly coming to a "unity of the faith" and a "fuller knowledge of the Son of God" are necessary ingredients in the development of a "mature personhood" that meets "the measure of the stature of the fullness of Christ" (verse 13).

It is important to remember that the mature "person" who is growing in unity, knowledge, and maturity is the church, the body (verse 16) of Christ. While it is true that all those goals are also important for individuals, Paul in verses 12 to 16 has in mind the need of the church as the body of Christ to mature so that it is does not get led astray by this charismatic voice or that forceful leader in the way that the wind and the waves drive a ship this way or that. Part of the function of the enabling/equipping gifts of verse 11 is to create and maintain doctrinal stability in God's church (verse 14).

Verse 15 adds an important dynamic to doing church when it mentions "speaking the truth in love." Here is a point at which the body of Christ often suffers. On the one hand there are those who are so adamant in defending doctrinal truth that they end up being meaner than the devil. They are right in desiring to protect God's truth, but wrong in their spirit. At the other extreme we find those who are so "loving" that they never want to speak up, even when others set aside or contradict God's word. They have missed the content side of the balance Paul so nicely sets forth in verse 15. God's ideal is to have both truth and love. It is also important to note that the word "speaking" is not explicit in the Greek text. The original implies speaking, but it goes beyond the verbal to a total living of the truth (see Lloyd-Jones, *Christian Unity,* pp. 241, 242). Speaking is good as far as it goes, but God wants His church not only to speak in love but to live in love. And such living is of major import in arriving at that "mature [perfect] personhood" that begins to measure up to "the stature of the fullness of Christ" (verse 13).

Ephesians 4:16 is complex in both Greek and English (as the variety of translations indicate), but the basic ideas are clear. Rudolf Schnackenburg insightfully points out that the verse "corresponds exactly to the development of thought in the whole section" (Schnackenburg, p. 189). Thus the decisive role of Christ is absolutely central. He is the one who gives all gifts (verse 7), including both those given to every church member and also the leadership gifts of verse 11. It is in Christ that the church body "is being joined together" (verse 16), but the ligaments (representing the special leadership gifts of verse 11) that hold it together He provides for the purpose of uniting the church. Lastly, the gifts of each saint serve to foster building up of the church. Thus the church "grows and builds itself up in love when each part is working properly" (verse 16b). Schnackenburg points out that in Paul's treatment "Christ's outstanding position is preserved" while "the whole Body is drawn [into] the process of growth" (*ibid.,* p. 190).

Before moving away from Ephesians 4:1-16 we should note the phrase that runs through this crucial passage—"in love." It first appears in verse 2, surfaces again in verse 15, and provides the last two words in the Greek sentence of verse 16.

The plain truth is that the "in love" witness of the church is the only thing that will hold it together and stimulate its growth. The problem with too many congregations and individual church members is that they lack the "in love" aspect of Christianity. But without it the church is only a caricature of Christianity and not the real thing. Both as individuals and as a corporate body the church's greatest need is the "in love" expression in all that it does and teaches.

15. Living in Newness of Spirit

Ephesians 4:17-24
   [17]*So this I say and testify in the Lord, that you are to walk no longer as the Gentiles walk, in the aimlessness of their minds,* [18]*being darkened in their understanding, alienated from the life of God because of the ignorance existing in them, because of the hardness of their hearts.* [19]*They have become callous and have given themselves to licentiousness for the practice of every kind of impurity with greediness.* [20]*But you did not so learn Christ,* [21]*if indeed you have heard Him and have been taught in Him, just as truth is in Jesus.* [22]*You have put off your former manner of life, your old man, the one corrupted in accordance with the lusts of deceit.* [23]*And you are to be continually renewed in the spirit of your mind,* [24]*having put on the new man, created after the likeness of God in righteousness and holiness of the truth.*

A Christian life is a radical change from the non-Christian. The center of that transformation is one's relationship to Christ and what He stands for.

A radical shift in a person's status was central to Ephesians 2. Once the Ephesians were under God's wrath "BUT NOW" (verse 4) they shelter under His grace (verse 8). They had been alienated from God's covenant people "BUT NOW" (verse 13) they are members of the household of God (verse 19).

Ephesians 4:17-24 again highlights the theme of radical change. Here we find a third BUT NOW, even though the passage does not use the actual words. Verses 17-19 speak to the pre-Christian condition of the Ephesians, while verses 20-24 reflect on their new life in Christ.

However, we find an essential difference in the BUT NOWs of chapter 2 and that of chapter 4. Those in chapter 2 speak to what God has done *for* the Ephesians while the BUT NOW implications in chapter 4 focus on what God has done and is doing *in* them. In Ephesians 4:17-24 the apostle lays the doctrinal foundation for the new life in Christ. Then from verse 25 up through Ephesians 6:9 he sets forth some concrete suggestions for living that new life.

The first half of Ephesians 4 dealt with the Holy Spirit, represented in other parts of the New Testament as the converting and energizing member of the Trinity. And verse 15 set the stage for Paul's discussion of the new life with its admonition to the Ephesians "to grow up in every way into him who is the head, into Christ" (RSV).

That "growing up . . . into him" means that they of necessity must maintain a radical break with their non-Christian past. Specifically, they are "to walk [live] no longer as the Gentiles walk" (verse 17). And how did they walk? Paul describes it as callousness toward their sins and as lives given over "to licentiousness for the practice of every kind of impurity with greediness" (verse 19).

And why did they live or walk that way? Paul, interestingly enough, emphasizes their intellectual deficits. They were "alienated from the life of God because" (verse 18):

1. their minds were aimless (verse 17),
2. their understanding was darkened (verse 18), and
3. they were ignorant (verse 18).

According to Ephesians 4 a large portion of their evilness had its base in intellectual deficit. But that wasn't the only factor. Verse 18 also lists hard hearts as a factor leading to corruption. Romans 1, as the following box demonstrates, outlines the same pathway from obstinacy and ignorance to moral corruption.

Paul pictures the new life in Christ as also rooted in intellectual terms. The Ephesian Christians had:

1. learned Christ (verse 20),
2. "heard Him" (verse 21), and
3. "been taught in Him" (verse 21).

It was that new intellectual understanding rooted in a disposition to accept what they had learned that set the stage for a new way of life.

The Downward Path in Romans and Ephesians

Romans 1:18-32		Ephesians 4:17-19
	Stage 1: Obstinacy	
18 "Men . . . by their wickedness suppress the truth" 21 "Although they knew God they did not honour him as God" 28 "They did not see fit to acknowledge God"		18 "Due to their hardness (pōrōsis) of heart"
	Stage 2: Darkness	
21 "They became futile in their thinking and their senseless minds were darkened 22 "They became fools" 28 "A base mind"		17 "The futility of their minds" 18a "They are darkened in" their understanding"
	Stage 3: Death or judgment	18b "The ignorance that is in them"
24 "Therefore God gave them up" 26 "For this reason God gave them up" 28 "God gave them up"		18 "They are . . . alienated from the life of God"
God gave them up to— 24 "Impurity" 26 "Dishonourable passions" 27 "Shameless acts" 28 "Improper conduct" 29-31 "All manner of wickedness . . ."	**Stage 4: Recklessness**	19 "They have become callous and have given themselves up to licentiousness (aselgeia, meaning public indecency of a shameless kind), greedy to practise every kind of uncleanness" (Stott, pp. 177, 178)

Education and educational preaching are important elements in conversion (see Rom. 10:14–17) and Christian living. Markus Barth points out that "the vocabulary and contents of 4:20-21 evoke the image of a school" (Barth, *Ephesians 4-6,* p. 504).

But what one learns in the school of Ephesians 4 is not just better things. To the contrary, Christ is absolutely central in every aspect of its instruction. When we follow Paul's words we discover that the Ephesians not only learned Christ or learned *about* Christ (verse 20), but that they *heard* Him (verse 21). That is, in Christian preaching and teaching Christ is not only the subject matter but, through the Holy Spirit (verse 11), the teacher Himself. Beyond that, the Ephesians had "been taught in Him" (verse 21), implying that Christ is not only the subject matter and the teacher but also the context of the Christian message. One of the tragedies of too much so-called Christian preaching and teaching is that it focuses on doctrine and morals without connecting them and immersing them in Christ. Along that line, Walter Liefeld highlights the fact that the kind of religious education that leads to genuine conversion "is pictured as an acceptance not merely of superior religious ideas or values but of Jesus himself. Without him, even theological precision is inadequate for salvation" (Liefeld, p. 114).

Paul is telling us in verses 21 and 22 that the big change in the lives of the Ephesians had taken place because they had heard Christ. And that hearing had led to three results in their lives:

1. they had put off their former manner of life (verse 22),
2. they had begun to be continually renewed in the spirit of their mind (verse 23), and
3. they had put on the new person (verse 24).

The verbs are important in those three points. The verbs I translated as "you have put off" (verse 22) and "having put on" (verse 24) are both infinitives, meaning they are most accurately rendered as "to put." They are also in the aorist tense, which "expresses the singleness of the act" (Abbott, p. 136). In other words, the putting on and off is something people generally only do once in their life. Many translations give the wrong sense of the verbs when they translate them as "put off your old nature" and "put on the new" (RSV, cf. KJV and NASB). That rendering implies that they are still something the Ephesians need to do. But that is not so. They had already done the putting on and putting off when they first came to Christ.

Andrew Lincoln captures that truth when he writes that "the readers had been taught that becoming believers involves a radical break with the past, the putting off of the old person. The imagery of putting off the old person and putting on the new is that of decisive change. Its meaning can be compared to that of the Synoptic language of repenting because of the coming of the kingdom" (Lincoln, p. 284). Repentance that leads to conversion is a past event in the life of the Christian. Thus the Ephesians had already cast off their old person and donned their new.

But something still had to be done in their lives after conversion. That is where the second verb of the three comes in. They needed to be "continually renewed" in the spirit of their mind (verse 23). Salvation is a process. It may have begun with conversion, with a putting on and a putting off, but day by day throughout our lives the Holy Spirit works to convict us of sin, lead us to righteousness (see John 16:8-11), and provide our minds with ever fuller knowledge of Christ and His will for us. Our minds are being "continually renewed" as the new identity that we have already put on continually deepens and develops. We can think of that mind-informed development of our new person as progressive sanctification.

B. F. Westcott sums up the significance of the three verbs when he writes that "the new life is realised by three processes: the putting off 'the old man,' the renewal of spiritual power, the putting on 'the new man.' The first and third are acts done once for all . . . ; and the second and third are connected together . . . so that the decisive change is apprehended little by little by growing spiritual discernment" (Westcott, p. 67).

The good news of Ephesians 4:17-24 is that God not only rescues us from the penalty of sin (see Eph. 2:5, 8), but that He saves Christians from the power and dominance of sin in their lives. The great reformer John Calvin notes that "he whose life differs nothing from that of unbelievers, has learned nothing of Christ; for the knowledge of Christ cannot be separated from the mortification of the flesh" (Calvin, p. 189).

What Calvin referred to as "mortification of the flesh" is what Paul called the putting off of the old man or the old nature. It is crucial to realize that "it is not just particular vices that are to be put off but the whole old person who was leading a life dominated by sin" (Lincoln, p. 284). The apostle in other places refers to that experience as becoming a new creation (2 Cor. 5:17) and as a crucifixion of the old way of life and a resurrection to a new (Rom. 6:1-11). Christ, Himself, called it a new birth through the Spirit (John 3:3, 5).

The central idea of Ephesians 4:17-24 is crystal clear. As Christians we have no business dallying with the sins of our old way of life because we have both met Christ and dedicated ourselves to Him who through a continual renewal of our minds enables us to walk ever more closely to the principles of His kingdom. His desire for each of us and the church as a whole is to become more and more like the Father as we grow in love (see verses 2, 16).

16. Specifics in Spiritual Living

Ephesians 4:25-32

[25]Therefore, having put off falsehood, let each one speak truth with his neighbor, because we are members of one another. [26]"Be angry but do not sin." Let not the sun set on your anger, [27]and do not give place in your life to the devil. [28]Let the thief no longer steal, but rather let him labor, working with his own hands at something good, so that he may have something to share with the one who has need. [29]No rotten word should come out of your mouth, but only good for edifying in accordance with the need, that it may impart grace to those listening. [30]And do not grieve the Holy Spirit, by whom you were sealed for the day of redemption. [31]Let all bitterness and anger and wrath and clamor and slander be put away from you, along with all evil. [32]And be kind to one another, tenderhearted, forgiving each other, as even God in Christ has forgiven you.

Therefore" is a key word in verse 25. It signals a shift between a discussion of the theological basis for the new life in Christ to practical exhortations regarding that transformed existence. As Peter O'Brien puts it, "the movement of thought is from the lofty heights of learning Christ and the new creation to 'the nitty-gritty of Christian behaviour'" (O'Brien, p. 334).

Ephesians 4:25-32 sets forth five of those nitty-gritties. John Stott outlines three features common to them all. First, they all concern our relationships with other people. "Holiness is not a mystical condition experienced in relation to God but in isolation from human beings. You cannot be good in a vacuum, but only in the real world of people" (Stott, p. 184).

Second, each of the five couples a negative prohibition to a positive command. "It is not enough to put off the old rags; we have to put on new garments. It is not enough to give up lying and stealing and losing our temper, unless we also start speaking the truth, working hard and being kind to people" *(ibid.)*. Contrary to much churchly mentality, there is no virtue in what a person has given up. Christianity is a positive not a negative. Christians will of necessity move beyond the negative to a positive reaching out in love to those around them.

Third, each of the five examples either gives or implies a theological reason for the command. "For in the teaching of Jesus and his apostles doctrine and ethics, belief and behaviour are always dovetailed into one another" *(ibid.)*.

Admonition #1: *"Having put off falsehood, let each one speak truth with his neighbor, because we are members of one another"* (Eph. 4:25).

The verb tense for putting off is the same as in verse 22. It suggests a past action. The Ephesians in their taking off of their old nature had managed to discard falsehood. That's good! After all, it is not easy to be strictly honest in a culture in which dishonesty is rampant. It is still difficult 2000 years later, as some discover as they find themselves tempted to fudge a bit on their tax returns or to pad their expense accounts in a "harmless" manner.

But while Paul suggests that the Ephesians had managed to achieve to some extent the negative of putting away falsehood, he also implies that they had fallen short in the positive duty of speaking the truth to their neighbors.

And here we have to recognize that the positive is always more difficult than the negative. Why? Because the limits of the negative are finite while the boundaries of the positive are infinite. It is easy for me, for example, to know when I have stopped beating my neighbor, but impossible to determine when I have loved him or her enough. The plain fact is that the progression of love has no end. Never can I say that I have loved enough so that now I can quit loving and be my real self. No, never. The positive virtues are infinite. And we will never truly be comfortable as Christians until the positive characterizes the very core of our being. That, of course, is what Paul meant when he defined Christians as those who have put off the old self and put on the new (verses 22-24). Having God's law of love written on our hearts characterizes the new (Matt. 22:36-40; Rom. 13:8-10; Gal. 5:14; Heb. 8:10).

Paul's theological reason for truthtelling is that "we are members of one another" (Eph. 4:25). Here he hints at a basic theme of Ephesians, the need for unity in the body of Christ (Eph. 4:4-6; 2:14-22). For that reason I almost entitled this section of my commentary as "Principles for Living the Mystery" (see 3:3-6).

Admonition #2: *"Be angry but do not sin"* (Eph. 4:26). Now here is some good news. It is ok to be angry, at least about some things. After all, Jesus was angry when He fashioned a whip to drive the money changers out of the Temple courts (John 2:13-17). And such anger at injustice as that expressed by William Wilberforce eventually eradicated the slave trade and finally slavery itself. Christians today need to be angry about the oppression of the poor and the needless destruction of the environment. It is our *Christian duty to be angry over all injustice.* There is not enough Christian anger in the world. We are too complacent.

But as the apostle's quotation from Psalm 4:4 plainly states, not all anger is good or healthy or helpful to the church body. Much of it is just downright sinful. Selfish anger, irritability, crossness, and a bad temper are always wrong.

Paul specifies two warnings about anger. First, "let not the sun set on your anger" (Eph. 4:26) or "don't go to bed angry" (Message). The basic idea is not that we have a right to be angry until bedtime, but that we should resolve our anger as soon as possible. As Andrew Fuller notes, "let us take the Apostle's meaning rather than his words . . . not understanding him so literally that we may take leave to be angry till sunset, then might our wrath lengthen with the days; and men in Greenland, where days last above a quarter of a year, have plentiful scope for revenge" (quoted in Kreitzer, p. 143).

For the sake of our community, our church, our marriage, and our self, we need to regard Paul's injunction seriously. It may be difficult to put away our pride, but we can save ourselves a multitude of problems if we refuse to let our selfish and self-centered anger fester. Here is a principle that you and I can put into practice today. Today and every day we need to make things right with others no later than bedtime (and preferably a great deal earlier). Not to do so is to give a massive place to the devil in our life (see verse 27).

Admonition #3: *"Let the thief no longer steal, but rather let him labor, working with his own hands at something good, so that he may have something to share with the one who has need"* (verse 28).

The Greek verse literally reads "let the one stealing no longer steal." Now a thief who no longer steals is obviously no longer a thief. And if such persons are no longer thieves, then they must be something else.

That is precisely what Christianity does to and for people. The power of the gospel transforms us (Rom. 12:2) into new beings. Of course, as in all Paul's admonitions in Ephesians 4:25-32, the negative is only the first step. True transformation of Christians always ends up in the positive realm. Thus verse 28 urges the thief to go to work so that he can give to those in need. As a result, the person is not merely an ex-thief but something like an anti-thief. He or she is no longer a taker but a giver. Such is the transforming power of God's love and grace. God wants to perform the anti-thief sort of miracle in each of us. The Lord longs to take our wickedest vices and transform them into our leading virtues. That is an essential part of the gospel according to Paul.

Admonition #4: *"No rotten word should come out of your mouth, but only good" for edification* (verse 29). Here is something that we all need to take to heart. After all, as James points out, nothing is more difficult to control than the human tongue (James 3:1-12). And, we might add, nothing is as destructive to the unity of the church as a loose tongue.

But, as we noted above, God is a specialist in transforming our problems into virtues if we will allow Him to do so. He can even take our unruly tongues and make them agents of blessing in every occasion. If we are willing, He is able.

Admonition #5: *"Let all bitterness and anger and wrath and clamor and slander be put away from you, along with all evil"* (Eph. 4:31). Here we have kind of a catch-all verse. God doesn't just want to clean up and transform a part of our life or even most parts. He seeks to remake us totally. Thus there is no way that Christians can feel good about harboring islands of evil in their lives. If we listen to the Holy Spirit as He seeks to "continually" renew us in the spirit of our minds (verse 23), God will reach into every corner of our lives and turn our vices into virtues one by one.

Of course we can always refuse the Spirit's wooing and guidance. To do so, however, is to "grieve the Holy Spirit, by whom you were sealed for the day of redemption" (verse 30).

Here is an important verse. God seals or marks us for final redemption when we first become Christians. It is as if the Holy Spirit puts a stamp on us signifying that we are God's possession and that He wants to take us home with Him at the Second Advent. That is good news.

But good news in a sinful world always has a flip side. Paul teaches that we can grieve the Holy Spirit. We do so, the context implies, when we refuse to follow the Spirit's lead as He comes to our consciences and warns us of sin and as we reject His transforming power. Matthew 12:31, 32 directly relates grieving the Holy Spirit to what Jesus called the unpardonable sin.

The plain truth is that God is willing and able to transform our lives from being self-centered and mean to being selfless and loving if we will allow Him to do so. If we refuse He will never force us. But of one thing we can be certain—heaven will have no liars, selfishly angry people, or thieves (Rev. 22:10-15). They wouldn't be happy there and would ruin it for everybody else. That is why God is so eager for us to let Him help us "put off" (Eph. 4:25) our self-centered evil and to transform us into His agents of love.

17. Walking in Love

Ephesians 5:1, 2
> *¹Therefore be imitators of God, as beloved children. ²And walk in love, just as Christ loved us and gave Himself up for us as a fragrant offering and sacrifice to God.*

Be imitators of God"! How arrogant. Who are we to try to act like the God of the universe? More to the point, given who He is as Lord of the universe and who we are as sinners, *how could we possibly emulate Him?*

We might as well face it up front. In most areas of God's being we cannot imitate Him. It is humanly impossible. Take His glory for example. There is no way a person can ever acquire His glory. The same goes for the eternity of the one who has existed from eternity in the past. None of us can have that quality of the perpetual I AM. And we certainly can't imitate His omnipotence, His omnipresence, or His omniscience. Such attributes belong to God alone. The plain fact is that He is so totally other that there is no way we can pattern ourselves after Him in most of His essential attributes. Perhaps that is why Ephesians 5:1 "is the only place in the Bible where that bold word 'imitate' is applied to the Christian relation to God" (Maclaren, p. 270).

Yet, as Alexander Maclaren points out, the idea of imitating God "underlies the whole teaching of the New Testament on the subject of Christian character and conduct. To be like God, and to set ourselves to resemble Him, is the sum of all duty; and in the measure in which we approximate thereto, we come to perfection" (*ibid.,* pp. 270, 271).

It is in the moral realm that we can be like God. More specifically, according to Ephesians 5:2, it is in the area of love that we may reflect Him. "May," however, is too soft a word for the book of Ephesians when it comes to love. The book's message and that of the New Testament as a whole is that we *must* be like God in loving other people. Living His love is at the heart of what it means to be a Christian. As a result, Paul has frequently used the word love in relation to Christian living thus far in Ephesians.

Love in Ephesians 1-4

- In Ephesians 1:15 Paul commends the Ephesians for their "love toward all the saints."
- In chapter 3, verse 17 he prays that they might be "rooted and grounded in love."
- In 4:2 he begs them to show "tolerance to one another in love."
- In verse 15 of chapter 4 Paul requests that they speak the truth in love.
- And in verse 16 he tells them that the church grows and becomes strong when it is loving.

Beyond the use of the word itself, the immediate context of Ephesians 5:1, 2, focuses on that virtue. Ephesians 4:31, 32, for example, tell us that the loving virtues of kindness, tenderheartedness, and forgiveness must replace bitterness, wrath, anger, clamor, and slander in those who have accepted Christ. And living the law of love is central to Paul's injunctions in Ephesians 5:3 and onward, becoming explicit in the command to love one's wife just as Christ loved the church and gave Himself for it (verses 28-33).

Thus Ephesians 5:1, 2, is a hinge text that connects the injunctions to live the life of the Spirit in the second half of chapter 4 and the continuing commands regarding Christian living in chapters 5 and 6. At the very center of the ethical section of Ephesians is Paul's command in the first two verses of chapter 5 to "be imitators of God" by walking in love. And that centrality should come as no surprise. After all, the apostle John tells us that the very essence of God's character is love: "God is love." He writes in the same verse that "He who does not love does not know God" (1 John 4:8). Jesus also taught the ethical centrality of *agapē* (love) when He noted that one could sum up the entire law in the injunctions to love God with all one's heart and mind and to love one's neighbor as one's self (Matt. 22:37-

40). Paul made those same connections explicit in Galatians 5:14 and Romans 13:8-10.

But, we need to ask, what does he mean in Ephesians 5:2, in which he commands us to "walk in love"? After all, love is a slippery word that has many connotations.

Once again the context to the command provides the answer. We are to love "just as Christ loved us and gave Himself up for us as a fragrant offering and sacrifice to God" (verse 2).

The verse presents two interconnected thoughts. One is an important statement on the doctrine of the atonement, while the second tells us how the doctrine should influence us as Christians in our daily lives. For Paul, doctrine and behavior are inextricably linked. Christian conduct flows out of doctrinal understanding. And one of the central doctrinal statements of the New Testament is that of Christ's atonement for sin.

In discussing the atonement Paul sets forth three great ideas. First, "Christ loved us and gave Himself up for us." Here the apostle claims that love motivated all that Christ did for us. That thought brings to mind one of the most well-known texts in the New Testament: "God so loved the world that he gave his only begotten Son, that whosoever believeth in him should not perish, but have everlasting life" (John 3:16, KJV).

Please note that Christ was not passive in His sacrificial work. The Bible does not teach that anything forced Him to come to earth and die on a cross. No! He *gave* Himself. "I lay down my life, that I may take it again. No one takes it from me, but I lay it down of my own accord" (John 10:17, 18, RSV).

Thus Christ is not a passive party in the work of atonement. To the contrary, He is active. In fact, He is an initiator. He expressed His love by the fact that He gave His self for us. And we can understand the magnitude of the gift and the depth of that love only as we begin to grasp the biblical doctrine of sin. It would not be totally out of the range of human logic if Christ had given Himself as a sacrifice for those who had been very good and had always tried to do the right thing. But that is not what Paul teaches on the topic. In Romans 5, for example, he tells us that Christ went to the cross when we still were sinners (verse 8). Now a sinner is in rebellion against God, His active enemy (verse 10). The wonder of Christ's gift is that it was bestowed on those who opposed or stood against Him. It is only in the light of that truth that we can grasp the magnitude of His gift and the love that inspired it.

And what did He give for us? Two things come to mind. First He left His place in heaven and became one like us in the incarnation. As Paul puts it in another place, Christ "emptied himself, taking the form of a servant, being born in the likeness of men. And being found in human form he humbled himself and became obedient unto death, even death on a cross" (Phil. 2:7, 8, RSV).

That brings us to the second great thought in Ephesians 5:2. Christ not merely loved us in a general sense, but rather in a very specific way. He "gave Himself up for us as a fragrant offering and sacrifice." The first word we want to look at in that passage is "for." "The preposition with a genitive," Harold Hoehner writes, "signifies that it was done 'for our sake, in our behalf'" (Hoehner, p. 648). Thus "for" implies that He became a sacrifice in our place. In other words, Christ became our substitute. As Ellen White so nicely put it, "Christ was treated as we deserve, that we might be treated as He deserves. He was condemned for our sins, in which He had no share, that we might be justified by His righteousness, in which we had no share. He suffered the death which was ours, that we might receive the life which was His" (White, *The Desire of Ages*, p. 25).

We can not fully understand Ephesians 5:2 unless we read it through the eyes of the Old Testament. When Paul says that Christ "gave Himself up for us as a fragrant offering and sacrifice," he is using language that comes straight out of the Jewish sacrificial system set forth in the book of Leviticus. A sacrifice generally consisted of an animal offered on the alter of the Jewish tabernacle/Temple. The slain animal received the punishment due for the guilt of the sins of the people. That is, the animal symbolically became the substitute for the guilty sinner. But only symbolically. In actuality, all of the sacrifices pointed forward to Jesus, who would die "once for all" for the sins of people on Calvary (Heb. 7:27; 9:26, 27; 10:10, 12, 14). John the Baptist recognized that the Levitical symbolism pointed to Jesus when he called Him the "Lamb of God, who takes away the sin of the world" (John 1:29, RSV). And Paul makes the substitutionary aspect of the "for" of Ephesians 5:2 explicit in Galatians 3:10-13, in which he asserts that all those who have sinned are under condemnation because of the broken law but that "Christ redeemed us from the curse of the law" by "having become a curse for us" on Calvary's tree (RSV). He sets forth that substitutionary idea a bit differently in 2 Corinthians 5:21, in which he writes that "for our sake he made him to be sin who knew no sin, so that in him we might become the righteousness of God" (RSV).

The substitutionary sacrifice of Christ is central to both testaments. It is not a negotiable aspect of Christian doctrine. To the contrary, it is bedrock to the plan of salvation as set forth in the New Testament. The fact that Christ's sacrifice was fragrant means that it was acceptable to God (Gen. 8:21).

That brings us to the third and final central thought in Ephesians 5:2: we who have accepted Christ are to "walk in love, just as Christ loved us." The key words are "just as" or "even as." "The precept is obvious," writes D. Martyn Lloyd-Jones. "Our love must flow from and correspond to that of our Lord Himself" (Lloyd-Jones, *Darkness and Light,* p. 311). Or as another author puts it, "it is because he laid down his life for us that we are to love others to the point of sacrifice" (Wood, p. 66). Eugene Peterson paraphrases the ethical essence of Ephesians 5:1, 2 nicely. "Watch what God does, and then you do it, like children who learn proper behavior from their parents. Mostly what God does is love you. Keep company with him and learn a life of love" (Message). God's sacrificial love is the foundation of Christian ethics. It is upon that foundation that we as Christians are to live our lives through the transforming and empowering gift of the Holy Spirit.

18. Walking in the Light, Part 1

Ephesians 5:3-14

³But sexual immorality and any impurity or greediness must not even be named among you, as is proper for saints. ⁴The same goes for shameful conduct and foolish talking or coarse jesting, which are not fitting. But rather let there be thanksgiving. ⁵For this you know with certainty, that no sexually immoral or impure person or greedy person (who is an idolator), has an inheritance in the kingdom of Christ and of God. ⁶Let no one deceive you with empty words, for because of these things the wrath of God comes upon the sons of disobedience. ⁷Do not, therefore, be partners with them, ⁸for you once were darkness, but now you are light in the Lord. Walk as children of light, ⁹(for the fruit of the light is made up of all goodness and righteousness and truth), ¹⁰seeking to discover what is well-pleasing to the Lord. ¹¹And do not participate in the unfruitful works of darkness, but rather even expose them. ¹²For it is shameful even to speak of the things they do in secret. ¹³But everything exposed by the light becomes visible, ¹⁴for everything that becomes visible is light. Therefore it says,

> *"Wake up sleeper,*
> *and rise from the dead,*
> *and Christ will shine on you."*

Walking in the light has never been easy. That is certainly the case in regard to sexual immorality. William Barclay points out that "the ancient world regarded sexual immorality so lightly that it was no sin at all. It was the expected thing that a man should have a mistress. In places like Corinth the great temples were staffed by hundreds of priestesses who were sacred prostitutes, and whose earnings went to the upkeep of the Temple. . . . Nothing could show the Greek point of view better than the fact that the Greeks saw nothing wrong in building a temple to the gods with the proceeds and the profits of prostitution" (Barclay, pp. 191, 192). Clinton Arnold adds that "adulterous relationships, men sleeping with their slave girls, incest, prostitution, 'sacred' sexual encounters in the local temples, and homosexuality were all a part of everyday life in that culture" (Arnold, "Ephesians," p. 329).

One of the most difficult challenges facing Paul was the need for a total reformation in sexual attitudes and actions among the Gentile populations he preached to. His converts came out of a world with a corrupted sexual ethic. Yet a reformation in sexual ethics was one of the greatest transformations accomplished by the early church. Barclay notes that "it has been said that chastity was the one new virtue which Christianity introduced into this world" (Barclay, p. 191).

But it was far from easy. That is the reason that Paul had to treat the topic so frequently in his epistles. So it is in Ephesians 5:3, in which he abruptly moves from the contemplation of "the self-giving, sacrificial love of Christ, to love's perversion in adultery and sexual abuse" (Foulkes, p. 148). The pull of the old ways was strong among Paul's Ephesian readers. "But sexual immorality," he pens, "and any impurity or greediness must not even be named among you." Speaking to the term "immorality," C. Leslie Mitton points out that "the Greek word *porneia* [from which we get our English pornographic] covers a wide range of sexual evils, and in a Christian context would mean any sexual indulgence outside the permanent relationship of marriage, in circumstances where the sexual appetites are used merely as a means of pleasure without any sense of responsibility and care for the partner. 'Impurity' would include sexual perversions of various kinds" (Mitton, p. 178).

Many readers have noted the seemingly strange reference to "greediness" in a list of vices dealing with sexual sins. Paul's intention probably had in mind coveting somebody else's body for self gratification.

Christians, says the apostle in Ephesians 5:3, should not even name or mention such things. And why? Undoubtedly because thinking and talking about them starts us on the road to doing them.

Paul goes on in verse 4 to warn against "foolish talking" and "coarse jesting." Apparently the Gentile society of the day cheapened God's gift of sexuality by making it the topic of jokes and crude language.

The apostle's counsel in verses 3 and 4, unfortunately, is just as much needed in the twenty-first century world as it was in the first. Christianity made a great move forward toward changing cultural ideas on the topic, but the last century has seen a return to a type of neo-paganism that has returned the larger culture to open greediness over the sexual ideals of the Greek/Roman world. One only has to look at the entertainment industry as a prime example. In nearly every case violence and illicit sex is the road to success for producers and script writers. Without those two ingredients most productions can't draw a crowd.

> ### Reflecting on the Media
>
> "Television talk shows, sit coms, and call-in radio have majored in the kind of coarse humor that Paul cautions us to avoid. Our 'old selves' are drawn to this form of entertainment, but it is destructive to our souls" (Arnold, "Ephesians," p. 329).

It is one of the tragedies of Christianity that many church members are among those who get drawn into the visual and verbal sewage of the media. Maybe things haven't changed as much as they should have. That is what makes the Bible a relevant book.

Fortunately, the Scriptures not only tell us what to avoid, but also what to run to. Paul's antidote for "foolish talking" and "coarse jesting" is thankful praise to God (Eph. 5:4). We as Christians need to let God transform not only our hearts, but also our tongues, eyes, and actions.

Peter O'Brien writes that "it is all too easy for believers to be influenced by the surrounding world and to succumb to its ways of thinking and behaving. The result is that what is acceptable to the culture of the day becomes acceptable in the church" (O'Brien, p. 364). Thus Paul sets forth some "incentives" toward rectitude for Christians, beginning in Ephesians 5:5-7. One of those is certainty of judgment on those who are sexual "idolators" (verse 5). Here he is not speaking to those who have a wayward thought or even deed that they repent of, but of those who cherish immorality of mind and action as a way of life. F. F. Bruce points out that the fact that the Ephesians "still have to be warned against such vices shows how strong, in a pagan environment, was the temptation to indulge in them even after conversion" (Bruce, *Epistles to the Colossians . . .* , p. 371).

Those who persist in sexual immorality of heart and mind, Paul asserts, will be condemned in the judgment.

The Bible is not hesitant about the concept of judgment, as are some modern Christians. And it was Jesus Himself who had the most to say on the topic. The gospel of Matthew, for example, has five of His sermons, four of them ending in three judgment scenes each and the fifth concluding with only one.

In spite of the negative aspect of judgment, however, its primary function is to get as many people into heaven as will be happy there. It vindicates the saints (see Dan. 7:22; Deut. 32:36; Ps. 135:14). But God doesn't want unhappy campers in the kingdom. He will not force those motivated by principles in opposition to His great law of love to live in a world of selfless giving to others for eternity. Those who greedily abuse and use others for their self-satisfaction will be quite uncomfortable in God's presence. For them the judgment will be one of exclusion from the kingdom (Eph. 5:5) and "wrath" (verse 6). God's wrath, we should note, is not some irrational anger, but rather His judgment on sin. His "wrath is not in opposition to His love," but "is the natural fruit of divine love" (Knight, p. 40). In His love God will not let the destructive principles of sin continue forever, but will put an end to sin and suffering. His wrath is His termination of those forces and principles that have been destroying the lives of His children and the peace of the universe.

With Ephesians 5:8 Paul raises a new thought: Christians are light rather than darkness. Please note that he is not saying that they used to live in darkness but are now living in the light. That is true, but the apostle asserts more than the fact that their environment has changed. To the contrary, their very lives and beings have been transformed (see Rom. 12:2) from darkness to light. We find an important lesson here. The Christian life is not a mere improvement of the old life, but rather a new one altogether, actuated by an entirely new set of spiritual principles. It is a life motivated by the love of God to give to others rather than taking from them sexually or in any other way.

As a result, Christians will desire to walk in God's ways (Eph. 5:8, 9) and will seek "to discover what is well-pleasing to the Lord" (verse 10) and to avoid participating "in the unfruitful works of darkness" (verse 11). Their very lives will "expose" those dark works for what they really are, in the sense that light makes visible their true implications (verses 11, 13). Thus a Christian life makes a difference, since that very life gives vision and an illustration of God's principle of love (verse 14).

Paul closes his thoughts on the Christian as light with a quotation from an unknown source. The quotation in verse 14 graphically portrays the fact that "conversion is nothing less than awakening out of sleep, rising from death and being brought out of darkness into the light of Christ. No wonder we are summoned to live a new life in consequence" (Stott, p. 201).

19. Walking in the Light, Part 2

Ephesians 5:15-21

[15]Watch carefully therefore as to how you walk, not as unwise but as wise, [16]making the most of the time, because the days are evil. [17]Do not be foolish, therefore, but understand what the will of the Lord is. [18]And do not get drunk with wine, which is dissipating, but be filled by the Spirit, [19]speaking to one another in psalms and hymns and spiritual songs, singing and making melody in your hearts to the Lord, [20]always giving thanks for all things in the name of our Lord Jesus Christ to God, even the Father, [21]being submissive to one another in the fear of Christ.

Watch carefully" or "walk carefully"? Both translations are possible and it is impossible to decide which is best. But in the end it may not matter all that much. The important thing to remember is that we are very careful about those things most important to us. If we don't care about something we become casual toward it. But when it is important we are careful, or full of care, as to how we frame our words about it and how we perform it. How much do we care about our Christian life? Enough to give it agonizing thought? Enough to desire with all our heart to do God's will? Paul's command to the Ephesians is that they "watch carefully . . . as to how you walk [live], not as unwise but as wise" (Eph. 5:15).

Tucked into the last part of that verse is the pregnant little word *sophoi,* meaning wise. Paul assumes that born-again Christians are already wise, that they have new hearts and minds, that they understand the ways of God—things that they lacked before their conversion. He doesn't so much question the fact that Christians are wise as he seems to fear that they might not use their wisdom, that they might act foolishly despite their status as children of God.

Paul appears to be especially concerned that they will be wise

1. in their use of time (verse 16) and
2. in discerning God's will (verse 17).

Concerning the first of those points, Ellen White writes that "our time belongs to God. Every moment is His, and we are under the most solemn obligation to improve it to His glory. Of no talent He has given will He require a more strict account than of our time" (White, *Christ's Object Lessons*, p. 342). That is probably true because it is so easily squandered and because each person has the same amount each day to use for either God's glory or in the service of evil.

F. F. Bruce suggests that it was of crucial importance for the Ephesians to use their time wisely because the days were "evil" (verse 16). That is, "persecution and distress threatened the churches throughout the Roman Empire; signs were not lacking of the impending fall of the Second Jewish Commonwealth, with all the incalculable implications which that might have for the Christian cause. The present opportunity for Christian life and work might not last much longer; Christians should therefore use it to the full while they could" (Bruce, *Epistle to the Ephesians*, p. 109). If that is so, Paul's message has the same import to those who live in the critical "evil" days of the beginning of the twenty-first century.

His second special concern is that his readers might discern God's will (verse 17), so that they will not act foolishly. Wise people by biblical definition are those who desire to know the divine will. John Stott argues that "nothing is more important in life than to discover and do the will of God" (Stott, p. 203). He goes on to point out that Christians need to understand both God's "general" and His "particular" will. The first is for all Christians at all times, that they might be more like Christ. His "general" will emerges in Bible study. God's "particular" will is His specific intent for our personal lives. While Scripture has certain principles to guide us in that personal search, "detailed decisions have to be made after careful thought and prayer and the seeking of advice from mature and experienced believers" *(ibid.)*. In order to maximize our knowledge of God's plan for us we need to understand both His general and His particular will. That entails both a search of His word and a personal interaction with the Holy Spirit.

With Ephesians 5:18 we come to a transition verse in which the apostle sets forth two commands closely related to the understanding of God's will.

- On the negative side: "do not get drunk with wine," which leads to dissipation.
- On the positive side: "be filled by the Spirit" (verse 18).

Clinton Arnold points out that "wine and drunkenness were central features of the worship of Dionysus (also known as Bacchus [the god of fruits and wine]). In the frenzied and ecstatic Dionysiac rituals, intoxication with wine was tantamount to being filled with the spirit of Dionysus. It is therefore conceivable that some of the new believers in Asia Minor were carrying this form of worship with them into the church by associating wine with the filling of the Holy Spirit," a practice Paul vigorously repudiates (Arnold, "Ephesians," p. 331).

The problem of drunkenness, of course, was a social problem in general in the ancient world, as it is in the modern. G. H. P. Thompson updates the application to our day when he writes that "the Christian is not to escape into a world of artificial gaiety by *drunkenness* . . . , or, as we might add today, by taking drugs of various kinds" (Thompson, p. 81).

Further Thoughts on Discovering God's "Particular" Will

In order to learn more fully God's plan for our personal lives, we need:
1. "To do our best in the work that lies nearest,"
2. "to commit our ways to God,"
3. "to watch for the indications of His providence."
(White, *Education*, p. 267).

D. Martyn Lloyd-Jones (who was both a physician and a pastor) points out that in actuality alcohol is a depressant rather than a stimulus. "What alcohol does is this; it knocks out those higher centres, and so the more primitive elements in the brain come up and take control; and a man feels better temporarily. He has lost his sense of fear, and he has lost his discrimination, he has lost his power to assess. Alcohol merely knocks out his higher centres and releases the more instinctive, primal elements; but the man believes that he is being stimulated. What is really true of him is that he has become more of an animal; his control over himself is diminished" (Lloyd-Jones, *Life in the Spirit*, p. 20; cf. p. 15).

To Paul the alternative is clear cut. If people want to be wise (verse

15) rather than foolish (verse 17) they need to turn away from drunkenness and "be filled by the Spirit" (verse 18).

Lessons From a Verb

We find at least four great lessons in the verb *(plērousthe)* that Paul uses for "filled."

1. "Filled" is an imperative. That is, it is a command to every Christian.
2. "Filled" is in the passive voice. We don't fill ourselves, but the Spirit takes the initiative as we open our hearts and lives.
3. "Filled" is a second person plural. The command is to the Christian community with which Paul has been so concerned throughout Ephesians.
4. "Filled" is in the present tense. That is, being filled with the Spirit is something we need continually. It is not a once-for-all experience.

Christians need more than anything else to be filled with the Spirit. If the filling with wine leads to dissipation or debauchery, the filling of the Spirit, according to Ephesians 5:19-21, has four positive results, signaled by four active present participles that flow out of the imperative command to be filled. The first two are "speaking to one another in psalms and hymns and spiritual songs" and "singing and making melody in your hearts to the Lord" (verse 19). Taken together, those two phrases imply the worshipful fellowship of the Christian community. It is God's desire for His people to unite together in praise. Worship is not merely a private affair between a person and God. Some people think it is, but Luther seems to have caught Paul's burden for the church as the body of Christ when he proclaimed that it is just as impossible to be a solitary Christian as it is to be a solitary adulterer.

The third attitude flowing out of a Spirit-filled Christian community is "giving thanks for all things in the name of our Lord Jesus Christ to God, even the Father" (verse 20). A complaining Christian is a contradiction in terms. Yet many congregations are full of such whining. But that is nothing new. The New Testament repeatedly teaches that the Jewish religious leaders murmured about Jesus. They complained about who He brought to church (Luke 15:1, 2), what He ate, and who He ate with (Matt. 11:19), and about what He said and how He said it (John 6:41).

Things haven't changed all that much. I still know people in the church who are always complaining about everything. Now it is true that some things in the church need correcting. But the way to move forward is not endless murmuring but constructive words and actions. The Pharisees of all ages, however, tend to focus on complaining rather than offering thanksgiving for what is positive and good. Such people certainly have a spirit, but according to the New Testament it is not the Holy Spirit.

The fourth important present participle flowing out of the command to be filled with the Spirit is "being submissive to one another in the fear of Christ" (Eph. 5:21). The church would be a happier place if more of its members deferred to one another rather than being self-assertive and aggressive for their "rights." It is all too easy to forget the meekness, humbleness, and gentleness of the Beatitudes and the life of Christ. There is a massive difference between being filled with self and being filled with the Spirit. And it is important to remember that those two cannot occupy the same space at the same time. Those diverse infillings might even be connected to being wise and unwise as outlined in verse 15 at the beginning of our paragraph. We truly do need to "watch carefully . . . because the days are evil" and it is tempting to walk in the wrong path (Eph. 5:15, 16).

20. Walking as Husband and Wife

Ephesians 5:22-33

²²Wives, submit yourselves to your own husband, as to the Lord, ²³because a husband is head of the wife even as Christ is head of the church, He Himself being the Savior of the body. ²⁴But as the church is submissive to Christ, so also wives ought to be to their husbands in everything. ²⁵Husbands, love your wives, just as Christ loved the church and gave Himself up for her, ²⁶so that He might make her holy, having cleansed her by the washing of water with the word, ²⁷so that He might present to Himself a glorious church, not having spot or wrinkle or any such things, but that she might be holy and blameless. ²⁸So ought husbands to love their own wives as their own bodies. He who loves his own wife loves himself, ²⁹for no one ever hated his own flesh, but nourishes and shows tender affection to it, just as Christ also does to the church, ³⁰because we are members of His body. ³¹"For this reason a man will leave his father and his mother and be joined to his wife, and the two will be one flesh." ³²This is a great mystery, but I am speaking with reference to Christ and the church. ³³In any case, let each one of you love his own wife as himself, and the wife respect her husband.

W ives, *submit* yourselves to your own husband" (verse 22). Not a politically correct way of saying things in the twenty-first century. But then the Bible is not always politically correct. It has its own agenda.

The first thing that we should note about Ephesians 5:22 is that the original Greek does not have the verb submit. In fact, it contains no verb. The verb, translators agree, must be supplied from the participle of to submit from verse 21. Verse 21 with its command of submission sets the stage for Ephesians 5:22-6:9 in which we find three categories of such submission: wives to husbands, children to parents, and slaves to master.

The verb for submission, Robert Bratcher and Eugene Nida point out, "is used in military contexts of a subordinate's relationship to his superior in the army hierarchy. It is used of a wife's relation to her husband in Colossians 3.18; Titus 2.5; 1 Peter 3.1; of servants to masters in Titus 2.9; 1 Peter 1.12; of people to state authorities in Romans 13.1. It means 'to be subject to, obey, be ruled by.' It carries the implication of subordination, reflecting the standards of the time, which no amount of special pleading can disguise" (Bratcher, p. 139).

Well, if we can't escape the word itself, we need to ask what it means in the context of Ephesians. One thing that we soon learn is that Paul uses it in terms of a loving relationship rather than in the framework of dominance or brutal authority, such as sometimes occurred in the military. As Peter O'Brien puts it, "Paul does not here, or elsewhere for that matter, exhort husbands to rule over their wives. They are nowhere told, 'Exercise your headship'! Instead, they are urged repeatedly to love their wives (vv. 25, 28, and 33). This will involve each husband showing unceasing care and loving service for his wife's entire well-being" (O'Brien, p. 419).

Contrary to the mistaken view that Ephesians 5:22-33 is a command for husbands to exercise authority over their wives, it is in actuality a warning against the improper use of authority that "forbids them to exploit their position, and urges them instead to remember their responsibilities and the other party's rights. Thus, husbands are to love their wives and care for them" (Stott, p. 219). Nowhere does Scripture tell men to rule or to dominate them.

The kind of submission that Paul is talking about was no stranger to Christianity. After all, central to the teaching of the New Testament is the fact that Christ placed Himself under the Father (1 Cor. 15:28). Submission, therefore, "can denote a functional subordination without implying inferiority, or less honour and glory" (O'Brien, p. 412). What we have in Ephesians 5 in regard to husband and wife are not implications of inferiority but of roles. As John Howard Yoder puts it, "equality of *worth* is not identity of *role*" (Yoder, p. 177). And that is just as true in the family as it is in the Godhead. The husband and wife are not subordinated in value in any way, even though they do have different roles, some of which derive from their very physiology.

The major reason that Paul supplies for a wife's submission to her husband reflects Christ's saving relationship to the church, which is submissive to Him. "Christ loved the church and gave Himself up for her" so that He might bless her (Eph. 5:26, 27). If we really want to see what Paul is implying when he speaks of headship, we need to look to Jesus, who focused on care rather than control.

That thought sets the stage for one of the New Testament's most profound passages on marriage. William Barclay, in commenting on Ephesians 5:22-33, writes that "no one reading this passage in the twentieth century can fully realize how great it is. Throughout the years the Christian view of marriage has come to be accepted" even if people often fall short of the ideal itself (Barclay, p. 199).

> ## An Abused Text
>
> Ephesians 5:22 "is surely one of the most abused and debated texts in the New Testament. Its focus is *not* on the privilege and dominance of the husband, and Paul never intended to suggest that wives were servants, compelled to follow any and every desire of the husband. The text does not tell women to *obey* their husbands, nor does it give any license for husbands to attempt to force submission" (Snodgrass, p. 294).

At the foundation of the problem of a low view of marriage in the pre-Christian world, Barclay notes, was a low regard for women. Jewish men, for example, daily thanked God that they were neither a Gentile, a slave, or a woman. And under Jewish law a woman had few rights. Her husband could divorce her for the most trivial offense, such as burning his dinner or speaking disrespectfully to him, but she, with a few extreme exceptions, had no right to divorce him. All that the lordly husband had to do was to hand her a bill of divorce in the presence of two witnesses and the divorce was complete.

Marriage was even more precarious in the Greek world. Prostitution was an ever present fact of life. Demosthenes had prescribed the accepted way of life when he penned: "We have courtesans for the sake of pleasure; we have concubines for the sake of daily cohabitation; we have wives for the purpose of having children legitimately, and of having a faithful guardian for all our household affairs" (quoted in Barclay, p. 201). A respectable Greek woman was never seen in public and had her own apartment separate from the quarters of her husband. A Greek wife had no rights and, given the fact that Greek society had no specified legal proceedings for divorce, the husband could dissolve a marriage at his whim, with no questions asked.

And in Rome the state of marriage was even more deplorable than in Greece or Palestine. By the time of Paul the institution was in a shamble, Seneca even going so far as to write that some women dated years by the names of their husbands. Fidelity was not practiced and one could best characterize the atmosphere as adulterous. It is in that context that Paul writes. (See Barclay, pp. 199-203 for a helpful discussion of marriage in the apostle's day.)

One of the tragedies of some people's use of Ephesians 5:22-33 is that they focus on subordination and miss the beautiful but radical picture of marriage that Paul paints in those few verses. Looking through the prism of Christ's love for the church, we discover at least five lessons about marriage and the husband's role in the relationship.

First, his love must be a sacrificial one. "Just as Christ loved the church and gave Himself up for her . . . , so ought husbands" to love their wives (verses 25, 28). The husband's role in a marriage is not to be served but to serve. He is even to give up, when necessary, those things that are dearest to him for the sake of his wife. Husbandly sacrifice is the high price and the demand of such headship. It is unfortunate that some men, not reading the passage very carefully, abuse the passage in a way that contradicts the principles that the Holy Spirit gave to us through Paul.

Second, a husband's love must be purifying. Just as Christ's aim was to make the church holy, "having cleansed her by the washing of water with the word, so that He might present to Himself a glorious church, not having spot or wrinkle or any such things, . . . so ought husbands to love their own wives" (verses 26-28). The husband's role is to build up his wife in every way. Anything that he does to degrade her or drag her down is out of harmony with God's command to him.

Third, a husband's love must be caring. He must love his wife just as much as he does himself and his own body (verse 28). That characteristic of husbandly love is not only an essential component of marriage, it also stands at the very foundation of the law of God (see Matt. 22:36-40). How many men pamper themselves and even use their wives to pamper them, while they in turn misuse and abuse their wives physically and in other ways. God's word is crystal clear that a husband is to have a caring love for his spouse.

Fourth, a husband's love is permanent. A married man has left his father and mother and united with his wife. The two have become "one flesh" (Eph. 5:31). His wife is not a disposable by-product or an exchangeable part. They are united in a permanent relationship by the very nature of the marriage experience.

Lastly, as Barclay points out, a husband marries his wife in the Lord. They are both a part of the body of Christ. Their marriage "is lived in the presence of the Lord; it is lived in the atmosphere of the Lord; its every motion is governed by the Lord; its every decision is taken in the Lord. In the Christian home Jesus is an ever-remembered, though an unseen, guest. In the Christian marriage there are not two partners, but three—and the third is Christ" (Barclay, p. 207).

21. Walking as Parent and Child

Ephesians 6:1-4

¹Children, obey your parents in the Lord, for this is right. ²"Honor your father and your mother," which is the first commandment with a promise, ³"so that it may be well with you and that you may live a long time on the earth." ⁴And fathers, do not provoke your children to anger, but raise them up in the discipline and instruction of the Lord.

Lists of the duties of various members of a household find their fullest expression in Paul's writings in Colossians 3:18-4:1 and Ephesians 5:22-6:9, even though 1 Timothy 2:1-15; 5:1-2; 6:1-2, 17-19; Titus 2:1-3:8, and 1 Peter 2:13-3:7 also contain teachings similar in tone and format. And such lists of duties were not restricted to the Bible. Household codes, in fact, formed a common part of the moral literature of the day. The difference between the lists found in the New Testament and those generated by the larger culture is that Scripture frames them within a Christian perspective.

From the duties of husbands and wives Paul turns in Ephesians 6:1 to the reciprocal duties of parents and children. And if his counsels reflected a high view of marriage and did much to give rights to women who had very few of them in the first-century world, he also put children and childhood on a higher plane. Most of us fail to realize how much of an impact Christianity has had on our views of women and children because we live in a world largely transformed by biblical values. We have only to examine the time in which Paul preached his gospel to see the contrast.

In his day traditional Roman notions of family life and education had deeply influenced the Greco-Roman world. The father in Roman culture had almost absolute legal power over the members of his household. Thus Dionysius of Halicarnassus could write, "The law-giver of the Romans gave virtually full power to the father over his son, whether he thought proper to imprison him, to scourge him, to put him in chains, and keep him at work in the fields, or to put him to death; and this even though the son were already engaged in public affairs, though he were numbered among the highest magistrates, and though he were celebrated for his zeal for the commonwealth" (Dionysius, *Rom. Ant.* 2.26.4, quoted in Lincoln, pp. 398-399).

Beyond powers over even their grown sons, the *paterfamilias* (ruling father) of the extended Roman family had the authority to expose an unwanted newborn child to the elements, command that deformed children be drowned, or sell unwanted daughters to be raised as slaves to furnish material for the next generation's brothels. Only his death terminated the control of the father over his children.

The Jews were years ahead of the Romans in their attitude toward children, but still they were not as enlightened as they should have been, as is evidenced by the disciples seeking to keep children away from Jesus, as if they weren't important enough for Him to spend time with (see Matt. 19:13-15). Then we encounter such counsel as that found in Ecclesiasticus 30:1-13, in which a father who loves his son is to whip him and beat him often while he is still a child (verses 1, 12), and which advises a father not to play with his son, share his laughter, or pamper him (verses 7-10).

The principles set forth in the life of Christ and in the writings of the New Testament would eventually transform cultural evaluations of children and how to raise them. Paul is at the forefront of that shift. The very fact that he even has a section on children indicates that young people had a part in the early Christian family of God. Certainly the principles of the one who had said "Whoever receives one such child in my name receives me" (Matt. 18:5, RSV) and "Let the children come to me, do not hinder them; for to such belongs the kingdom of God" (Mark 10:14, RSV) were having their impact on the young Christian community in Ephesus.

Paul's counsel to parents and children falls into two parts. The first, and the most extended, is to children. "Obey your parents" is his command (Eph. 6:1). Please note that he did not say that to wives. He never ordered wives to obey their husbands, but rather that they should be submissive to them and respect them (5:22, 33). In his counsel to children we find a note of authority absent in his admonitions to wives. Theirs was a self-giving to one who loved and cared for them, but here we find a command to obey.

But even that obedience was not to be unlimited, as it might first appear from Colossians 3:20 ("obey your parents in everything," RSV). It was to be "in the Lord" (Eph. 6:1). That is an important qualification, because not all parents were Christians and not all those who were believers were correct in what they told their children to do. Obeying "in the Lord" signaled the fact that even in the family "we must obey God rather than men" (Acts 5:29, RSV). Thus if a parent commands a child to steal or disobey the Lord's commands in some other way, that child is duty bound to refuse on the basis of principle.

But it appears that the apostle sees such situations to be in the minority in a Christian household. He provides three reasons why children should obey their parents. First, that it is "right" (Eph. 6:1). And Paul is certainly correct on that point. In a society in which children cease to obey their parents all order breaks down, because the family is the foundation of society. In other places the apostle lists disobedience to parents as the sign of a decadent culture (see Rom. 1:28-30; 2 Tim. 3:1-5). Colossians 3:20 expands upon the implications of Ephesians 6:1 when it states, "children, obey your parents in everything, for this pleases the Lord" (RSV).

Even the natural mind without God's word can conclude that obedience is right and pleasing, since we find child obedience a concern in every society. But Paul moves on in Ephesians 6:2, 3, to provide his readers with a revealed reason. There he quotes the fifth commandment of the Decalogue from the Septuagint (Greek) version of Exodus 20:12 or Deuteronomy 5:16, inserting "which is the first commandment with a promise" into the reading. The fifth command, as we might expect, had been an oft-mentioned one among Jewish writers. In fact, the New Testament quotes it in five other places (Matt. 15:4; 19:19; Mark 7:10; 10:19; Luke 18:20). Klyne Snodgrass makes a pertinent aside when he notes that Paul's "use of this command and of other Old Testament texts as motivation throughout the ethical teaching of Ephesians shows that the law has not been set aside. We may find Paul's teaching on the law difficult, but *he* did not think he was abolishing the law" in spite of some people's misunderstanding of what he taught in Ephesians 2:15 (Snodgrass, pp.

321, 322). For Paul there was no doubt that even for Christians the Ten Commandments provided a motivational foundation for Christian living. The keeping of them, he asserts in Ephesians 6:2, 3, results in a blessing.

His third motivation for children to obey their parents we find in the words "in the Lord" (verse 1). While these words, as we noted earlier, imply a limitation on obedience, John Stott is quite right in arguing that such a restriction "does not exhaust their meaning." They also "bring child-obedience into the realm of specifically Christian duty, and lay upon children the responsibility to obey their parents because of their own personal relationship to the Lord Jesus Christ" (Stott, p. 244). All of a Christian's relationships are transformed at the time of conversion to Christ. Thus a Christian young person obeys not only because it is right and the Old Testament commands it, but also because of a love relationship with Jesus Christ as Lord and Savior.

The apostle not only has counsel for children in Ephesians 6, but also for fathers, a word that can and should in principle include both parents. "Fathers," he pens, "do not provoke your children to anger, but raise them up in the discipline and instruction of the Lord" (verse 4). Paul approaches the topic with a two edged sword. First comes the negative edge: do not provoke them to anger. Colossians 3:21 is helpful here when it adds "lest they become discouraged" (RSV).

Andrew Lincoln, in commenting on Ephesians 6:4 and Colossians 3:21, writes that "fathers are made responsible for ensuring that they do not provoke anger in their children. This involves avoiding attitudes, words, and actions which would drive a child to angry exasperation or resentment and thus rules out excessively severe discipline, unreasonably harsh demands, abuse of authority, arbitrariness, unfairness, constant nagging and condemnation, subjecting a child to humiliation, and all forms of gross insensitivity to a child's needs and sensibilities" (Lincoln, p. 406).

Ellen White is on the same wavelength when she writes that "an atmosphere of unsympathetic criticism is fatal to effort. Flowers do not unfold under the breadth of a blighting wind." "Suspicion," she pens in another connection, "demoralizes, producing the very evils it seeks to prevent." Thus "the wise educator," in dealing with children, "will seek to encourage confidence and to strengthen the sense of honor. Children and youth are benefited by being trusted. . . . The true object of reproof is gained only when the wrongdoer himself is led to see his fault and his will is enlisted for its correction. When this is accomplished, point him to the source of pardon and power. Seek to preserve his self respect" (White, *Education,* pp. 289-292).

In child rearing the positive always supercedes the negative. Thus it is with Paul's command to parents in Ephesians 6:4. Beyond not provoking children to anger lest they become discouraged, he points parents to their positive role in developing self-discipline or self-control (the only truly effective discipline in the long run) in their children and in providing "instruction of the Lord" that they might grow up to be healthy members of the body of Christ.

22. Walking as Employer and Employee

Ephesians 6:5-9

*5Slaves, obey your masters according to the flesh with fear and trem-
bling, in the sincerity of your heart, as to Christ, 6not by way of eyeser-
vice as men-pleasers, but as slaves of Christ, doing the will of God from
the heart. 7With good will do service to the Lord and not to men, 8know-
ing that whatever good thing each one does, this he will receive again from
the Lord, whether he is a slave or free. 9And masters, do the same things
to them, let up on threatening, knowing that both their Master and yours
is in heaven, and that there is no partiality with Him.*

Now I know that Ephesians 6:5-9 refers to slaves and masters rather
than employees and employers. But modern cultures are rather short
on real slaves. Yet the principles that Paul lays down apply equally to the
modern world of employment. However, before moving to our day we
should take a look at slavery in the Roman Empire and to the original implications of his counsel.

In writing to the churches in and around Ephesus Paul was undoubtedly addressing a large number of Christian slaves. Approximately one-third
of the population in such Roman cities consisted of slaves. And we might
assume that even a higher proportion of slaves were in the church than in
the culture at large, given the fact that Christianity with its message of hope
has always had a special appeal to the downtrodden and dispossessed.

Writers in the Greco-Roman world variously referred to slaves as "a
living tool" and "a beast who happens to be able to talk" (see Barclay, p.
213). Masters possessed, if they chose to use it, the power of life and death

over their slaves. But then, we should not forget, a father had the same power over his sons and daughters. Slaves could be bought and sold, and they definitely had fewer rights than those who were free.

On the other hand, we need to see Roman slavery in a different light than the more recent African slavery. For one thing, slaves belonged to all races. More importantly, "persons in slavery under Roman law in the 1st cent. A.D. could generally count on being set free by age thirty." And "by no means was the slave's position always 'subordinate,' for in Greco-Roman households slaves served not only as cooks, cleaners, and personal attendants, but also as tutors of persons of all ages, physicians, nurses, close companions, and managers of the household. In the business world, slaves were not only janitors and delivery boys; they were managers of estates, shops, and ships, as well as salesmen and contracting agents. In the civil service slaves were not only used in street-paving and sewer-cleaning gangs, but also as administrators of funds and personnel and as executives with decision-making powers" (S. S. Bartchy in Bromiley, vol. 4, pp. 545, 544).

In short, the slaves of the empire did its work and included workers in positions of high status as well as low. Slaves were, in fact, often well educated (sometimes at the master's expense) and better off in every way than the free poor. As a result, "for many, self-sale into slavery with anticipation of manumission was regarded as the most direct means to be integrated into Greek and Roman society. As such, in stark contrast to New World slavery in the 17th-19th cents., Greco-Roman slavery functioned as a process rather than a permanent condition, as a temporary phase of life by means of which an outsider obtained 'a place within a society'" (*ibid.,* p. 544). Thus in many ways ancient slavery resembled more a system of indentured servants than the more recent slavery of Africans by Whites.

It is because of the non-racial aspects, the temporariness, and the relative moderation of Roman slavery that we read of no slave revolts in the first century. Slavery was the economic system Rome used to get its work done.

Yet it still represented a social system less than ideal, one in which a slave was subject to arbitrary abuse by a master.

It was with that realization in mind that Paul wrote his counsel to slaves and masters. As in the sections on marriage and parenting, he addresses the subordinate group first. "What is remarkable," Peter O'Brien notes, "is that Paul directly exhorts slaves in a manner that is unprecedented, for in traditional discussions of household management the focus of attention was on how a master should rule his slaves." But in the Pauline admonitions "slaves, like wives and children, are treated as ethically responsible persons (cf. Col. 3:22-25)" (O'Brien, pp. 448, 449). His remarks to slaves also indicate that they were full members of the body of Christ in the congregations of the Ephesian community.

We also need to note the Christocentric implications set forth in each of the five verses in this section. Whether the instruction is to slaves or masters, each of them refers to Christ.

- obey sincerely, *"as to Christ"* (Eph. 6:5)
- obey as "slaves *of Christ"* (verse 6)
- service to be rendered as *"to the Lord"* (verse 7)
- slaves will receive recompense *"from the Lord"* (verse 8)
- "masters" ("lords" in Greek) also have a *"Master"* ("Lord" in Greek, verse 9)

Christians in the Workplace

"Paul's instructions encourage responsibility and integrity on the job. Christian employees should do their jobs as if Jesus Christ were their supervisor, and Christian employers should treat their employees fairly and with respect. Can you be trusted to do your best, even when the boss is not around? Do you work hard and with enthusiasm? Do you treat your employees as people, not machines? Remember that no matter whom you work for and no matter who works for you, the One you ultimately should want to please is your Father in heaven" (Barton, p. 125).

Like all other aspects of life, the roles of slave and master and employee and employer all take place within the context of a person's relation to God through Christ. In other words, our occupations in the everyday world are a part of our religious life and responsibility (rather than being something in the so-called "secular" realm).

With that context in mind, Paul presents several guidelines for slaves in the ancient world and, by implication, employees in the modern. First (verse 5), employees are to respect their employers. While modern employees might not fear and tremble in the same manner as a slave of old, it is true that employers do hold, in a sense, our jobs and future advancement in their hands. And without respect for leadership and management businesses tend to break down and lose their direction. The God of the Bible is a deity of order, even in the workplace. A Christian employee is to do his or her work as if doing it for Christ Himself.

Second (verse 6), Christian employees should be faithful at their work even though no one is watching. As George Stoeckhardt puts it, "Christian servants . . . should consider themselves servants of Christ and should therefore, in the service which they render their masters, seek to fulfill the will of God, whose eye beholds also those actions and omissions which masters according to the flesh cannot see" (Stoeckhardt, p. 252). Thus Christians are not merely doing service as "men-pleasers" for the eyes of the boss, but are servants of Christ in the workplace.

Third (verse 7), as servants of Christ, their true Master, Christians will seek to do God's will while on the job. And fourth (verse 8), faithful work, even though it may get overlooked on earth, will receive its reward in the future. Thus Paul reminds his readers that "nothing is unwitnessed by the Lord in heaven, nothing well done is ever done in vain. There may be no thanks on earth. A person may reap only criticism and misunderstanding. But there is an unfailing reward for faithful service (cf. Lk. 6:35; 1 Pet. 1:17; Rev. 22:12)" in God's final accounting of the business of life (Foulkes, p. 175).

It is with the thought of judgment that Paul brings in the phrase "whether he is a slave or free" (Eph. 6:8). Here slave and master, employee and employer, stand on equal ground. Eventually the all-seeing Master will evaluate everyone.

Verse 9 finds Paul transitioning from slaves to masters. And in the process he makes a play on words. The Greek word he uses for master is "lord," the very same word that he employs for the master's Master. In the end all of us, no matter what our status here on earth, stand on level ground. We will all be evaluated and judged by the Lord of lords (and the Lord of slaves), who will show "no partiality" between slave and master.

It is in that context that Paul sets forth a few guidelines for Christian employers. First, he urges them to apply the golden rule to the work place—the master should "do the same things to them" (verse 9). Thus, in the context, if employers desire to receive respect, they should show respect to their employees; if they expect service, they should provide it for those who work for them; and if they expect honesty, they should act honestly. Beyond that, they should not behave in an arrogant or threatening manner toward others less powerful than themselves. After all, both Christian employers and Christian employees all serve the same ultimate Master. And both groups "will receive again from the Lord" (verse 8) according to their work relationships when the great Master in heaven passes out the final rewards (cf. Matt. 16:27; Rev. 22:12).

23. Fighting the Powers of Darkness

Ephesians 6:10-17

> *10Finally, be strong in the Lord and in the strength of His might. 11Put on the whole armor of God, so that you will be able to stand against the craftiness of the devil. 12For we are not struggling against flesh and blood, but against the rulers, against the authorities, against the world powers of this darkness, against the spiritual forces of evil in the heavenly places. 13Therefore, take up the whole armor of God, so that you will be able to resist in the evil day, and having done everything, to stand. 14Stand therefore, having girded your loins with truth, and having put on the breastplate of righteousness, 15and having shod your feet with the solid foundation of the gospel of peace. 16Besides all these things, take up the shield of faith, by which you will be able to extinguish all the flaming arrows of the evil one, 17and take the helmet of salvation, and the sword of the Spirit, which is the word of God.*

With Ephesians 6:10-17 we come to the climax of the epistle. It is one thing to read about the high ideals that Paul has presented in his intense letter, but it is quite another to carry them out in everyday life. After all, in this life Christians face serious opposition. While Ephesians has alluded to that opposition several times, the heart of chapter 6 makes it quite explicit, as is the call for vigorous resistance to the forces of evil.

Three forceful imperatives dominate verses 10-17:

1. "be strong" (verse 10),
2. "put on the whole armor of God" (verse 11), and
3. "stand" (verse 11, 13, 14).

The basic idea underlying each of them is that Christian victory doesn't come about by accident, but must be planned for in an intelligent manner. Ephesians 6:10-17 vividly describes Christian living as spiritual warfare.

The situation is that "many converts were streaming into the churches—converts who were formerly affiliated with the Artemis cult [headquartered in Ephesus], practiced magic, consulted astrologers, and participated in various mysteries. Underlying the former beliefs and manner of life of all these converts was a common and deepset fear of the demonic 'powers'" (Arnold, *Ephesians,* p. 122). Ephesians 6 addresses that fear and instructs believers in how to resist.

In the process, Paul makes it clear that as Christians we are facing evil forces that are both real and powerful. Not a mere figment of disturbed imaginations or fictional superstitions, they exist and are active in people's lives. Even though they may have lost control of the Ephesians' hearts and lives because of their conversion to Christ, such "demonic 'powers,'" Clinton Arnold writes, "are bent on regaining their control in the lives of believers. Through a variety of means they attempt to block the progress of the gospel and cause believers to walk according to the pattern of their former manner of life." The lesson of Ephesians 6 is that "victory over the 'powers' is not assured apart from the appropriation of the power of God" (*ibid.,* p. 121).

"Be strong" Paul exclaims in his first great imperative. The Greek word underlying the word strong is *dunamis,* from which we get our word dynamite. Christians need power if they are to succeed, but it is not something that we get from being good or wise or from anything within ourselves. To the contrary, the emphasis in verse 10 falls on God's *dunamis* not ours: "Be strong in the Lord and in the strength of His might."

Now the people in the area of Ephesus were well aware, Arnold points out, of their need for spiritual power, but they had "been accustomed to receiving it from the wrong means—through helper spirits, incantations, rituals, formulas, and calling on their gods and goddesses" (Arnold, "Ephesians," p. 336). In that they were not all that different from those in our day who utilize New Age channelers for power and access to the transcendent world, or who seek guidance for their lives through seances or horoscopes.

But, according to the apostle, such sources are exactly the problem. Behind all of them lurks "the craftiness of the devil" (verse 11). Paul is dead serious here. The problems that we face do not result from evil people ("flesh and blood"), but rather from "rulers, . . . authorities, . . . world powers of this darkness, . . . spiritual forces of evil in the heavenly places" (verse 12). The apostle is not playing word games here. To the contrary, he could not be more serious. One of the greatest weaknesses of many Christians is that they consider the devil to be fictional or some sort of medieval superstition. But that is a part of the "craftiness" of the evil one. It is, so to speak, his trump card. After all, if he isn't a real power then we don't have to be vigilant. We can live in our own human strength because we have nothing more to fear than ill-willed or twisted people. But according to Paul, a powerful devil not only exists, but is also crafty. Part of that craftiness, Klyne Snodgrass points out, is that he works by "trickery and subterfuge" to enter our lives. "Evil rarely looks evil until it accomplishes its goal; it gains entrance by appearing attractive, desirable, and perfectly legitimate. It is a baited and camouflaged trap. As Paul puts it in 2 Corinthians 11:14, Satan masquerades as an angel of light" (Snodgrass, p. 339).

It is in that context that we read the thrice repeated command to "stand" (Eph. 6:11, 13, 14). The context makes it explicitly clear that individual Christians and the church as a whole will not be able to resist in their human power. If they seek to do so, the church as the body of Christ will fragment and be overcome. The only way either the church or individuals within it can stand "against the craftiness of the devil" is in the Lord's strength and might (verses 10, 11), and they can only have victory by putting "on the whole armor of God" (verses 11, 13).

Please note that the emphasis is on the divine nature of the armor. Paul does not command us to put on *our* armor but *God's*. Thus even though Harold Hoehner suggests that "it is quite possible that Paul's vivid description of the armor may stem from the fact that, while writing this letter, he was in prison being guarded by Roman soldiers (cf. Acts 28:16, 20)," he is also quick to add that "the words *tou theou* [of God] are genitives of origin, indicating that God provides the armor." After all, "this is not a physical battle, but rather a spiritual one. Thus it requires supernaturally provided spiritual armor" (Hoehner, p. 823).

The armor is "of God" in at least one additional way. Each of the six spiritual weapons listed in Ephesians 6:14-17 the Old Testament describes as being the armor of God and of His Messiah. That is especially evident in Isaiah. "The Isaianic references," Peter O'Brien points out, "depict the

Lord of hosts as a warrior dressed for battle as he goes forth to vindicate his people. The 'full armour of God' which the readers are urged to put on as they engage in a deadly spiritual warfare (v. 11) is Yahweh's own armour, which he and his Messiah have worn and which is now provided for his people as they engage in battle" (O'Brien, p. 457). We see that parallelism portrayed in the following box.

God's Armor Is to Be Our Armor

Image	Old Testament Background	Spiritual Weapon
1. Belt . . . buckled around your waist	Isa. 11:5	Truth
2. Breastplate	Isa. 59:17	Righteousness
3. Feet fitted	Isa. 52:7	Gospel of peace
4. Shield	(Isa. 21:5; Ps. 35:2)—23 times in the OT	Faith
5. Helmet	Isa. 59:17	Salvation
6. Sword	(Isa. 49:2)—178 times in the OT	Spirit/Word of God/Prayer

(adapted from Arnold, "Ephesians," p. 337).

That Paul primarily based his discussion of armor on the Old Testament rather than on Roman soldiers is also evident from the fact that he makes no mention of certain weapons generally used by the Romans, such as the javelin. Nor does he refer to the typical leg armor.

While the armor metaphors are important in Ephesians 6, it is the spiritual gifts and virtues associated with them that are central to the passage. Earlier chapters of Ephesians have previously featured all of them.

- Truth in Ephesians 1:13; 4:15, 21, 24, 25; 5:9
- Righteousness in Ephesians 4:24; 5:9
- Peace in Ephesians 1:2; 2:14–18; 4:3
- The gospel in Ephesians 1:13; 3:6
- The word of God in Ephesians 1:13; 5:26
- Salvation in Ephesians 1:13; 2:5, 8; 5:3

• Faith in Ephesians 1:1, 13, 15, 19; 2:8; 3:12, 17; 4:5, 13

Thus the spiritual gifts and virtues connected with the armor in Ephesians 6:14-17 represent theological themes of Ephesians that are "recapitulated in relation to the weaponry believers are to employ in their spiritual warfare" (O'Brien, p. 459).

The armor comes in two aspects: defensive and offensive. Among the defensive is the belt of truth. While it is not clear if the belt is an allusion to the Old Testament's girding up of the loins (a tying up of long robes around the waist) as a designation of readiness for action or a reference to the leather-like apron worn by Roman soldiers to protect the lower abdomen, it is obvious that the reception of God's truth and acting upon it in daily life are essential to spiritual health.

A second defensive item is the breastplate of righteousness. It suggests that the covering of Christ's righteousness protects a Christian's vital regions, and that as Christians reflect the righteous character of God in their daily actions or walk it further guards them. A third item is the helmet of salvation, which represents the ultimate assurance of God's protection. In Ephesians, salvation is both a past event (2:5, 8) and a future hope (4:30). That is, believers have already been saved, but God still has a fuller blessing for them in the future. Those two assurances are affirming and stabilizing as Christians face life's challenges.

With the shield of faith we are dealing with an article that serves both defensive and offensive functions. If Paul has in mind the large Roman infantry shield, it would have been four feet tall and two-and-one-half-feet wide. Covered in leather stretched over wood, soldiers often soaked such shields in water to stop burning arrows that had been dipped in pitch and set alight. Snodgrass notes that "when overlapped with the shields of soldiers on either side, they provided effective protection. They were not merely defensive, however, for a line of soldiers with interlocked shields and weapons poised could push right through enemy ranks" (Snodgrass, p. 343). Here we may have a side lesson. After all, it is only when church members are linked together in Christ's body that they can be effective in either defensive or offensive spiritual warfare.

The two strictly offensive weapons of the church, feet shod with the gospel of peace (Eph. 6:15) and "the sword of the Spirit, which is the word of God" (verse 17), represent an aggressive taking of God's word into the territory of the enemy. The preaching of that word brings peace between people and their God and also amongst the people themselves as on the basis of salvation by grace the wall of separation vanishes from between them and they become a part of the body of Christ (see Eph. 2:5-22). The paradox of offensive Christian warfare is that its ultimate aim is to bring peace to the world.

But that peace is at present far from universal. To the contrary, Paul refers to the current wartorn condition of the world as "the evil day" (verse 13). As noted previously, believers at present live in an already but not yet condition. That is, God has already saved them in Christ (2:5, 8), but their ultimate redemption still awaits them (see 1:14; 4:30). Until that time they live in the "evil day," during which the spiritual forces of darkness still hope to win professed Christians back to their way of thinking and living. Christians, therefore, must "resist" and "stand" firm (6:11, 13, 14). But they can only hope to be successful by doing so in "the strength of His might" and in "the whole armor of God" (verse 10, 11). To seek to engage in our own strength in combat with the spiritual forces of evil is the certain route to defeat.

24. Praying Is a Two-way Street

Ephesians 6:18-20

¹⁸With all prayer and petition pray at all times in the Spirit, and be watchful to that very thing with all perseverance and petition concerning all the saints, ¹⁹and pray on my behalf, that words may be given to me in opening my mouth to make known in boldness the mystery of the gospel, ²⁰of which I am an ambassador in chains, that I might proclaim it boldly, as I ought to speak.

Prayer, suggests William Barclay, is "the greatest weapon of all" (Barclay, p. 218). It is with the topic of prayer that Paul closes his discussion of the Christian's warfare with the powers of evil. That is clear enough. But the question arises, is prayer merely another piece of a Christian's armor—the seventh in the list, or does prayer qualitatively stand apart from the six pieces of a Christian's armor?

We find arguments to support both sides of that question. On the one hand, the author maintains a structural continuity with the previous list of the armor by employing the participle of the verb to pray. Thus praying is a part of what it means to stand against the devil (Eph. 6:11, 13, 14). Just as one is to gird up one's loins, to put on the breastplate of righteousness, and so on, so a Christian is to pray. From that perspective, praying is central to resisting and standing against the devil and his kingdom. Thus from one point of view praying is merely another weapon.

But, on the other side of the issue, Paul seems to give a special place to prayer. As Clinton Arnold observes, "the author seems to highlight the importance of prayer by a two-fold departure from the pattern of the preceding manner of listing the weapons" (Arnold, *Ephesians,* p. 112). First, he does not use a military metaphor to illustrate prayer. And second, he elaborates on prayer and emphasizes its meaning in a way that differs from the six items of armor.

In short, it appears that prayer has a strategic place in the warfare with the forces of evil. While it is related to the items of armor, it also is in some ways more basic to them in Paul's thinking. As John Stott notes, prayer is "to pervade all our spiritual warfare" (Stott, p. 283). Arnold puts it more succinctly when he writes that "in 6:18-20, prayer is seen as essential to the arming of believers with the power of God in order to resist the diabolic 'powers' who would seek to prevent them from living according to Christian ethics. . . . The writer *thus wants his readers to understand prayer as an essential spiritual weapon, but more than a weapon, it is foundational for the deployment of all the other weapons*" (Arnold, *Ephesians,* p. 112, italics supplied).

Paul emphasizes the strategic importance of prayer in spiritual warfare by employing the word "all" four times in verse 18, as seen in the following box.

The Four Alls of Prayer

1. We are to pray "with all prayer and petition."
2. We are to pray "at all times."
3. We are to pray "with all perseverance."
4. We are to pray "concerning all the saints."

Falling short of that ideal, John Stott suggests that "most Christians pray sometimes, with some prayers and some degree of perseverance, for some of God's people" (Stott, p. 283). But God wants us to replace that "some" with the biblical "all" in each case.

That means that prayer needs to be constant. Victorious Christians live in an atmosphere of prayer. Rather than praying merely when a crisis arrives, or at meals, or in the evening and the morning, prayer must become a part of our life throughout the day. That doesn't mean that we are on our knees all day long, but rather than we can utter a prayer to God as we drive down the road or as we meet a person and aren't quite sure what to say in a particular situation. It is from a life of constant and consistent prayer that we gain strength and wisdom to live the Christian life.

A second thing to note about victorious prayer is that it has a manysid-edness. We are to pray with all "prayer and petition." I know people who only pray when they want something. They too often forget the prayer of thankfulness, or the prayer of praise to God for His blessings, or the prayer for forgiveness of their sin, or the prayer of deliverance, or the prayer for guidance in the small and large decisions of the day, or the prayer of sup-plication for others, or the prayer of just communing with God as with a friend. A healthy prayer life will be comprehensive and well-rounded.

A third mark of a healthy prayer life is that it perseveres. It is all too easy to pray without intensity. Momentary prayer has its place in life, but so does the prayer of intensity and concentration. At times prayer is even sleepless in its demands. So it was with Jesus, who at times forgot sleep al-together as He wrestled with God in the face of the enemy.

Finally, Christian prayer is unselfish. We need to learn to pray "con-cerning all the saints" and not just those whom we like or who like us. Jesus described perfect, God-like people as those who can love their ene-mies and pray for those who persecute them (Matt. 5:44; see all of 5:43-48). If Jesus could pray for Judas and for those who put Him on the cross, it seems to me that I should be able to pray for the Judases in my life (whether I *feel* like it or not).

In living the Christian life it is crucial to remember the strategic role of prayer. The defensive and offensive aspects of a Christian's armor are wonderful, but, in Paul's understanding, without prayer they will be inef-fective. After all, "prayer . . . is foundational for the deployment of all the other weapons" (Arnold, *Ephesians,* p. 112).

It is the importance of prayer that leads the apostle to request that the Ephesians pray for him. Here is a wonderful truth. Prayer is a two-way street. Already Paul has uttered two heart-felt prayers for his Ephesian readers. In Ephesians 1:15-23 he prayed that they might have a greater awareness of the divine power available to them. And in the third chapter he again prayed that they might truly understand their resources in God through Christ (verses 14-21).

Well, you may be saying to yourself, *we can understand those prayers. Paul has a direct connection to God. We expect him to pray for those who he is ministering to.*

But wonder of wonders, the great apostle needs our prayers also. It might be difficult for us to imagine such a prominent leader being intimidated by anyone or of ever being at a loss for words. But Paul knows the truth of his own fears and weaknesses. As a result, he asks the Ephesians to pray for him on two counts:

- That he might be given correct words to preach the gospel (6:19).
- That he might receive boldness to preach that gospel (verse 20).

Even great people feel their need. In fact, sensing one's need and being able to verbalize it are two of the marks of greatness, in contrast to the arrogant shallowness of those who do not have enough spiritual sense to grasp their limitations in the warfare against the powers of darkness in the heavenly places.

Here is another universal lesson concerning prayer. We need to pray for the leaders of the church on earth. It is all too easy to criticize them. And maybe they deserve it. But even if they do—especially if they do—they require our prayers. To listen to some church members you would think that they have a divine commission to cannibalize leadership. They do have a divine commission all right, but it is to pray for every church leader. As Barclay writes, "we would do well to remember that no Christian leader and no Christian preacher can go on unless his [or her] people are ever upholding his [or her] hands in prayer" (Barclay, p. 219). And while you are praying, don't forget the "cannibals." They need it, even though, unlike Paul, they don't recognize that fact.

The apostle closes his request for prayer by noting that he is "an ambassador in chains" (Eph. 6:20). Now there is a paradox for you. As Markus Barth points out, "Paul coins an oxymoron when he calls himself an 'ambassador in chains'" (Barth, *Ephesians 4-6*, p. 782). An ambassador by definition is the representative of one kingdom to another. It is a position of great honor that carries diplomatic immunity. That is, by mutual international agreement ambassadors are not subject to arrest. If war breaks out a nation gives the ambassadors of the enemy country their papers and sends them home, but they do not arrest them.

But not so with Paul. He is truly the ambassadorial representative of the kingdom of God to Caesar, to whom he has appealed to hear his case (Acts 25:10-12), but he has been imprisoned. In fact, it is those very chains that he trusts will eventually give him an audience with the Roman emperor. No wonder he asks for the prayers of the Ephesians that he might have boldness to preach with clarity when the opportunity comes. Even the rulers of this world need to hear the "mystery of the gospel."

Jesus had predicted that His followers would someday present the good news to kings and rulers (Matt. 10:18). And such preaching is not finished. It will continue to the end of the world. Each time they give the gospel message, whether it be to high or low, God's servants require boldness and clarity of thought. They are always in need of the prayers of all of God's saints as they face the forces of the powers of darkness in heavenly places (Eph. 6:12).

And that means you and me. We are all God's ambassadors in a world of sin. All of us must have the whole armor of God (verse 14-17). And we all must have the prayers of God's people if we are to navigate life as victorious Christians. The implications of Ephesians are that leaders need to earnestly pray for church members, that church members need to pray for church leaders, and that all Christians need to pray for all other Christians as we individually and collectively face the "spiritual forces of evil in the heavenly places" (verse 12).

Part IV

Saying Goodbye

Ephesians 6:21-24

25. Personal Report and Final Greeting

Ephesians 6:21-24

²¹Now in order that you also may know about me and what I am doing, Tychicus, the beloved brother and faithful minister in the Lord, will make everything known to you. ²²I have sent him to you for this very thing, that you may know about us and that he might encourage your hearts.

²³Peace to the brethren, and love with faith from God the Father, and the Lord Jesus Christ. ²⁴Grace be with all those loving our Lord Jesus Christ with an undying love.

We have come to the end of the tightly packed letter that we call the Epistle to the Ephesians. The letter itself, as you will recall, falls into two quite distinct halves. The first three chapters, outside of a brief introduction, deal with doctrinal matters, while the last three focus on practical exhortations. In Paul the practical always rests upon and flows out of the theological.

The epistle's final four verses fall into two sections. The apostle in verses 21 and 22 tells his readers that Tychicus will give them a full report of his condition. That was undoubtedly important to the Ephesians, since the only up-to-date biographical information in the letter occurs in verse 20, in which the apostle describes himself as being in chains (*i.e.*, a prisoner). Then in verses 23 and 24 he closes off his letter with a final prayer/blessing.

Tychicus is central to verses 21 and 22. In 2 Timothy 4:12 Paul notes that he sent Tychicus to Ephesus during his imprisonment. And Luke tells us that the faithful coworker, who may have penned the letter at Paul's dictation, was an Asian and links him with Trophimus (Acts 20:4), whom he later refers to as an Ephesian (21:29). Thus it may be that Paul was sending Tychicus back to his home region with both his letter and an oral report on his current status as a Roman prisoner.

As we noted in the introduction, Tychicus most likely had more than the letter to the Ephesians to deliver on this particular mission. It appears that Paul composed Ephesians and Colossians about the same time, since the two letters overlap so much in their content and wording. Beyond that, in Colossians 4:7 the apostle gives Tychicus the same teaching mission about his current status to the church at Colossae as he did to the recipients of Ephesians. The evidence points to the probability that Tychicus delivered the letters to the Ephesians and to the Colossians on the same trip.

Also of interest is that Colossians 4:9 tells us that Paul was sending Onesimus with Tychicus on the mission to Asia Minor. Thus it is probable that the apostle's letter to Philemon was also in the letter packet that he was sending by the hand of the trusted Tychicus.

Paul describes Tychicus by two phrases that capture his appreciation of the man:

- "beloved brother" and
- "faithful minister in the Lord" (Eph. 6:21).

Perhaps we have here an implied contrast with Demas, who had deserted Paul because of his love of "this present world" about the same time that he commissioned Tychicus to go to the Ephesians (see 2 Tim. 4:10-12). At any rate, it is clear that the apostle had full confidence in the man.

Tychicus was not only to deliver the letter to the Ephesians, but he also had another task when he visited them. Three times the apostle tells us of what it was:

1. that "you also [the "also" may be a reference to the Colossians, who were to get the same report (cf. Col. 4:7-9)] may know about me and what I am doing" (verse 21),
2. "Tychicus . . . will make everything known to you" (verse 21), and
3. "I have sent him to you for this very thing, that you may know about us" (verse 22).

The threefold repetition indicates Paul's sense of the importance that the Ephesians be aware of what was taking place in his life. Of course, we wish that he would have written it out so that we could know also. But perhaps some of his information was best put in oral form, since that data may have been problematic for some of his fellow workers in some way if the wrong people intercepted the letter. Our imagination strains a bit here, but the unfortunate fact is that the written record is largely silent on what Paul was going through. Whatever it was, however, we recognize that the apostle believed that Tychicus' report to the Ephesians and Colossians would encourage their hearts both as congregations and as individuals (Eph. 6:22; Col. 4:8).

The last two verses of Paul's Epistle to the Ephesians flash forth four of Paul's favorite theological words:

- Peace   - Faith
- Love   - Grace

Grace and peace both appear in the letter's introduction, in which he writes "grace to you and peace from God our Father and the Lord Jesus Christ" (Eph. 1:2, RSV). Peace has been central to the epistle. Ephesians 2:14, for example, calls Jesus "our peace." Chapter 2 goes on to note that in breaking down the dividing wall between Jew and Gentile he made peace (verses 14, 15) and that He "preached peace" to both groups (verse 17). And in chapter 4 the apostle begs the church to maintain unity and the "bond of peace" (verse 3).

Of course, the Ephesians also had a uniting peace with God because of His saving grace (cf. Rom. 5:1). Grace is the key word in two of Paul's most explicit statements on salvation in the epistle. Twice he asserts that "by grace you have been saved" (Eph. 2:5, 8). The glory of the gospel is that salvation is a gift and that it is a current possession. It is that gift that brings both peace with God and with other believers. In fact, it is grace which unites them as a community of the saved in the body of Christ.

And then there is faith. In Ephesians Paul helps us see that faith is the way that the church and individuals within it receive God's gift of grace (see 2:8). Beyond that, those who "have faith in Christ" (1:1) are those who follow Christ through life by walking the way that He walked.

Closely connected with the other three words is love. The Ephesians were to be without blame before Him in love (1:4); they were commanded to express "love toward all the saints" (1:15); Paul's desire for them was that they be "rooted and grounded in love" (3:17); they were to forbear one another in love (4:2); they were to speak the truth in love

(4:15); the church was to edify itself in love (4:16); the Ephesians were to walk in love (5:2); and love was to be central in the marriage relationship (5:25, 28, 33).

Paul's four great words run throughout his letter. It should not surprise us, therefore, that we find them in his last prayer-wish for his readers. And that prayer-wish is not merely for those who lived 2,000 years ago. The apostle's prayer-wish for me and you in the twenty-first century is that peace, grace, faith, and love might be at the very center of our personal and corporate lives.